ARCO WITH

MASTER THE
AMERICAN FOREIGN
SERVICE OFFICER
EXAM

4th Edition

Elaine Bender

Larry Elowitz

Arva C. Floyd

Philip J. Lane

Steven Petersen

Eve P. Steinberg

University of Alaska Anchorage
Career Services Center
3211 Providence Drive, BEB-122
Anchorage, Alaska 99508-8279

THOMSON

PETERSON'S

Australia • Canada • Mexico • Singapore • Spain • United Kingdom • United States

An ARCO Book

ARCO is a registered trademark of Thomson Learning, Inc., and is used herein under license by
Thomson Peterson's.

About Thomson Peterson's

Thomson Peterson's (www.petersons.com) is a leading provider of education information and advice, with
books and online resources focusing on education search, test preparation, and financial aid. Its Web site offers
searchable databases and interactive tools for contacting educational institutions, online practice tests and
instruction, and planning tools for securing financial aid. Peterson's serves 110 million education consumers
annually.

For more information, contact Peterson's, 2000 Lenox Drive, Lawrenceville, NJ 08648; 800-338-3282; or find
us on the World Wide Web at www.petersons.com/about.

© 2005 Thomson Peterson's, a part of The Thomson Corporation
Thomson Learning™ is a trademark used herein under license.

Previous editions © 1988, 1992, 2001

An American BookWorks Corporation Project

Petersons.com/publishing
Check out our Web site at www.petersons.com/publishing to see if there is any new information regarding the
test and any revisions or corrections to the content of this book. We've made sure the information in this book
is accurate and up-to-date; however, the test format or content may have changed since the time of publication.

Editor: Joe Krasowksi; Production Editor: Teresina Jonkoski; Manufacturing Manager: Judy Coleman;
Composition Manager: Melissa Ignatowski; Cover Design: Christina Chattin

ALL RIGHTS RESERVED. No part of this work covered by the copyright herein may be reproduced or used in
any form or by any means—graphic, electronic, or mechanical, including photocopying, recording, taping, Web
distribution, or information storage and retrieval systems—without the prior written permission of the publisher.

For permission to use material from this text or product, submit a request online at www.thomsonrights.com

Any additional questions about permissions can be submitted by e-mail to thomsonrights@thomson.com

ISBN 0-7689-1835-9

Printed in the United States of America

10 9 8 7 6 5 4 3 2 1   07 06 05

Fourth Edition

Contents

PART III: APPENDICES

Before You Begin

HOW TO USE THIS BOOK

If you already know what to expect from a career in the Foreign Service, this book will help you prepare for the written and oral exams. If you don't know what's in store from such a career choice, this book will also help you. Not only will you be able to prepare for your exam, but you will also find information here about various options within the State Department and other agencies.

There are three parts to this book. **Part I** covers careers representing the U.S. abroad within the Foreign Service. There are lots of ways to represent your country abroad, and there's bound to be one path that's right for you! It also provides an overview of the application process. We will show you how to apply, whether on-line or by mail. By walking you through the forms, giving you information you will need to fill them out, and preparing you for the questions you will have to answer about yourself, your past, and your goals for the future, you will be assured of a complete and thorough application for this exam.

In addition, we offer study hints and give you all the information you'll need to feel confident on the day of your exam. We know this is an intimidating process and we're here to make it a little less scary for you. We've also given you a review section so that you can practice on a variety of different question types. We suggest you go through this chapter to get an idea of where your strengths lie and what weaknesses you'll have to deal with on the actual test.

Part II provides real written examinations, or official sample examinations; others are model examinations closely patterned on the actual exams. Timing, level of difficulty, question styles, and scoring methods all conform closely to the examination for which they are meant to prepare. In addition, as a special feature of this book, we explain the answers to all practice questions.

Part III provides appendices to help you out with any questions you may have while working your way through this book and to provide other ideas of careers representing the United States abroad. **Appendix A** offers the essentials of English grammar to help you on both the written and oral exams. Even if your major in college was English, there may be a few points here that can be useful. **Appendix B** delivers background information on careers in the Foreign Commercial Service and the Foreign Agriculture Service. Each of these career tracks also allows people to be part of the U.S. Government while living and working abroad.

CAN YOU PREPARE FOR THE TEST?

You want to pass this test. That's why you bought this book. Used correctly, your "self-tutor" will show you what to expect and will give you a speedy brush-up on the subjects tested in your exam. Some of these are subjects not taught in schools at all. Even if your study time is very limited, you should:

- Become familiar with the type of examination you will take
- Improve your general examination-taking skill
- Improve your skill in analyzing and answering questions involving reasoning, judgment, comparison, and evaluation
- Improve your speed and skill in reading and understanding what you read—an important part of your ability to learn and an important part of most tests

ARCO Master the American Foreign Service Officer Exam will prepare you by

- **Presenting every type of question you will get on the actual test.** This will put you at ease come test day.

- **Analyzing your weaknesses.** Once you know what subjects you're weak in, you can get right to work and concentrate on those areas. This kind of selective study yields maximum test results.

- **Giving you confidence *now*.** It will build your self-confidence while you are preparing for the test. As you proceed, it will prevent the kind of test anxiety that causes low test scores.

- **Stressing the multiple-choice type question because that's the majority of what is on the written test.** You must not be satisfied with merely knowing the correct answer for each question. You must find out why the other choices are incorrect.

- **Perfecting your oral presentation skills.** You will need to prepare for and deliver oral presentations so that you are ready for the Oral Assessment day. We want you to be confident when you walk in there to sell yourself to the State Department.

After testing yourself, you may find that you are weak in a particular area. You should concentrate on improving your skills by using the specific practice sections in this book that apply to you.

When you do take the sample exams, try to set aside the full measure of time to take the exam in one sitting. Time yourself accurately (a stop watch or a kitchen timer will work well) and stop working when the time is up. If you have not completed all of the questions when the time expires, stop anyway. Check your answers against the provided correct answers and score your exam. Continue with the remaining questions to get in all the practice you can. Carefully study all the answer explanations, even those for questions that you answered correctly. By reading all of the explanations, you can gain greater insight into methods of answering questions and the reasoning behind the correct choices.

One very important suggestion: We strongly believe that regardless of the career path you want to follow you should try to take *all* of the exams in this book. It may seem like a lot of extra work, but you never know where you may end up. You may think you're interested in a job in one area but end up serving somewhere completely different. Keep an open mind and be prepared for the unknown. This can be a fun process if you walk into it knowing what to expect!

The most important thing is to use this book. By going through all of the sections and reading them, reviewing question types, and taking the practice exams, you will be using what you learned here to the best of your ability to succeed in your intended career path.

PART I

CAREERS IN THE FOREIGN SERVICE

What Is the Foreign Service?

OVERVIEW

- **What are the advantages of a Foreign Service career?**
- **Is the Foreign Service for you?**
- **Profile of entry-level offices**

WHAT ARE THE ADVANTAGES OF A FOREIGN SERVICE CAREER?

The Foreign Service of the United States is America's diplomatic, consular, commercial, and overseas cultural and information service. It assists the President and the Secretary of State in planning, conducting, and implementing our foreign policy at home and abroad. Approximately 4,000 Foreign Service Officers (FSOs) of the Department of State serve as management, consular, economic, political, and public diplomacy officers in more than 230 U.S. embassies and consulates in over 160 nations, in Washington, D.C., and with other government agencies. More than 3,500 Foreign Service Specialists serve as secretaries, communications technicians, financial and personnel managers, and physicians and nurses, and in other fields of expertise needed to meet Foreign Service responsibilities around the world.

The Foreign Service offers challenging and important work, variety, the chance to grow, and the pride and satisfaction of representing America abroad.

If you are looking for this very special type of career satisfaction, and you think you can shoulder some of the responsibilities that come with the rewards, you may be a candidate for the Foreign Service of the United States of America.

IS THE FOREIGN SERVICE FOR YOU?

A Foreign Service career is more than a job. It involves uncommon commitments and occasional hardships, as well as unique rewards and opportunities. A decision to enter this career must involve unusual motivation and a firm dedication to public service. Foreign Service personnel are committed to supporting U.S. policy publicly, even if it conflicts with their private views. The Foreign

chapter 1

NOTE

Overseas service
may involve security
risks to personnel and
their families.

TIP

To find out if this is a
good career fit for
you, we suggest
trying an interactive
tool set up by the
State Department at
www.careers.state.gov/
officer/right.html.

Service is a mobile profession. Personnel must agree to serve at any U.S. diplomatic or consular post abroad or in any domestic position, according to the needs of the Foreign Service. Personnel spend an average of 60 percent of their careers abroad, moving at two- to four-year intervals. This imposed mobility presents challenges to family life and raising children that are not found in more settled careers. Many overseas posts are in small or remote countries where harsh climates, health hazards, and other discomforts exist and where American-style amenities frequently are unavailable.

However, careers in the Foreign Service offer special rewards, too: the pride and satisfaction of representing the United States and protecting American interests abroad; the challenge of working in a demanding, competitive, action-oriented profession; opportunities for change and growth; contact with stimulating American and foreign colleagues in government, business, the press, and other professions; frequent travel; and the enriching cultural and social experience of living abroad.

PROFILE OF ENTRY-LEVEL OFFICES

Entry-level Officer Career Candidates typically enter the Foreign Service (FS) in Class 6 or 5. (Expression of pay grades in the Foreign Service is precisely the reverse of that in the more familiar General Schedule (GS) scale. While the GS begins at an entry level of GS-1, GS-2, or GS-3 and has a top of GS-15, the FS scale begins with FS-9 and rises to the top level of FS-1.) Recent candidates have ranged in age from the early twenties to the middle fifties, with a median age around 31. Of those officers recently appointed, some 54 percent had Master's degrees, 11 percent had law degrees, and 6 percent had Ph.D.s. Many have some years of professional work experience as well. All have a keen awareness of the significance of current events and trends, breadth of knowledge of domestic and international affairs, and a wide range of interests. Some 45 percent of the recently appointed Officer Career Candidates possessed acceptable skills in at least one foreign language; 7 percent qualified in two or more foreign languages. The principal areas of study of these officers included international relations, political science, history, economics, foreign languages, English/American literature, and law.

What Foreign Service Officers Do

OVERVIEW

- **The Foreign Service "cones"**
- **Prerequisites for performing well in the cones**

Foreign Service Officers (FSOs) can be sent anywhere in the world, at any time, to serve the diplomatic needs of the United States. They are the frontline personnel of all U.S. embassies, consulates, and other diplomatic missions.

Historically, FSOs are generalists who are assigned to various kinds of jobs in different parts of the world throughout the course of their careers. For most FSOs, this is still the case.

However, the field of international affairs has changed. Today, the Foreign Service seeks candidates interested in more than political science or international relations to help guide American diplomacy in the twenty-first century; people who can manage programs and personnel are needed. Also, transnational issues will characterize the diplomacy of the future. Among these new priorities are counterterrorism, nonproliferation, science, and technology, including the global fight against diseases such as AIDS; efforts to save the environment; anti-narcotics efforts; and trade.

THE FOREIGN SERVICE "CONES"

The U.S. Department of State also has an increasing need for candidates with training and experience in administration and management. The Department of State requires that applicants select a functional area of specialization, or "cone" when applying to take the written examination. The Foreign Service cones are

- Management
- Consular
- Economic
- Political
- Public Diplomacy

5

Regardless of your choice, all officers may represent the U.S. at selected official functions, ceremonies, and meetings and will likely participate in varied activities such as serving as duty officer; assisting with high-level visits; providing assistance to VIPs; reporting to Washington; and assisting the Ambassador in assessing U.S. policies and programs and developing policy proposals.

The choice of a cone is the first important decision potential Foreign Service Officers must make. Career candidates can expect to spend most, if not all, of their Foreign Service careers in the cone that is selected when registering for the exam. Prospective candidates are urged to carefully read the following descriptions of the five cones before making a decision.

Management Cone

The Department of State is the nation's oldest "multinational corporation," with representation in more than 160 countries, supported by a relatively small staff of professionals headquartered in Washington, D.C. Officers who work in the management cone exhibit and develop the same skills and abilities their counterparts do in a private-sector multinational company: resourcefulness, initiative, and leadership, as well as organizational and negotiating skills. Unlike their private-sector colleagues, FSOs report to a Chief Operating Officer and Chief Executive Officer who are known throughout the world: the Secretary of State and the President of the United States.

Management Officers are the resource managers for the Foreign Service. They manage the property, financial, and human resources that keep our diplomatic and consular missions functioning. Most Management Officers often have greater and broader contacts with host country officials earlier in their careers than do officers working in other sections of the embassy. Supervising the host country's national employees in an embassy, they have an excellent opportunity to either use the language skills they bring to the service or develop new foreign language skills.

These officers interact with every section and every agency at a mission, gaining more insight than most into the inner workings of that mission, as well as a greater understanding of how all the elements must work together to accomplish U.S. foreign policy objectives in the most efficient, effective, and economical manner. Based on information received from embassy colleagues, the Management Officer identifies resource requirements for achieving foreign policy objectives and directs preparation of budget submissions and staffing plans. They do this by utilizing their knowledge of mission goals and available resources.

General Duties

The Management Officer serves as manager of the post's human and material resources and as adviser to the Chief of Mission (Ambassador), Deputy Chief of Mission, or

Principal Officer—as well as heads of other agencies represented at the mission who make up the embassy's country team—on all aspects of management and post administration. The Management Officer is a key member of the Ambassador's management team. This person must have the ability to develop new perspectives and directions in management practices (often in response to complex or sensitive situations) and learn to find resolution among offices competing for limited resources.

A typical management section is comprised of the following units: general services, budget and fiscal, personnel, communications, and security (including Marine Guards, where applicable). The responsibilities include, but are not limited to, financial analysis; leasing, buying, and constructing of facilities; supervision, maintenance, and upgrade of buildings and fleets of vehicles; procurement of goods and services; issuance of travel orders for official travel; management of high-level official visits; and updating of computers and telecommunications. The FSO must learn the labor laws of the country regarding employment of local personnel as well as U.S. regulations governing salaries and benefits.

Management Officers must establish and maintain contact with officials at all levels in the local and national governments, other diplomatic missions, banks, airlines, and local business organizations on a variety of official matters. Officers solve problems or achieve mission objectives concerning customs regulations, immunities and privileges, tax laws, contracts, leases, and high-level visits. Management Officers also use such contacts to stay abreast of exchange rates, banking laws, and local employment practices.

Another duty of Management Officers is to develop and direct a wide variety of staff support activities designed to promote the morale and well-being of U.S. Government employees and their dependents. Such activities may include recreation, health care, and U.S. Government-supported schools and commissaries. The Management Officer also negotiates management support arrangements with the chiefs of other U.S. agencies serviced by the management section and resolves any questions arising from services requested and services received. These officers play a leadership role in the local American community (both official and private) to foster goodwill and cooperation on matters of mutual interest. This is especially important for employee morale at posts where living conditions are difficult and community facilities are limited. The Management Officer may also perform a similar function in the larger international community when it is in the best interest of the mission.

Consular Cone

Consular work is one of the oldest forms of diplomatic service. Traditionally, Consular Officers were appointed to look after U.S. commercial and shipping interests overseas. Gradually, this role evolved into looking after the interests of U.S. citizens abroad, issuing visas to foreign applicants, and monitoring migration issues.

Consular Officers provide both emergency and nonemergency services to American citizens residing or traveling abroad. They help with replacing a passport, finding medical assistance, securing funds from family members for citizens in need, locating citizens in an emergency, visiting an arrested American, making arrangements in the event of the death of an American citizen, and helping in the event of a disaster or evacuation. The Consular Officer serves as a "life raft" for American citizens who experience problems while overseas.

In nonemergency situations, the Consular Officer reports the birth of American citizens abroad and issues a Consular report that serves as proof of citizenship. Consular Officers distribute federal benefits checks, such as social security or pension; assist in child custody disputes; issue U.S. voting registration materials; supply tax forms; and serve in other ways that make overseas living easier for American citizens. Consular Officers also play leadership roles in the local American community (both official and private) to foster goodwill and cooperation on matters of mutual interest.

Consular Officers must master a complex set of laws and regulations, develop the interpersonal and investigative skills to be able to combat fraud, understand and manage new technologies, and write clearly and persuasively on a wide variety of issues. The officer often meets a broad range of host country residents and maintains official contacts not only with the foreign ministry, but also with people in the immigration, justice, customs, health, and social service ministries. Important contacts are also nurtured within local business, trade, legal, education, and religious institutions, as well as with the expatriate, immigrant, or refugee populations.

A Consular Officer's daily workload may appear formidable, with large numbers of visa or U.S. citizen services applications and inquiries to process. Good Consular Officers must be resourceful and know how to prioritize and make technical and personnel resources available to cover the workload. In many cases, professional-level foreign language skills are required in order to interview clients or speak in public. An ability to read documents in the local language is always beneficial. Knowledge of one's locale and the ability to quickly analyze and report on situations within or outside the office are essential. In addition to routine duties, the Consular Officer works with embassy colleagues on the visits of U.S. officials, international conferences, and meetings. Logistics, as well as preparing information for and working with the principal visitors, fall within each officer's duties on these occasions.

Many consular functions, such as the provision of passports, visas, and federal benefits payments, follow strict guidelines and regulations. Other functions, such as assisting American citizens in distress, depend on judgment, ingenuity, common sense, cultural sensitivity, and strong interpersonal skills. Consular work combines the skills of lawyers, judges, social workers, reporters, and investigators in addressing the vast range of human interactions and problems that require a consular response. The Consular Officer is often the only U.S. official with whom foreign nationals or U.S. citizens come into contact and, thus, has an important public, representational role.

General Duties

Consular Officers at U.S. missions oversee a variety of tasks, many involving the provision of services to U.S. citizens. The officer must determine whether or not the applicant is eligible for the consular services requested and explain any legal and documentary requirements.

Consular Officers review applications for passports and passport renewals, extensions, and amendments. They verify the information presented and provide or refuse to provide the requested passport service based on all available facts, applicable laws, and regulations.

Consular Officers register births and marriages of U.S. citizens, maintain locator information on resident American citizens in compliance with the post's emergency and evacuation requirements, visit U.S. citizens in prison, provide services in connection with illness and death, aid destitute Americans, and may serve as a notary.

Almost all Foreign Service Officers serve their first tour as Vice Consuls adjudicating visa applications. Consular Officers review visa applications (usually by conducting a brief interview with the applicant), verify the information presented, and issue or refuse visas based on all the available facts, applicable U.S. laws, and regulations.

After a morning of adjudicating visas, a Consular Officer will likely spend the afternoon drafting replies to inquiries regarding consular activities from U.S. citizens, attorneys, U.S. government agencies, members of Congress, and other interested parties. Consular Officers may confer with the appropriate host government officials on consular matters, maintain cordial relations with officials and consular officers of other nations, and establish and maintain working relationships with the resident American community in general.

Finally, a Consular Officer advises embassy colleagues on significant developments in current consular work. An officer also provides appropriate advice regarding all areas of consular affairs, including local immigration laws and all other pertinent laws, policy regulations, and processing procedures that affect U.S. citizens. A Consular Officer prepares, as appropriate, written reports on matters affecting U.S. citizens in the host country, such as travel warnings or instances of mistreatment of U.S. citizens.

Economic Cone

Economic Officers concentrate on issues such as money and banking, trade and commerce, communication and transportation, economic development, and government finance, reporting significant developments to the State Department. Economic Officers also deal with environmental, scientific, and technology matters such as ocean fisheries, cooperation in space, acid rain, global warming, population, health, biodiversity, and intellectual property rights. In addition to dealing with these issues bilaterally, they also deal with them multilaterally when assigned to or attending international organizations or conferences.

These officers are alert to the promotion of U.S. national interests in many areas and intervene with foreign governments and multilateral organizations when circumstances warrant. Sometimes they are given precise instructions on an intervention; sometimes they are left to their own ingenuity.

Economic Officers may also accompany more senior embassy officials as note-takers at high-level meetings. Economic Officers are expected to be knowledgeable in all aspects of economics and how economic systems work, in policy issues that are important in an economic context, in how the U.S. economy and U.S. government function, and in the host country's commercial practices and opportunities. They must understand the culture of the host country and be conversant in its language in order to see the world through its eyes. Trade within the country may also be involved. Economic Officers stationed abroad are both information gatherers and analysts, informing Washington agencies of important developments and their implications.

In Washington, Economic Officers work with various policy elements of the State Department and with other agencies (Treasury, U.S. Trade Representative, the White House, Commerce, Energy, Interior, Environmental Protection Agency, Federal Aviation Agency, the Congress, etc.) and organizations such as the World Bank, the International Monetary Fund, the local and/or U.S. Chamber of Commerce, and other trade entities. At home and abroad, Economic Officers need to develop extensive public and private sector contacts to be effective in their work. To do this well, they need good interpersonal skills and common sense in addition to formal training in economics.

General Duties

Economic Officers are responsible for providing the post and Washington with information and analysis on significant economic developments in the host country and for advancing U.S. economic and commercial policies, interests, and goals, including assistance to U.S. business representatives.

General duties of an Economic Officer include developing published and unpublished sources of information on significant economic and commercial developments in the host country and establishing and maintaining contacts with knowledgeable host country officials and key members of public and private institutions and enterprises. Economic Officers also engage in in-depth economic analyses of macro- and microeconomic problems involving important sectors of the host economy and report to other post officers and to Washington through cables, memoranda, and oral briefings. An Economic Officer recommends alternative courses of U.S. Government action and new policy directions in order to meet changing economic and commercial circumstances in the host country. An Economic Officer serves as the post's working-level expert from whom senior officers at the post seek information and guidance on economic and commercial developments.

Economic Officers are often required to convey official U.S. Government statements or requests for information to officials of the host government. The proper handling of the message is among the most important duties an Economic Officer has. The message must be presented accurately and completely, and the response must be reported precisely to avoid potential international misunderstanding. If negotiation is required, the Economic Officer must carefully adhere to instructions from Washington.

The Economic Officer provides assistance to the local American and foreign business communities and is often the first contact for local business representatives who are interested in doing business with the U.S. He or she may brief visiting American business representatives on economic and commercial conditions and developments in the host country and assist them in developing their marketing and investment goals. The Economic Officer speaks for the U.S. Government on economic and commercial issues to host government officials, private sector interests, and media representatives.

Economic Officers may support or conduct bilateral negotiations on economic and commercial issues; participate in the development of the Embassy's export promotion efforts; provide support for specific U.S. trade promotion programs; supervise the Embassy's commercial library; and participate in other post activities. The Economic Officer works with the Political Officer and the Public Diplomacy Officer at the post to evaluate local media reports, to develop programs to influence public opinion, and to identify actual and potential local leaders to be reached through the post's International Visitors Program. Economic Officers write analytical reports on the significance and influence of economic, financial, and business figures and travel with the host country to establish and maintain contact with local officials and others in order to report significant economic developments.

Political Cone

A Political Officer's primary responsibility is to follow political events within the host country and to report significant developments to the State Department. These officers are alert to the promotion of U.S. national interests in many areas and intervene with foreign governments and entities when circumstances warrant. Political Officers also convey official communications from the U.S. Government to host country officials and may accompany more senior officials of the Embassy as note-takers when they meet with host government officials. Similar functions are performed within multilateral organizations.

General Duties

Political Officers must know the people and customs of the host country, travel widely within that country, and speak the local language. They need not only to report accurately what happens but also to explain why events unfold as they do. Reporting is often done under considerable time pressure. To report successfully, a Political Officer must know informed host country individuals in politics, government, academia, journalism, the legal profession, business, and labor, to name only some sources of political information. A good Political Officer must be able to distinguish among the many opinions he or she will encounter, to analyze developments thoughtfully, and to provide accurate advance information.

Political Officers are often required to convey official statements or requests for information from the U.S. Government to officials of the host government. The proper handling of the message is among the most important duties a Political Officer has. It must be presented accurately and completely, and the response must be reported precisely to avoid potential international misunderstanding. If negotiation is required, the Political Officer must carefully adhere to instructions from Washington.

Finally, a Political Officer must be prepared to assist visiting U.S. officials. Every aspect of a visit, from hotel reservations to requested meetings to social events, must be planned and executed. The official visitor may be of any rank, including the President and/or Secretary of State. If the visit is at such a high level, the Political Officer will be a vital part of a coordinated embassy effort.

General Duties

Political Officers follow, analyze, and report political developments in the host country or in multilateral organizations. They promote U.S. policy objectives with key government officials, members of influential organizations, leaders in the private sector, and counterparts in international multilateral organizations. Political Officers maintain contact at an appropriate level with host government officials, political party leaders, trade unionists, other diplomatic missions, and private individuals.

The Political Officer monitors and/or consults with host government officials and reports information and recommendations on international and bilateral agreements or programs in which the U.S. participates or has an interest. Political Officers negotiate, as required, with appropriate officials in the host government on issues of concern to the U.S. Government.

The Political Officer works with Economic Officers and Public Diplomacy Officers at the post to evaluate local media reports, to develop programs to influence public opinion, and to identify actual and potential local leaders to be reached through the post's International Visitors Program. Political Officers write analytical reports on the significance and influence of political figures and travel within the country to establish and maintain contact with local officials and others in order to report significant political developments.

Public Diplomacy Cone

Officers who serve in the Public Diplomacy cone are charged with building bridges of communication between the United States and the host country in support of U.S. national interests. They carry out both cultural and information programs to explain to foreign audiences the complexities of U.S. society and culture and the current

Administration's foreign policy agenda. The overall management of the public diplomacy program at an embassy is in the hands of the Public Affairs Officer (PAO). The Information Officer (IO) is charged with explaining and defending the content of U.S. foreign policy. The Cultural Affairs Officer (CAO) provides audiences with an understanding of the social and cultural context of U.S. foreign policy by presenting a fuller picture of the values, beliefs, and principles held by Americans that influence not only domestic political life but foreign policy decisions as well.

General Duties

Much of what a Public Diplomacy Officer does depends on the size and location of the Embassy in which the officer is serving. Many posts around the world are staffed by just one Public Diplomacy Officer, the PAO, who handles both information and cultural affairs functions, and who, with the assistance of locally hired staff, carries out the entire range of public diplomacy programs in the host country. The PAO in any post is responsible for advising the Ambassador and the country team on the effect of public opinion on U.S. interest and on ways that public diplomacy can advance those interests. The PAO works with the Political and Economic Officers at the post to evaluate local media reports, to develop programs to influence public opinion, and to identify actual and potential leaders to be reached through the post's International Visitors Program.

The Information Officer (IO), sometimes also known as the Press Attaché, serves as the Embassy spokesperson and handles all media inquiries concerning official U.S. government policy. Information Officers set up and conduct press conferences for the Ambassador and other high-level officials; place material with local TV, radio, and print media; and maintain an active dialogue with both information media officials and opinion-makers and the wider public of the host country. The IO frequently writes speeches for the Ambassador and sets up media coverage of events in which the Ambassador or other high-level U.S. government officials take part. During bilateral negotiations, international conferences, or VIP visits, the IO becomes the main point of contact for both the host country media and the traveling U.S. press who accompany the President or the Secretary of State.

Information Officers must be prepared to respond to questions from the local media on a variety of issues, most of them germane to U.S. policy in the host country. The IO closely follows local media coverage as it pertains to U.S. presence in the host country and keeps the Embassy's country team, as well as appropriate offices in Washington, abreast of media reaction. Successful IOs must have a good grasp of the local language, a solid understanding of the customs and culture of the host country, and an ability to get out and meet personally with reporters, editors, news anchors, officials at the Ministry of Information or equivalent institution, and others who can be potentially influential in presenting the U.S. point of view to a mass audience.

It is also the responsibility of the Cultural Affairs Officer (CAO) to put U.S. foreign policy into context. The CAO arranges and conducts programs that address specific themes

NOTE

The KSAs are considered essential for success on the job, regardless of which cone is selected.

identified at the beginning of the programming year as key issues in either a bilateral or multilateral context. Traditionally, the CAO employs visiting American lecturers with special expertise to speak directly to selected audiences on these topics. American academic or cultural specialists also work with specific universities or organizations on programs lasting from two to twelve weeks. CAOs are increasingly employing electronic means to meet the challenges of the new telecommunications environment. Officers routinely use Worldnet Dialogues—audio and video linkups between the host country and the United States—and other forms of both audio and video teleconferencing to interpret and explain U.S. policy for both elite and mass audiences. Public Diplomacy Officers have also pioneered the use of the World Wide Web as a direct and efficient communications tool for reaching self-selecting audiences. The public diplomacy section is responsible for maintaining and coordinating the home pages for all embassy offices and functions, and the CAO's input is important in shaping the overall U.S. message in a way that will be intelligible to an overseas audience.

Because a fundamental role of the CAO is to establish links at personal, institutional, and governmental levels, exchanges are a primary area of interest on the CAO agenda. Among the most important programs managed directly or indirectly from the Cultural Affairs Office are

NOTE

The Job Analysis also identified the following skills and abilities as important in the work of a Foreign Service Officer across all cones: strong interpersonal and communication skills, adaptability and stress tolerance, good problem solving and decision making, integrity and dependability, ability to plan and set priorities, and initiative and leadership.

- The International Visitors Program. This program sends selected Embassy contacts—current or potential leaders in government, politics, economics and business, the media, education, labor relations, the arts, and other fields—to the United States on 30-day programs to learn more about U.S. government, institutions, and society. They also meet with their professional counterparts.

- The Fulbright Program. This program provides opportunities for U.S. and host country professors and graduate students to spend an academic year in each other's country for study or research.

- The Humphrey Fellows Program. This program brings accomplished host country professionals at a midpoint in their careers to the U.S. for a year of study and related professional experiences.

- English Language Programs. These programs promote the development of English-teaching curricula, textbooks, and teacher training, while stimulating and reinforcing academic exchange programs.

The overarching goal of all such exchange programs is a multiplier effect: the CAO seeks to build relationships, to encourage the expansion of bilateral networks, and to develop influential support for programs linking the U.S. with the host country. The CAO meets many challenges, from obtaining support for cross-cultural communications to seeking out private-sector cosponsors for programs ranging from speakers to performing artists.

The work of a Public Diplomacy Officer is varied and demanding. It involves a high degree of outside contact work across a wide spectrum of endeavors, dealing with the independent media, Ministry of Information, universities, cultural and arts institutions, libraries, think tanks, and nongovernmental organizations. A good Public

Diplomacy Officer must be resourceful, politically sensitive, and flexible, with the ability to understand a culture quickly and to deal easily with a variety of people. Strong interpersonal skills are vitally important for success in the Public Diplomacy cone.

PREREQUISITES FOR PERFORMING WELL IN THE CONES

A recent job analysis of the Department of State identified certain knowledge, skills, and abilities (KSAs) that prospective Foreign Service Officers should possess prior to entry into the Foreign Service.

Knowledge of the following areas was identified as essential for success on the job across all cones: proper English usage; a thorough understanding of U.S. society, culture, history, government, political systems, and the Constitution; and knowledge of world geography, historical antecedents of international affairs, and world political and social issues. In addition, all Foreign Service Officers should understand basic accounting, statistics and mathematics, principles of management, interpersonal communication, and basic economic principles and trends.

How to Apply and What to Expect

chapter 3

OVERVIEW

- Becoming an American Foreign Service Officer
- Career status and development
- Compensation and benefits
- Information for family members

BECOMING AN AMERICAN FOREIGN SERVICE OFFICER

The Foreign Service needs qualified men and women who reflect the breadth and variety of American society. To be truly representative of the United States, the Foreign Service must reflect the diversity of the American people. The Foreign Service needs men and women from all backgrounds—Americans of all racial and ethnic origins and from all regions of the country. The Foreign Service also seeks officers from diverse educational backgrounds. Approximately 750 American colleges and universities are represented by today's FSOs. They come from every state in the union. Most officer candidates enter the Foreign Service after attending college or graduate school, with degrees in a variety of subjects. A few do not have university degrees. Others have worked in teaching, business, law, science, journalism, the military, government, or other fields, bringing valuable skills and experience to the Foreign Service. Most officer candidates have backgrounds in history, political science, economics, or management, but needs are increasing in foreign affairs for scientists, systems analysts, language and area experts, business managers, industrial development specialists, and others. Today, the Foreign Service seeks diversity of education, talents, and experience to handle the complex and multifaceted tasks of foreign affairs.

The primary resource for a career in the American Foreign Service is the U.S. Department of State. The easiest way to get information about becoming a Foreign Service Officer or any of the other related Foreign Service careers is to go directly to www.careers.state.gov. Here you will find everything you need to start a career with the Department of State.

Now that you know where to look for a job, it's important to understand the procedure. The procedure you must follow to get a government job varies little from job to job and from one level of government to another. There are variations in details, of course, but certain steps are common to all.

Once you have found a Notice of Examination (it may be called an Announcement), read it very carefully. If you can get a copy for yourself, do so. Make sure you have written down all of the details. The Notice of Examination will give a brief job description. It will tell the title of the job and describe some of the job duties and responsibilities. On the basis of the job description, you will decide whether or not you want to apply for a particular job. If the job appeals to you, you must concentrate on:

NOTE

Government service is very popular; many people apply. The government has more than enough applicants from which to choose. It will not waive requirements for you.

- **Education and experience requirements.** If you cannot meet these requirements, do not bother to apply.

- **Age requirements.** Discrimination on the basis of age is illegal, but a number of jobs demand so much sustained physical effort that they require retirement at an early age. For these positions there is an entry age limit. If you are already beyond that age, do not apply. If you are still too young, inquire about the time lag until hiring. It may be that you will reach the minimum age by the time the position is to be filled.

- **Citizenship requirements.** Many jobs are open to everyone who is eligible to work in the United States, but all law enforcement jobs and most federal jobs are limited to citizens. If you are well along on your way toward citizenship and expect to be naturalized soon, inquire as to your exact status with respect to the job.

- **Residency requirements.** If there is a residency requirement, you must live within the prescribed limits or be willing to move. If you are not willing to live in the area, do not waste time applying.

- **What forms must be filed.** The Announcement of the position for which you are applying will specify which application you must complete. For most federal jobs, you may submit either the Optional Application for Federal Employment (OF-612) or a resume that fulfills the requirements set forth in the pamphlet "Applying for a Federal Job (OF-510)." To apply for a Foreign Service Officer position, you must complete the Application for Employment (DS-1950). You can obtain Form DS-1950 online at www.careers.state.gov/res_forms.html. A sample Application for Employment can be found on pages 19–26. A sample optional Application for Federal Employment (OF-612) is given on pages 27–28.

- **For positions other than federal jobs, the Notice of Examination may tell you whom to contact to get the necessary form(s).** Be sure you secure them all. The application might be a simple form asking nothing more than your name, address, citizenship, and social security number, or it may be a complex Experience Paper. An Experience Paper, as its title implies, asks a great deal about education,

U.S. Department of State

Instructions for Completing Application for Employment

Carefully Read the Following Instructions and the Vacancy Announcement Before You Complete this Application

THIS APPLICATION IS REQUIRED FOR CERTAIN EMPLOYMENT OPPORTUNITIES IN THE DEPARTMENT OF STATE. TYPE OR PRINT CLEARLY IN BLACK INK. NOTE: Illegible statements on the application form may hinder full consideration of your application. Data on the application form are read by computer. Using care while filling in the form will speed processing of your application. **TYPING IS PREFERRED**. If you plan to type this application, **first fill in the boxes** (items #10, 11, 12, etc.) with black ink. If you plan to handwrite, print carefully and close letters.

Before completing this application, determine from the appropriate office if applications are being accepted for the position in which you have an interest and, if so, obtain a vacancy announcement from that office. In addition to describing the job, the announcement will help you determine if you have the appropriate qualifications and how to present them, advise whether any additional application documents are needed, and explain how to submit the application and any supplemental documents.

You must submit at least the following parts of this application (refer to the vacancy announcement for complete instructions on what to submit): one Page 3, one Page 4, and one Page 5. On each Page 4 and 5 you submit, enter your Social Security Number and up to the first 18 characters of your last name. You may submit more than one Page 4 depending on the number of experience blocks you need, but only one Page 5.

When completing date (except item # 18- "Date of Diploma/GED" and items #19 & 20 - "Date of Degree"), use the following format: 03-08-1994.

Answer all questions fully and correctly. Otherwise, you may delay the review of your application and exclude yourself from consideration for employment. See the vacancy announcement for the fax number and/or mailing instructions and for any required additional submissions and attachments. You must keep a copy of this application with an original signature. At some point in the selection process, you may be asked to submit original copies of your application and attachments. If you plan to make copies of your application, we suggest you leave items #9, 24 and 25 blank, so you can use this application for future vacancies. Complete these blank items each time you apply. YOU MUST SIGN AND DATE, IN INK, EACH COPY YOU SUBMIT.

SPECIFIC INSTRUCTIONS

Page 3
#5. If applicable, include your apartment number at the end of your street address.

#6, 7. Include area codes for all phone numbers. Use the following format: 202-555-1234.

#12. If you are a male and were born prior to December 31, 1959, you should NOT answer item # 12.

#13. DO NOT LEAVE ITEM #13 BLANK. If you do not claim veterans' preference, mark the "No Preference" box. You cannot receive veterans' preference if you are retired or plan to retire at or above the rank of major or lieutenant commander, unless you are disabled or retired from the active military Reserve. To receive veterans' preference, your separation from active duty must have been under honorable conditions. This includes honorable and general discharges. A clemency discharge does not meet the requirements of the Veterans' Preference Act. Active duty for training in the military Reserve and National Guard programs is not considered active duty for purposes of veterans' preference.

To qualify for preference, you must meet ONE of the following conditions:
1. Served on active duty anytime between December 7, 1941 and July 1, 1955; (If you were a Reservist called to active duty between February 1, 1955 and July 1, 1955, you must meet condition 2, below.)   **or**
2. Served on active duty any part of which was between July 2, 1955 and October 14, 1976 or a Reservist called to active duty between February 1, 1955 and October 14, 1976 and who served more than 180 days;   **or**
3. Entered on active duty between October 15, 1976 and September 7, 1980 or a Reservist who entered on active duty between October 15, 1976 and October 13, 1982 and received a Campaign Badge or Expeditionary Medal or are a disabled veteran; **or**
4. Enlisted in the Armed Forces after September 7, 1980 or entered active duty other than by enlistment on or after October 14, 1982 **and:**
   a. Completed 24 months of continuous active duty, or the full period called, or ordered to active duty, or were discharged under 10 U.S.C.1171, or for hardship under 10 U.S.C. 1173, **and** received or were entitled to receive a Campaign Badge or Expeditionary Medal;   **or**
   b. Are a disabled veteran.

If you meet one of the previous four conditions, you qualify for 5-Point Preference. If you want to claim 5-Point Preference and do not meet the requirements for 10-Point Preference, mark the box next to "5-Point Preference."

U.S. Department of State

Instructions for Completing Application for Employment (Con't)

(Item #13 continued)

If you think you qualify for "10-Point Preference", review the requirements described in Standard Form (SF) 15, Application for 10-Point Veterans' Preference. The SF-15 is available from any Federal Job Information Center. If you claim "10-Point Preference", mark the box next to "10-Point Preference." The 10-Point Preference groups are:

Non-Compensably Disabled or Purple Heart Recipient.
Compensably Disabled (less than 30%).
Compensably Disabled (30% or more).
Spouse, Widow(er) or Mother of a deceased or disabled veteran.

To receive "10-Point Preference", you must send in a completed SF-15 with the proof requested in the SF-15.

#16, 17. Mark only one box per item. For # 16, indicate the highest level of education you have completed. For # 17, mark the box that most closely indicates your present status.

#18, 19, 20. List the most recently attended schools for each of these items. On Page 5, you have more space to list schools where you received additional degrees or certificates, such as from Vocational/Technical programs. Use the following format for "Date of Diploma/GED" and "Date of Degree": mm-yyyy (e.g. 04-1994). For "Date From" and "Date To" use mm-yyyy (e.g. 04-2000).

#22. Rate your proficiency for speaking and reading languages other than English. Be sure to include the two languages in which you have the highest proficiencies. If you wish to list more than two languages in which you have proficiency, give details in the "Continued Items" area on Page 5. Rate your proficiency using the codes listed below:

Proficiency Code	Speaking Definitions	Reading Definitions
0-No Practical Proficiency	No practical speaking proficiency	No practical reading proficiency.
1-Elementary Proficiency	Able to satisfy routing travel needs and minimum courtesy requirements.	Able to read some personal and place names, street signs, office and shop designations, numbers and isolated words and phrases.
2-Limited Working Proficiency	Able to satisfy routine social demands and limited work requirements.	Able to read simple prose, in a form equivalent to typescript or printing, on subjects within a familiar context.
3-Minimum Professional Proficiency	Able speak the language with sufficient structural accuracy and vocabulary to participate effectively in most formal and informal conversations on practical, social, and professional topics.	Able to read standard newspaper items addressed to the general reader, routine correspondence, reports, and technical materials in the individual's special field.
4-Full Professional Proficiency	Able to use the language fluently and accurately on all levels pertinent to professional needs.	Able to read all styles and forms of the language pertinent to professional needs.
5-Native or Bilingual Proficiency	Equivalent to that of an educated native speaker.	Equivalent to that of an educated native.

Pages 4 & 5

Fill in your employment, unemployment, and education activities, **beginning with the present and working backwards 10 years.** Label each experience with a consecutive letter (A, B, C, D, etc.) beginning with the letter "A" in the first "Experience Block". **INCLUDE ALL:** full-time work, part-time work, temporary work, paid work, unpaid work, active military duty, self-employment, periods of unemployment, educational activities (for unpaid activities, leave the salary blocks blank). You may also include any other experience prior to the past 10 years which you feel would be relevant to the position for which you are applying. If you had a significant change of duties or responsibilities while you worked for the same employer, describe each major change as a separate experience. If specific experience continues to the present, mark the box for "Present" **and do not mark the "Date To" blocks.**

PRIVACY ACT STATEMENT

Section 1104 of Title 5 of the U.S. Code allows Federal agencies to rate applicants for Federal jobs. We need the information you put on this application form to see how well your education and work skills qualify you for a Federal job. We also need information on matters such as citizenship and military service to see whether you are affected by laws we must follow in deciding who may be employed by the Federal Government.

Executive Order 9397 authorizes solicitation of your Social Security Number (SSN) for use as an identifier in personnel records management, thus ensuing proper identification of applicants throughout the selection and employment process. The information we collect by using your SSN will be used for employment purposes and also may be used for studies, statistics, and computer matching to benefit payment files. Furnishing your SSN or any of the other data specified in the vacancy announcement, is voluntary. However, failure to do so may prevent timely processing of your application or may prevent consideration for the vacancy.

Note: If you receive the application form by fax and the four corner boxes are cut off at the top or bottom of any page, please contact the sending office to resend the fax or request a form by mail. The form may not read properly if the boxes are not intact.

U.S. Department of State
Application for Employment

*OMB Approved No. 1405-0139
Expires 05-31-2005
Estimated Burden 30 Minutes

☐ Mr.
☐ Mrs.   1. Name *(Last, First, MI)*
☐ Ms.

2. Other Names Ever Used *(maiden, nicknames, etc.)*   3. Date of Birth *(mm-dd-yyyy)*   4. Social Security Number

5. Currrent Address *(include apartment number, if any)*

5a. City   5b. State (2 Letters)   5c. ZIP/Postal Code *(ZIP +4)*   5d. E-Mail Address

5e. Country *(if not United States)*   6. Current Home Phone *(include Area Code)*   6a. Current Work Phone *(include Area Code)*

7. Permanent Address *(include apartment number, if any)*

7a. Permanent City   7b. State (2 Letters)   7c. ZIP/Postal Code *(ZIP +4)*

7d. Permanent Country *(if not United States)*   7e. Permanent Home Phone *(include Area Code)*

8. Indicate Title, Position or Program you are applying for.   Job Announcement Number   9. Lowest Acceptable Annual Salary   Or Grade Level

10. Are you available for: *(Select all appropriate)*	11. Are you a U.S. Citizen? ☐ Yes ☐ No	12. If you are a male born	13. Veteran's Preference

10. Are you available for: *(Select all appropriate)*
☐ Full-Time?   ☐ Shift Work?
☐ Temporary/Part-Time?   ☐ Flexible Work Schedule?
☐ Overtime?   ☐ World Wide Assignment?

11. Are you a U.S. Citizen? ☐ Yes ☐ No
Is your spouse/cohabitant a U.S. Citizen?
☐ Yes ☐ No
If "NO", enter the country of his/her citizenship.

12. If you are a male born after December 31, 1959, have you registered with the Selective Service? ☐ Yes ☐ No

13. Veteran's Preference
☐ No Preference
☐ 5-Point Preference
☐ 10-Point Preference

14. Were you ever employed as a civilian by the ☐ Yes ☐ No Federal Government? If "YES" mark all that apply.
☐ Temporary ☐ Career-Conditional ☐ Career ☐ Excepted
Do you receive, or have you ever applied for retirement pay, pension or other pay based on military, Federal civilian, or District of Columbia Government service? ☐ Yes ☐ No

15. Do you have a relative working for the Agency for which you are applying? If "YES", give details on Page 5.
☐ Yes ☐ No

16. Highest Education Level Completed
☐ 10   ☐ College: 2   ☐ Graduate Studies
☐ 11   ☐ College: 3   ☐ Masters
☐ 12/GED   ☐ College: 4   ☐ Professional Degree
☐ Vo/Tech Prog.   ☐ College: AA   ☐ JD/other law degree
☐ College: 1   ☐ College: BA/BS   ☐ Doctorate

17. Current Student Status
☐ Full-Time Student
☐ Part-Time Student
☐ Not a Student

18. High School Name   City, State, ZIP Code   Date of Diploma/GED *(mm-yyyy)*

19. Undergraduate Institution	Date of Degree *(mm-yyyy)*	20. Graduate Institution	Date of Degree *(mm-yyyy)*
City, State, ZIP Code, Country *(if not U.S.)*	Grade Point Avg. (on 4.0 scale)	City, State, ZIP Code, Country *(if not U.S.)*	Grade Point Avg. (on 4.0 scale)
Major Minor	Number of credit hours completed	Major Minor	Number of credit hours completed
Date From *(mm-yyyy)* Date To *(mm-yyyy)*	☐ Quarter hours completed ☐ Semester hours completed	Date From *(mm-yyyy)* Date To *(mm-yyyy)*	☐ Quarter hours completed ☐ Semester hours completed

21. Do you have or have you had a Security Clearance?
☐ Yes ☐ No
If "YES", what type of clearance and who issued the clearance?

22. First Foreign Language Proficiency *(See Codes Page 2)*   Second Foreign Language Proficiency *(See Codes Page 2)*

Speaking Proficiency   Reading Proficiency   Speaking Proficiency   Reading Proficiency
S   R   S   R

23. List any special skills (e.g. computer), experiences, current licenses, honors,awards, special accomplishments, and/or training (with date completed) **relating to the position for which you are applying.** Continue on Page 5, if necessary.

24. Original Signature *(SIGN IN INK)* I certify that all of the information on and attached to this application is true, correct, complete, and made in good faith.

Signature

25. Date Signed *(mm-dd-yyyy)*

*The response time is an estimated average including the time needed to look for, get and provide the information required. You do not have to provide the information requested if the OMB approval has expired. We would appreciate any comments on the estimated responses and cost burdens, and recommendations for reducing them. Please send your comments to A/RPS/DIR, U.S. Department of State, Washington, DC 20520.

DS-1950   An Equal Opportunity Employer   **Page 3 of 7**

U.S. Department of State
Application for Employment (Con't)

Social Security Number	Last Name
_____	

Experience Block	Type of Experience	Full-Time/Part-Time	Exact Title of Your Job	Starting Salary	per	Ending Salary	per

Experience Block [ ]

Type of Experience
- [ ] Paid
- [ ] Unpaid
- [ ] Unemployed
- [ ] Education

Full-Time/Part-Time
- [ ] Full-Time
- [ ] Part-Time If P/T, hours per week [ ][ ]

Exact Title of Your Job

Date From *(mm-dd-yyyy)*
_____   **To**

Starting Salary
_____
per
- [ ] Hr
- [ ] Wk
- [ ] Mo
- [ ] Yr

If present experience, mark box and leave "Date To" blank. [ ] Present

Ending Salary
_____
per
- [ ] Hr
- [ ] Wk
- [ ] Mo
- [ ] Yr

Date To *(mm-dd-yyyy)*
_____

Employer's Name and Address *(include ZIP Code, if known)*

If Federal employment, civilian or military, list series, grade or rank, and if promoted in this job, indicate the date of your last promotion.

Supervisor's Name, Area Code and Telephone Number

Describe your duties and accomplishments *(include any knowledge, skills, and abilities listed in the vacancy announcement that you have gained from this work experience).*

Experience Block [ ]

Type of Experience
- [ ] Paid
- [ ] Unpaid
- [ ] Unemployed
- [ ] Education

Full-Time/Part-Time
- [ ] Full-Time
- [ ] Part-Time If P/T, hours per week [ ][ ]

Exact Title of Your Job

Date From *(mm-dd-yyyy)*
_____   **To**

Starting Salary
_____
per
- [ ] Hr
- [ ] Wk
- [ ] Mo
- [ ] Yr

If present experience, mark box and leave "Date To" blank. [ ] Present

Ending Salary
_____
per
- [ ] Hr
- [ ] Wk
- [ ] Mo
- [ ] Yr

Date To *(mm-dd-yyyy)*
_____

Employer's Name and Address *(include ZIP Code, if known)*

If Federal employment, civilian or military, list series, grade or rank, and if promoted in this job, indicate the date of your last promotion.

Supervisor's Name, Area Code and Telephone Number

Describe your duties and accomplishments *(include any knowledge, skills, and abilities listed in the vacancy announcement that you have gained from this work experience).*

DS-1950   An Equal Opportunity Employer   Page 4 of 7

U.S. Department of State
Application for Employment (Con't)

Social Security Number   Last Name

_____   _____

Experience Block	Type of Experience	Full-Time/Part-Time	Exact Title of Your Job	Starting Salary	per	Ending Salary	per

Experience Block [ ]

Type of Experience
- [ ] Paid
- [ ] Unpaid
- [ ] Unemployed
- [ ] Education

Full-Time/Part-Time
- [ ] Full-Time
- [ ] Part-Time

If P/T, hours per week [ ][ ]

Exact Title of Your Job

Date From (mm-dd-yyyy) _____ **To**

Starting Salary _____
per
- [ ] Hr
- [ ] Wk
- [ ] Mo
- [ ] Yr

If present experience, mark box and leave "Date To" blank. [ ] Present

Ending Salary _____
per
- [ ] Hr
- [ ] Wk
- [ ] Mo
- [ ] Yr

Date To (mm-dd-yyyy)

Employer's Name and Address (include ZIP Code, if known)

If Federal employment, civilian or military, list series, grade or rank, and if promoted in this job, indicate the date of your last promotion.

Supervisor's Name, Area Code and Telephone Number

Describe your duties and accomplishments (include any knowledge, skills, and abilities listed in the vacancy announcement that you have gained from this work)

Continued Items from Page 3

Item 15 continued. Include: *father, mother, husband, wife, son, daughter, brother, sister, uncle, aunt, first cousin, nephew, niece, father-in-law, mother-in-law, son-in-law, daughter-in-law, brother-in-law, sister-in-law, stepfather, stepmother, stepson, stepdaughter, stepbrother, stepsister, half brother, and half sister.*

Items 19 & 20 continued. Other schools and/or certificate programs where degrees were received or vocational, technical or armed forces schools where certificates were received and not listed in blocks #19 or 20. Include all information as requested in blocks #19 & 20.

Name	Relationship

Item 22 continued.

Language	Speaking Proficiency	Reading Proficiency

Item 23 continued. List special skills, awards, accomplishments and/or training .

AUTHORIZATION TO FURNISH INFORMATION

I hereby authorize the U.S. Department of State to furnish to any organization or individual who is a potential funding source or organization all the information I have furnished on this form, any official financial aid statement from any college or university, and any other information I have provided with respect to my application for this position with the U.S. Department of State.

_____   _____
Signature   Date (mm-dd-yyyy)

U.S. Department of State
Application for Employment (Con't)
Employment Data

General instructions: The information from this survey is used to help ensure that agency personnel practices meet the requirements of Federal law. Your responses are voluntary. Please answer each of the questions to the best of your ability. Please print entries in pen. Be sure to read each item thoroughly before completing this form.

☐ Mr.   1. Name *(Last, First, MI)*
☐ Mrs.
☐ Ms. _____

2. Social Security Number   3. Position for which you are applying

_____

4. Job Announcement Number

_____

5 (a). Is this a Student Program position?   ☐ Yes ☐ No

(b). If "YES", do you intend to enroll or continue to be enrolled in a
college or university immediately after completing the program?   ☐ Yes ☐ No

6. Have you ever taken the Foreign Service Officer Examination?

☐ Yes ☐ No

7. Race and Ethnicity Identification (Voluntary). The race and ethnic categories for federal statistics and administrative reporting are defined below. Please identify yourself in terms of one or more of the following categories by marking the appropriate box(es).

☐ (1) American Indian or Alaska Native   ☐ (4) Hispanic or Latino
☐ (2) Asian   ☐ (5) Native Hawaiian or Other Pacific Islander
☐ (3) Black or African American   ☐ (6) White

Note: Race is defined by the Equal Employment Opportunity Commission as follows:

1. American Indian or Alaska Native — A person having origins in any of the original peoples of North America and South America (including Central America), and who maintains tribal affiliation or community attachment.

2. Asian — A person having origins in any of the original peoples of the Far East, Southeast Asia, or the Indian subcontinent including, for example, Cambodia, China, India, Japan, Korea, Malaysia, Pakistan, the Philippine Islands, Thailand, and Vietnam.

3. Black, or African American — A person having origins in any of the black racial groups of Africa. This category includes terms such as "Haitian" or "Negro" as well as "Black" or "African American."

4. Hispanic or Latino — A person of Cuban, Mexican, Puerto Rican, South or Central American, or other Spanish culture or origin, regardless of race. This category includes the term "Spanish origin," as well as "Hispanic" or "Latino."

5. Native Hawaiian or Other Pacific Islander — A person having origins in any of the original peoples of a Hawaii, Guam, Samoa, or other Pacific Islands.

6. White — A person having origins in any of the original peoples of Europe, the Middle East, or North Africa.

8. Do you have a Disability? (Voluntary)   ☐ Yes ☐ No   ☐☐ *(see Page 7 for codes)*

Self-identification of disability status is essential for effective data collection and analysis. The information you provide will be used for statistical purposes only. While self-identification is voluntary, your cooperation in providing accurate information is critical.

Definition of a Disability: A person is disabled if he or she has a physical or mental impairment which substantially limits one or more major life activities; has a record of such impairment; or is regarded as having such impairment. Those disabilities that are to be reported are listed on page 7. In the case of multiple impairments, choose the code which describes the impairment that would result in the most substantial limitation on this job.

9. If employed, describe Field of Work. (Mark the appropriate box(es))

☐ Administrative/Management   ☐ Media/Journalism
☐ Economics/Marketing   ☐ Fine Arts
☐ Banking/Finance   ☐ Scientific/Technical
☐ International Trade   ☐ Clerical and Related
☐ Law   ☐ Sales/Service
☐ Teaching   ☐ Military
☐ Federal Government   ☐ Other _____
☐ Foreign Affairs   *(Please specify)*

10. Years of Full-Time Work Experience ☐☐

11. Years of Overseas Experience ☐☐

12. Overseas Experience

☐ Student   ☐ Military
☐ Dependent   ☐ Government
☐ Peace Corps   ☐ Other _____
(Please specify)

13. How did you learn about the job for which you are applying? *(You may select up to 3 choices)*

☐ Private Information Service   ☐ State Employment Office (Job Service)   ☐ Agency Diplomat-in-Residence
☐ Magazine   ☐ Agency Human Resources Dept. (Bulletin Board or Other Announcement)   ☐ School or College Counselor or other official
☐ Newspaper   ☐ Military Transition Assistance Program   ☐ Federal, State or Local Job Information Center
☐ Radio   ☐ Agency or other Federal Government Recruiter at School or College   ☐ Friend or Relative Working for Agency
☐ TV   ☐ Agency Web site   ☐ Friend or Relative not Working for Agency
☐ Poster   ☐ Other Web site (Please specify) _____   ☐ Religious organization
☐ Private Employment Office   ☐ Other *(Please specify)* _____

DS-1950   An Equal Opportunity Employer   Page 6 of 7

U.S. Department of State
Application for Employment (Con't)
Employment Data Self-Identification of Disability

01. I do not wish to identify my disability.	
05. I do not have a disability.	
06. I have a disability but it is not listed below.	

SPEECH IMPAIRMENTS

13. Severe speech malfunction or inability to speak; hearing is normal (Example: defects of articulation [unclear language sounds]; stuttering; aphasia [impaired language function]; larynegectomy [removal of the "voice box"])

HEARING IMPAIRMENTS

15. Hard of hearing (Total deafness in one ear or inability to hear ordinary conversation, correctable with a hearing aid)
16. Total deafness in both ears, with understandable speech
17. Total deafness in both ears, and unable to speak clearly.

VISION IMPAIRMENTS

22. Ability to read ordinary size print with glasses, but with loss of peripheral (side) vision (Restriction of the visual field to extent that mobility is affected -"Tunnel vision")
23. Inability to read ordinary size print, not correctable by glasses (Can read oversized print or use assisting devises such as glass or projector modifier)
24. Blind in one eye
25. Blind in both eyes (No usable vision, but may have some light perception)

MISSING EXTREMITIES

27. One hand
28. One arm
29. One foot
32. One leg
33. Both hands or arms
34. Both feet or legs
35. One hand or arm and one foot or leg
36. One hand or arm and both feet or legs
37. Both hands or arms and one foot or leg
38. Both hands or arms and both feet or legs.

NONPARALYTIC ORTHOPEDIC IMPAIRMENTS

(Because of chronic pain, stiffness, or weakness in bones or joints, there is some loss of ability to move or use a part or parts of the body.

44. One or both hands	47. One or both legs
45. One or both feet	48. Hip or pelvis
46. One or both arms	49. Back
57. Any combination or two or more parts of the body	

PARTIAL PARALYSIS

(Because of brain, nerve, or muscle problem, including palsy and cerebral palsy, there is some loss of ability to move or use a part of the body, including legs, arms, and/or trunk.

61. One hand	64. Both hands
62. One arm, any part	65. Both legs, any part
63. One leg, any part	66. Both arms, any part

67. One side of body, including one arm and one leg	68. Three or more major major parts of the body (arms and legs)

COMPLETE PARALYSIS

(Because of a brain, nerve, or muscle problem, including palsy and cerebral palsy, there is a complete loss of ability to move or use a part of the body, including legs, arms, and/or trunk.)

70. One hand	76. Lower half of body, including legs.
71. Both hands	
72. One arm	77. One side of body, including one arm and one leg.
73. Both arms	
74. One leg	78. Three or more major parts of the body (arms and legs)
75. Both legs	

OTHER IMPAIRMENTS

80. Hear disease with no restriction or limitation of activity (History or heart problems with complete recovery)
81. Heart disease with restriction or limitation of activity
82. Convulsive disorder (e.g., epilepsy)
83. Blood diseases (e.g., sickle cell anemia, leukemia, hemophilia)
84. Diabetes
86. Pulmonary respiratory disorders (e.g., tuberculosis, emphysema, asthma)
87. Kidney dysfunctioning (e.g., if dialysis [Use of an artificial kidney machine] is required)
88. Cancer-a history of cancer with complete recovery
89. Cancer-under surgical and/or medical treatment
90. Mental retardation (A chronic and lifelong condition involving a limited ability to learn to be educated, and to be trained for useful productive employment as certified by a State Vocational Rehabilitation agency under section 213.3102(t) of Schedule A
91. Mental or emotional illness (A history of treatment for mental or emotional problems.
92. Severe distortion of limbs and/or spine (e.g., dwarfism, kyphosis [severe distortion of back])
93. Disfigurement of face, hands, or feet (e.g., distortion of features on skin, such as those caused by burns, gunshot injuries, and birth defects [gross facial birthmarks, club feet, etc])
94. Learning disability (A disorder in one or more of the processes involved in understanding, perceiving, or using language or concepts [spoken or written]; e.g., dyslexia).

Instructions for Optional Application for Federal Employment - OF 612

You may apply for most Federal jobs with a resume, an Optional Application for Federal Employment (OF 612), or other written format. If your resume or application does not provide all the information requested on this form and in the job vacancy announcement, you may lose consideration for a job. Type or print clearly in black ink. Help speed the selection process by keeping your application brief and sending only the requested information. **If essential to attach additional pages, include your name and Social Security Number on each page.**

• For information on Federal employment, including alternative formats for persons with disabilities and veterans' preference, contact the U.S. Office of Personnel Management at 478-757-3000, TDD 478-744-2299, or via the Internet at www.USAJOBS.opm.gov.

• If you served on active duty in the United States Military and were separated under honorable conditions, you may be eligible for veterans' preference. To receive preference, if your service began after October 15, 1976, you must have a Campaign Badge, Expeditionary Medal, or a service-connected disability. Veterans' preference is not a factor for Senior Executive Service jobs or when competition is limited to status candidates (current or former career or career-conditional Federal employees).

• Most Federal jobs require United States citizenship and also that males over age 18 born after December 31, 1959, have registered with the Selective Service System or have an exemption.

• The law prohibits public officials from appointing, promoting, or recommending their relatives.

• Federal annuitants (military and civilian) may have their salaries or annuities reduced. Every employee must pay any valid delinquent debt or the agency may garnish their salary.

• Send your application to the office announcing the vacancy. If you have questions, contact the office identified in the announcement.

Privacy Act Statement

The U.S. Office of Personnel Management and other Federal agencies rate applicants for Federal jobs under the authority of sections 1104, 1302, 3301, 3304, 3320, 3361, 3393, and 3394 of title 5 of the United States Code. We need the information requested in this form and in the associated vacancy announcements to evaluate your qualifications. Other laws require us to ask about citizenship, military service, etc. In order to keep your records in order, we request your Social Security Number (SSN) under the authority of Public Law 104-134 (April 26, 1996). This law requires that any person doing business with the Federal government furnish an SSN or tax identification number. This is an amendment to title 31, Section 7701. Failure to furnish the requested information may delay or prevent action on your application. We use your SSN to seek information about you from employers, schools, banks, and others who know you. We may use your SSN in studies and computer matching with other Government files. If you do not give us your SSN or any other information requested, we cannot process your application. Also, incomplete addresses and ZIP Codes will slow processing. We may confirm information from your records with prospective nonfederal employers concerning tenure of employment, civil service status, length of service, and date and nature of action for separation as shown on personnel action forms of specifically identified individuals.

Public Burden Statement

We estimate the public reporting burden for this collection will vary from 20 to 240 minutes with an average of 40 minutes per response, including time for reviewing instructions, searching existing data sources, gathering data, and completing and reviewing the information. Send comments regarding the burden statement or any other aspect of the collection of information, including suggestions for reducing this burden to the U.S. Office of Personnel Management (OPM), OPM Forms Officer, Washington, DC 20415-7900. The OMB number, 3206-0219, is currently valid. OPM may not collect this information and you are not required to respond, unless this number is displayed. Do not send completed application forms to this address. Follow directions provided in the vacancy announcement(s).

THE FEDERAL GOVERNMENT IS AN EQUAL OPPORTUNITY EMPLOYER

OPTIONAL APPLICATION FOR FEDERAL EMPLOYMENT – OF 612

Form Approved
OMB No. 3206-0219

Section A – Applicant Information

★ Use Standard State Postal Codes (abbreviations). If outside the United States of America, and you do not have a military address, type or print "OV" in the State field (Block 6c) and fill in the Country field (Block 6e) below, leaving the Zip Code field (Block 6d) blank.

1. Job title in announcement	2. Grade(s) applying for	3. Announcement number
4a. Last name	4b. First and middle names	5. Social Security Number

6a. Mailing address ★

7. Phone numbers (include area code if within the United States of America)

7a. Daytime

6b. City	6c. State	6d. Zip Code	7b. Evening

6e. Country (if not within the United States of America)

8. Email address (if available)

Section B – Work Experience

Describe your paid and nonpaid work experience related to this job for which you are applying. Do not attach job description.

1. Job title (if Federal, include series and grade)

2. From (mm/yyyy)	3. To (mm/yyyy)	4. Salary per $	5. Hours per week

6. Employer's name and address

7. Supervisor's name and phone number
7a. Name
7b. Phone

8. May we contact your current supervisor?   Yes ☐   No ☐
If we need to contact your current supervisor before making an offer, we will contact you first.

9. Describe your duties and accomplishments

Section C – Additional Work Experience

1. Job title (if Federal, include series and grade)

2. From (mm/yyyy)	3. To (mm/yyyy)	4. Salary per $	5. Hours per week

6. Employer's name and address

7. Supervisor's name and phone number
7a. Name
7b. Phone

8. Describe your duties and accomplishments

U.S. Office of Personnel Management
Previous edition usable

NSN 7540-01-351-9178
50612-101

Page 1 of 2

Optional Form 612
Revised December 2002

www.petersons.com/arco

Section D – Education

1. Last High School (HS)/GED school. Give the school's name, city, state, ZIP Code (if known), and year diploma or GED received:

2. Mark highest level completed: Some HS ☐   HS/GED ☐   Associate ☐   Bachelor ☐   Master ☐   Doctoral ☐

3. Colleges and universities attended. Do not attach a copy of your transcript unless requested.

	Total Credits Earned Semester Quarter	Major(s)	Degree (if any), Year Received
3a. Name			
City State Zip Code			
3b. Name			
City State Zip Code			
3c. Name			
City State Zip Code			

Section E – Other Qualifications

Job-related training courses (give title and year). Job-related skills (other languages, computer software/hardware, tools, machinery, typing speed, etc.). Job-related certificates and licenses (current only). Job-related honors, awards, and special accomplishments (publications, memberships in professional/honor societies, leadership activities, public speaking, and performance awards). Give dates, but do **not** send documents unless requested.

Section F – General

1a. Are you a U.S. citizen?   Yes ☐   No ☐   ➔   1b. If no, give the Country of your citizenship

2a. Do you claim veterans' preference?   No ☐   Yes ☐   ➔   If yes, mark your claim of 5 or 10 points below.

2b.   5 points ☐   ➔   Attach your *Report of Separation from Active Duty* (DD 214) or other proof.

2c.   10 points ☐   ➔   Attach an *Application for 10-Point Veterans' Preference* (SF 15) and proof required.

3. Were you ever a Federal civilian employee?   No ☐   Yes ☐   ➔   If yes, list highest civilian grade for the following:

3a. Series	3b. Grade	3c. From *(mm/yyyy)*	3d. To *(mm/yyyy)*

4. Are you eligible for reinstatement based on career or career-conditional Federal status?   No ☐   Yes ☐
   If requested in the vacancy announcement, attach *Notification of Personnel Action* (SF 50), as proof.

Section G – Applicant Certification

I certify that, to the best of my knowledge and belief, all of the information on and attached to this application is true, correct, complete, and made in good faith. I understand that false or fraudulent information on or attached to this application may be grounds for not hiring me or for firing me after I begin work, and may be punishable by fine or imprisonment. I understand that any information I give may be investigated.

1a. Signature	1b. Date *(mm/dd/yyyy)*

Print Form   Save Form   Clear Form

job training, job experience, and life experience. Typically, the Experience Paper permits no identification by name, sex, or race; the only identifying mark is your social security number. The purpose of this procedure is to avoid permitting bias of any sort to enter into the weighting of responses. The Experience Paper generally follows a short form of application that does include a name. When the rating process is completed, the forms are coordinated by means of the social security number.

- **Filing dates, location, and fee.** For some positions you can file your application at any time. Others have deadlines. If you file too early or too late, your application will not be considered. More often, your application must be received by the last date. If you are mailing your application, allow five full business days for it to get there on time. Place of filing will be stated right on the Notice. Get the address right! Most applications may be filed by mail, but occasionally in-person filing is specified. Follow directions. Federal and postal positions require no filing fee. Most, but not all, other government jobs do charge a fee for processing your application. The fee is not always the same. Be sure to check this out. If the Notice specifies "money order only," plan to purchase a money order. Be sure the money order is made out properly. If you send or present a personal check, your application will be rejected without consideration. Of course, you would never mail cash; but if the announcement specifies "money order only," you cannot submit cash even in person.

- **How to qualify.** This portion of the Notice will tell you the basis on which the candidate will be chosen. Some examination scores consist of a totaling up of weighted education and experience factors. This type of examination, called "an unassembled exam" because you do not come to one place to take the exam, is based upon your responses on the application and supplementary forms. Obviously, these must be very complete for you to get full credit for all you have learned and accomplished. The Notice may tell you of a qualifying exam, an exam you must pass in addition to scoring high on an unassembled, written, or performance test. Or, the Notice may tell you of a competitive exam, written, performance, or both. The competitive exam may be described in very general terms or may be described in detail. It is even possible that a few sample questions will be attached. If the date of the exam has been set, that date will appear on the Notice.

The Application Process

The first step to becoming a Foreign Service Officer is taking the Foreign Service Written Exam. The written examination is given throughout the United States and at Foreign Service posts abroad. Application forms for the examination (DS-1950), Form OF-612, and the form on which applicants must write a "Statement of Interest" are included in a separate booklet, which may be obtained from college and university placement offices, from regional offices of the Office of Personnel Management, or by logging on to www.careers.state.gov/officer/register.html. Candidates whose applications are accepted are sent tickets of admission that provide the address of their assigned examination site at least two weeks before the examination date.

Sometimes it is
sufficient to have
your application
postmarked by the
last day for filing.

The exam measures your knowledge of subjects determined to be necessary for performing the tasks required of a Foreign Service Officer. There are multiple-choice questions on topics ranging from U.S. Government to psychology to American culture to management and finance. The exam includes an English usage section, a biographic inventory, and an essay exercise.

No other examination can be substituted for the Foreign Service written examination. However, the U.S. Department of State will provide reasonable accommodations for qualified applicants with disabilities. Accommodation may include a reader, a person to record answers, a separate testing room, extra testing time, a Braille or cassette version of the test, and/or large-print versions of the exam. Decisions for these and other accommodations are made on a case-by-case basis.

NOTE

Makeup
examinations cannot
be authorized, no
matter how valid an
applicant's reason
for missing the
scheduled
examination.

Also, applicants whose religious beliefs preclude them from taking the examination on a Saturday may apply to test on Sunday. The request for a candidate to take the exam on Sunday must be sent in writing. You must send a letter from your cleric to confirm your affiliation with a recognized body that observes its Sabbath throughout the year on Saturday. This letter should be sent with the completed paper registration form using the pre-addressed envelope in the registration book. For this request, please do not choose online registration as the method for registering as it will delay processing and possibly not meet registration deadline dates. The required documentation needs to accompany and be submitted at the same time as the paper registration form. Saturday Sabbath observers may register to take the exam on a Sunday. Alternate dates for the examination will not be authorized for any reason other than for Saturday Sabbath observance. For more information, go to www.careers.state.gov/officer/register.html.

Filing Your Application

You may apply for most jobs with a resume or the Optional Application for Federal Employment (OF-612). It is essential that you follow the instructions carefully for applying, and that your application contains the following:

- **Job Information:** The announcement number, title, and grade

- **Personal Information:** Full name, mailing address (with Zip Code,), day and evening phone numbers (with area code), social security number, country of citizenship, veterans' preference, reinstatement eligibility, highest Federal civilian grade held

- **Education:** High school name, city and state; colleges or universities, name, city, and state; majors and type and year of any degrees received (if no degree, show total credits earned and indicate whether semester or quarter hours)

- **Work Experience:** Job title, duties and accomplishments, employer's name and address, supervisor's name and phone number, starting and ending dates (month and year), hours per week, salary and whether or not your current supervisor may be contacted (prepare a separate entry for each job)

- **Other Qualifications:** Job-related training courses (title and year), job-related skills, job-related certificates and licenses, job-related honors, awards, foreign language proficiency, and special accomplishments

Statement of Interest

The Board of Examiners for the Foreign Service requires that all applicants for the Foreign Service Written Examination submit a brief (one typed page maximum) Statement of Interest in a career in the Foreign Service. The statement should be TYPED or WRITTEN NEATLY in ink, with the applicant's name in the upper right-hand corner of the page. The Statement of Interest should explain the applicant's motivation for taking the Foreign Service Written Examination and comment on the quotation reproduced at the top of the form provided. A reduced facsimile of this form appears below.

Name: _____
Address: _____
_____

Statement of Interest

Former Secretary of State James A. Baker III has called for "a new generation of diplomats who understand the policy implications of science, oceanography and the environment, and economics and economic statesmanship, who can and will think broadly about the impact of computers, agricultural technology, and nuclear science in a changing world. At the same time, Foreign Service officers will continue to perform their traditional functions of political and economic reporting, administrative management, and providing consular services to American citizens and foreign residents." In the space below, describe your interest in such a career.

Select a Career Track

Foreign Service Officers are considered Generalists, but, as discussed in Chapter 2, all Officers enter in one of five career tracks: Management, Consular, Economic, Political, and Public Diplomacy. This is an important decision, and applicants should carefully inform themselves before making a career track choice in the registration for the exam. Successful candidates will take the second step—an Oral Assessment with reference to their chosen career track. Hiring is based on requirements in each of the five career tracks, and candidates compete for appointment from their chosen career track, where their composite Oral Assessment score determines their relative position on the career track register. In FY 2004, the Department of State's goal was to hire 103 Management Officers, 81 Consular Officers, 113 Economic Officers, 119 Political Officers, and 124 Public Diplomacy Officers. The Written Examination covers job knowledge in each of these career tracks but does not test specifically in any one area.

The Foreign Service Written Examination

Upon receipt of your registration, you will be notified of the exact time and location of the exam, and you will receive an admission ticket. You must bring your admission ticket with you to the test location. The introductory process and exam will take all day. You might be nervous about taking the exam, but that is normal and quite understandable. When you think about it, you have nothing to lose and everything to gain. When you show up to take your exam, make sure you have your admission ticket, a black pen, several No. 2 pencils, and valid identification such as a photo ID card or a driver's license with photo.

Out of the 15,000 persons who take the examination each year, approximately 250 may eventually be appointed as Foreign Service Officer (FSO) Career Candidates of Classes 6, 5, or 4, depending on their qualifications and experience. Regardless of age and experience, appointments under this program cannot be made at a level higher than Class 4 (FS-4).

Eligibility Requirements

To be eligible for the written examination, the applicant must be:

1. Between 20 and 59 years old on the date of examination. Appointment to the Foreign Service must take place before the candidate's 60th birthday
2. A citizen of the United States
3. Available for worldwide assignment, including Washington, D.C.

No specific educational background is required. Success in the written examination and the subsequent oral assessment requires a broad knowledge of foreign and domestic affairs and U.S. history, government, foreign policy, and culture.

Most, but not all, successful candidates have earned at least a bachelor's degree. In recent years, about 65 percent have had advanced degrees in international relations, economics, business administration, law, journalism, and other fields. Foreign Service Officers have graduated from hundreds of large and small colleges and universities, and many have had work experience in various fields before their appointments.

Content

The written examination consists of the following multiple-choice tests for all candidates:

A *Knowledge* test designed to measure a candidate's breadth of understanding of the institutions and concepts that are basic to the development of the United States and of other countries, and knowledge of subjects basic to the functions of the Foreign Service.

The candidates will likely be tested on the following subjects:

- Knowledge of the historical antecedents of international affairs to aid understanding of foreign governments and societies
- Knowledge of world geography to understand the geographic context of foreign relations and U.S. foreign policy
- Knowledge of major events, institutions, and movements in the history of the United States to facilitate understanding the U.S. system of government
- Knowledge of the history of U.S. intellectual, artistic, and cultural life to interpret U.S. cultural life for foreign nationals
- Knowledge of social, cultural, political, and economic trends in the U.S.
- Knowledge of the U.S. political process and its impact on policy
- Knowledge of the U.S. Constitution and the structure of the U.S. Government
- Knowledge of the U.S. economic systems, their institutions and philosophical principles, to aid in interpreting U.S. policies and actions to foreign nationals
- Knowledge of the U.S. educational system
- Knowledge of the basic principles of economics
- Knowledge of major contemporary international economic and commercial issues to understand the impact of economic conditions on the host country and on U.S. programs and policy interests
- Knowledge of foreign political systems

A specialized knowledge of Foreign Service procedures and operations is not required, and no particular course of study or preparation is expected. Rather, the best background for the test is a good general education, political and cultural sensitivity, and the habit of reading widely.

An *English Expression* test measures skill in written English. It contains four sections of questions that test ability to correct sentences, express ideas clearly and accurately, revise sentences according to instruction, and organize information logically.

Success in the Foreign Service requires a strong command of the English language. All Foreign Service Officers must be able to speak and write clearly, concisely, and correctly. The success of much of their work depends on their ability to speak and write

TIP

The best preparation for the Knowledge section of the exam is a good general education, including courses in history, government, geography, economics, literature, international relations, and business and public administration.

persuasively and to analyze and defend policies and proposals. The Departments of State and Commerce give high priority to English-language skills in selecting officers and evaluating their performance.

The *Biographical Questionnaire*, which constitutes the third part of the written exam, is set up to look like a multiple-choice test and is timed like a test, but it is not a test at all. There are no right or wrong answers. The only way to prepare for the test is to gather statistical records from your school career and recall what you have achieved in your post-student years.

The section consists of 120 questions to be answered in 30 minutes. Some questions will refer to your high school days. They ask about your best and worst grades, your favorite courses, extracurricular activities, etc. A series of questions similar to the high school questions in their scope and in the topics they cover will refer to college days. The remaining questions refer to your working life or college relationships. These questions ask for your assessment of the impression you make upon others. About half of the questions ask what you think your peers think of you; the other half ask similar questions with respect to your supervisors or teachers. You will not have much time to dwell on these questions. Just do your best to answer candidly and consistently.

In a nutshell, the Biographical Questionnaire measures the candidate's experience, skills, and achievements in school, employment, and other activities. The questionnaire does not penalize candidates who have not gone to college, have no previous work experience, are younger or older, or have other varied patterns of education and experience, but rather credits candidates for what they have achieved relative to the opportunities they have had. The questionnaire is based on research on the actual characteristics of successful people in federal government professional and administrative occupations. It is designed to supplement the other portions of the examination by providing an assessment of additional job-related characteristics gained through experience, skills, and achievements.

Knowledge of foreign languages is not required for appointment, but once hired, all new officers must demonstrate professional competency in at least one foreign language before the end of their initial probationary period. If necessary, an officer attends classes at the Foreign Service Institute, which offers training in over 40 languages. Those who enter with language abilities are tested within 30 days of appointment and, if found proficient in certain designated languages, may receive a higher salary. The Department of State particularly seeks persons with knowledge of "hard" or "exotic" languages (e.g., Arabic, Chinese, Russian). Candidates without prior foreign language ability are appointed as language probationers, and must acquire acceptable language competency before tenure can be granted.

In addition to the multiple-choice tests, an *Essay* is used to evaluate the candidate's ability to analyze a topic, organize and develop appropriate ideas, and then express these ideas in a cogent essay. The candidate chooses one topic from a list of five. These topics cover U.S. and/or International social systems, customs, culture, history, education, religion, employment, and so on. The candidate's ability to analyze the subject is just as important as the correct use of grammar. (See Appendix A for the "The Essentials of English Grammar.") The Essay is scored only for those candidates who pass the three multiple-choice tests.

It is also recommended that you have at least one college course in each of the following subjects:

- Comparative Politics
- English Composition
- Geography
- International Affairs
- International Trade/World Finance/Economic Development
- Non-Western History
- Principles of Economics
- U.S. Economic, Social, and/or Intellectual History
- U.S. Foreign Policy and International Relations
- U.S. History
- U.S. Political System (Legislative Process, Role of President, PACs, etc.)
- U.S. Political Systems
- Western Civilization

The official sample questions later in this book are included in order to give candidates an indication of the types of questions asked in the written examination and the rationale for each. Three full-length simulated Foreign Service Exams are provided in Part II of this book. The number of candidates who pass the examination each year is determined by the number of officers needed by the Foreign Service in subsequent years. Those who do not pass may take the examination again the following year, if they wish to do so. No limit is imposed on the number of times a candidate may compete.

Preparing for the Exam

If your application is accepted, you will be assigned an exam date. The exam might be either a paper-and-pencil exam or a performance exam. The exam depends on the nature of the job. Applicants for most jobs will take only a written test. The written test is most frequently a multiple-choice test, one in which the test-taker chooses the best of four or five answer choices and marks its number on a separate answer sheet. Multiple-choice tests are machinescored. Machine scoring insures accuracy and objectivity. No one can misinterpret your answers. Machine scoring also allows for many applicants to be rated at the same time. It speeds up the process, though if you are waiting to hear about your job you may doubt this fact.

Occasionally, the written test will consist of an essay portion along with the multiple-choice section or even of essays alone. Essays usually appear at levels above initial entry level where there are fewer applicants and fewer papers to score. On an essay, the examiners are looking for indications that you can organize your thoughts and can express them effectively in writing.

If you are called for an exam, arrive promptly and dress appropriately. Neatness is always imperative. However, you do not need to "dress up" for a performance exam or a written exam. If you will do manual work for your performance exam, wear clean work clothes. For a written exam, neat, casual clothing is fine.

Test-Taking Techniques

It goes without saying that you cannot learn the subject matter of the Foreign Service Officer Exam in a week's time, much less during an all-night cram session. Your success on the Knowledge portion of the exam is based on a lifetime of learning, reading, discussing, and thinking.

TIP

Some brushing up on the principles of punctuation, grammar, and English usage will raise your score on the English Expression questions.

Many factors enter into a test score. The most important factor should be ability to answer the questions, which in turn indicates the ability to learn and perform the duties of the job. Assuming that you have this ability, knowing what to expect on the exam and familiarity with techniques of effective test-taking should give you the confidence you need to do your best on the exam.

There is no quick substitute for long-term study and development of your skills and abilities to prepare you for doing well on tests. However, there are some steps you can take to help you do the very best that you are prepared to do. Some of these steps are done before the test, and some are followed when you are taking the test. Knowing these steps is often called being "test-wise." Following these steps may help you feel more confident as you take the actual test.

"Test-wiseness" is a general term that simply means being familiar with some good procedures to follow when getting ready for and taking a test. The procedures fall into four major areas:

❶ Being prepared
❷ Avoiding careless errors
❸ Managing your time
❹ Guessing

BE PREPARED

Don't make the test harder than it has to be by not preparing yourself. You are taking a very important step in preparation by reading this book and taking the sample tests that are included. This will help you to become familiar with the tests and the kinds of questions you will have to answer.

As you use this book, read the sample questions and directions for taking the test carefully. Then, when you take the sample tests, time yourself as you will be timed in the real test.

As you are working on the sample questions, don't look at the correct answers before you try to answer them on your own. This can fool you into thinking you understand a question when you really don't. Try it on your own first. Then compare your answer with the one given. Remember, in a sample test, you are your own grader; you don't gain anything by pretending to understand something you really don't.

On the examination day assigned to you, allow the test itself to be the main attraction of the day. Do not squeeze it in between other activities. Be sure to bring your admission card, identification, and pencils, as instructed. Prepare these the night before so that you are not flustered by a last-minute search. Arrive rested, relaxed, and on time. In fact, plan to arrive a little bit early. Leave plenty of time for traffic tie-ups or other complications that might upset you and interfere with your test performance.

In the test room, the examiner will hand out forms for you to fill out. He or she will give you the instructions that you must follow in taking the examination. The examiner will tell you how to fill in the grids on the forms. Time limits and timing signals will be explained. If you do not understand any of the examiner's instructions, ASK. It would be ridiculous to score less than your best because of poor communication.

At the examination, you must follow instructions exactly. Fill in the grids on the forms carefully and accurately. Misgridding may lead to loss of veterans' credits to which you may be entitled or misaddressing of your test results. Do not begin until you are told to begin. Stop as soon as the examiner tells you to stop. Do not turn pages until you are told to do so. Do not go back to parts you have already completed. Any infraction of the rules is considered cheating. If you cheat, your test paper will not be scored, and you will not be eligible for appointment.

The answer sheet for most multiple-choice exams is machine scored. You cannot give any explanations to the machine, so you must fill out the answer sheet clearly and correctly.

HOW TO MARK YOUR ANSWER SHEET

❶ Blacken your answer space firmly and completely.

❷ Mark only one answer for each question. If you mark more than one answer, you will be considered wrong, even if one of the answers is correct.

❸ If you change your mind, you must erase your mark. Attempting to cross out an incorrect answer will not work. You must erase any incorrect answer completely. An incomplete erasure might be read as a second answer.

④ All of your answering should be in the form of blackened spaces. The machine cannot read English. Do not write any notes in the margins.

⑤ Answer each question in the right place. Question 1 must be answered in space 1; question 52 in space 52. If you should skip an answer space and mark a series of answers in the wrong places, you must erase all those answers and do the questions over, marking your answers in the proper places. You cannot afford to use the limited time in this way. Therefore, as you answer each question, look at its number and check that you are marking your answer in the space with the same number.

AVOID CARELESS ERRORS

Don't reduce your score by making careless mistakes. ALWAYS read the instructions for each test section carefully, even if you think you already know what the directions are. You will notice that we stress throughout the book the importance of reading and fully understanding directions for the different question types before you go into the actual exam. It will not only reduce errors, but it will also save you time.

What if you don't understand the directions? You risk getting the answers wrong for a whole test section. As an example, vocabulary questions can sometimes test synonyms (words that have similar meanings), and sometimes, test antonyms (words with opposite meanings). You can see how a mistake in following directions could lead to a whole section of incorrect answers.

If you have time, reread any complicated instructions after you do the first few questions to check that you really understand them. Of course, whenever you are allowed, ask the examiner to clarify anything you don't understand.

Other careless mistakes affect only the response to particular questions. This often happens with arithmetic questions, but can happen with other questions as well. This type of error, called a "response error," usually stems from a momentary lapse of concentration.

Here is one example:

The question reads: "The capital of Massachusetts is ...." The answer is (D) Boston, and you mark (B) because "B" is the first letter of the word "Boston."

Here is another example:

The question reads: "$8 - 5 = ...$" The answer is (A) 3, but you mark (C) because it is the third letter in the answer choices.

A common error in reading comprehension questions is bringing your own information into the subject. For example, you may encounter a passage that discusses a subject you know something about. While this can make the passage easier to read, it can also tempt you to rely on your own knowledge about the subject. You must rely on information within the passage for your answers. In fact, sometimes the "wrong answer" for the questions is based on true information about the subject not given in the passage. Since the test-makers are testing your reading ability, rather than your general knowledge of the subject, an answer based on information not contained in the passage is considered incorrect.

MANAGE YOUR TIME

Although you are usually not expected to finish all of the questions, you should at least get an idea of how much time you should spend on each question in order to answer them all. For example, if there are 60 questions to answer and you have 30 minutes, you will have about 30 seconds to answer each question.

Keep track of the time on your watch or the room clock, but do not fixate on the time. Your task is to answer questions. Do not spend too much time on any one question. If you get stuck, do not take the question as a personal challenge. Either guess or skip the question entirely, marking the question as a skip and taking care to skip the answer space on the answer sheet. If there is time at the end of the exam or section, you can return and answer any questions you skipped.

MULTIPLE-CHOICE QUESTIONS

Almost all of the tests given on civil service exams are given in a multiple-choice format. This means that you normally have four or five answer choices. There is a basic technique to answering these types of questions. Once you master this technique, you will find the questions much less stressful.

First, there should only be one correct answer. Since these tests are given time and again, and the test-developers have a sense of which questions work and which questions don't work, it is rare that your choices will be ambiguous. They may be complex and somewhat confusing, but there will still be only one right answer.

The first step is to look at the question without looking at the answer choices. Now answer the question. Once you have come up with the answer, look at the answer choices. If your answer is one of the choices, you're probably correct. Usually, your first choice is the correct one. If you go back and change your answer—unless you are 100 percent sure that the change is correct—you will more than likely end up with the wrong answer. The bottom line is to follow your instinct. It's not 100 percent infallible, but there is a strong possibility that you've selected the right answer.

When answering math questions, you should first solve the problem. If your answer is among the choices, you're probably correct. Don't ignore things like the proper function signs (addition, subtraction, multiplication, and division), negative and positive numbers, and so on.

TIP

Before you begin the exam, take a moment to plan your progress through the test.

Suppose you don't know the correct answer. You can then use the "process of elimination." It's a time-honored technique for test-takers. There is always one correct answer. If an answer choice seems highly unlikely, eliminate it. By eliminating as many answer choices as possible, you can increase your odds of getting the correct answer. If you have to pick an answer from five answer choices, you only have a 20 percent chance of being correct. With four choices, you have a 25 percent chance. But if, after eliminating some answer choices, you are left with only two answers, you now have a 50 percent chance of getting it right.

SHOULD YOU GUESS?

You may be wondering whether or not it is wise to guess when you are not sure of an answer (even if you've reduced the odds to 50 percent) or whether it is better to skip the question when you are not certain. The wisdom of guessing depends on the scoring method for the particular examination. If the scoring is "rights only," that is, one point for each correct answer and no subtraction for wrong answers, then by all means you should guess. Read the question and all of the answer choices carefully. Eliminate those answer choices that you are certain are wrong. Then guess from among the remaining choices. You cannot gain a point if you leave the answer space blank; you may gain a point with an educated guess or even with a lucky guess. In fact, it is foolish to leave any spaces blank on a test that counts "rights only." If it appears that you are about to run out of time before completing such an exam, mark all the remaining blanks with the same letter. According to the law of averages, you should get some portion of those questions right.

If the scoring method is "rights minus wrongs," a wrong answer counts heavily against you. In this case, do not rush to fill answer spaces randomly at the end. Work as quickly as possible while concentrating on accuracy. Keep working carefully until time is called. Then stop and leave the remaining answer spaces blank.

When guessing the answers to multiple-choice questions, take a second to eliminate those answers that are obviously wrong, then quickly consider and guess from the remaining choices. As discussed, the fewer choices there are from which to guess, the better the odds of guessing correctly. Once you have decided to make a guess, whether an educated guess or a wild stab, do it right away and move on. Don't keep thinking about it and wasting time. You should always mark the test questions at which you guess so you can return later and try to answer them more confidently.

For those questions that are scored by subtracting a fraction of a point for each wrong answer, the decision as to whether or not to guess is really up to you. A correct answer gives you one point; a skipped space gains you nothing at all, but costs you nothing except the chance of getting the answer right. A wrong answer costs you 1/4 point. If you are really uncomfortable with guessing, you may skip a question, BUT you must then remember to skip its answer space as well. The risk of losing your place if you skip questions is so great that we advise you to guess even if you are not sure of the answer. Our suggestion is that you answer every question in order, even if you have to guess. It is better to lose a few 1/4 points for wrong guesses than to lose valuable seconds figuring out where you started marking answers in the wrong place, erasing, and remarking answers. On the other hand, do not mark random answers at the end. Work steadily until time is up.

QUICK TIPS

1. Get to the test center early.

2. Listen to the test administrator and follow all instructions carefully.

3. Read every word of the instructions. Read every word of every question.

4. Mark your answers completely. Do not use the test paper to work out your answers.

5. Mark only ONE answer for each question, even if you think that more than one answer is correct. If you mark more than one answer, the scoring machine will consider you wrong.

6. If you change your answer, erase it completely.

7. If your exam permits you to use scratch paper or the margins of the test booklet as scratch paper, don't forget to mark the answer on the answer sheet. Only the answer sheet is scored.

8. Check often to ensure that the question number matches the answer space and that you have not skipped a space by mistake.

9. Guess appropriately based on how the test will be scored.

10. Stay alert. Be careful not to mark a wrong answer just because you were not concentrating.

11. Do not panic. If you cannot finish any part before time is up, do not worry. If you are accurate, you can do well even without finishing. It is even possible to earn a scaled score of 100 without entirely finishing an exam part if you are very accurate. At any rate, do not let your performance on any one section affect your performance on another section.

12. Check and recheck, time permitting. If you finish before time is up, use the remaining time to check that each question is answered in the right space and that there is only one answer for each question. Return to the difficult questions and try to answer them more confidently.

NOTE

Prior to the exam, ask the test administrator what scoring method will be used. You can then adjust your test-taking strategy accordingly.

Scoring

If your exam is a short-answer exam such as those often used by the private sector, your answers will be graded by a personnel officer trained in grading test questions. If you blacken spaces on the separate answer sheet accompanying a multiple-choice exam, your answer sheet will be machine scanned or hand scored using a punched card stencil. Then a raw score will be calculated using the scoring formula that applies to that test or test portion—rights only, rights minus wrongs, or rights minus a fraction of wrongs. Raw scores on test parts are then added together for a total raw score.

A raw score is not a final score. The raw score is not the score that finds its way onto an eligibility list. The civil service testing authority, Postal Service, or other testing body converts raw scores to a scaled score according to an unpublicized formula of its own. The scaling formula allows for slight differences in level of difficulty of questions from one exam to another and allows for equating the scores of all candidates. The entire process of converting from a raw to scaled score is confidential information. The score you receive is neither your number right, your raw score, nor a percentage. It is a scaled score. If you are entitled to veterans' service points, these are added to your passing scaled score to boost your rank on the eligibility list. Veterans' points are added only to passing scores. A failing score cannot be brought to passing level by adding veterans' points. The score earned plus veterans' service points, if any, is the score that finds its place on the rank order eligibility list. Highest scores go to the top of the list.

Oral Assessment

Candidates who pass the written examination at the designated level are eligible for a day-long Oral Assessment that includes a variety of simulation techniques, examinations, and appraisals. Candidates are not in direct competition with each other. Rather, they are judged by a panel of trained Foreign Service examiners against a uniform and consistent set of standards. Relevant observations about each candidate are reported, discussed, scored, and integrated by the examiners. The assessment day concludes with a personal interview.

The assessment procedures are based on current job analyses of Foreign Service work and the knowledge, skills, abilities, and personal characteristics necessary to perform that work. These procedures measure:

- **Written Communication.** To write concise, well-organized, grammatically correct, effective, and persuasive English in a limited amount of time.

- **Oral Communication.** To speak fluently in a concise, grammatically correct, organized, precise, and persuasive manner; to convey nuances of meaning accurately; to use appropriate styles of communication to fit the audience and purpose.

- **Information Integration and Analysis.** To absorb and retain complex information drawn from a variety of sources; to draw reasoned conclusions from analysis and synthesis of available information; to evaluate the importance, reliability, and usefulness of information; to remember details of a meeting or event without the benefit of notes.

- **Planning and Organizing.** To prioritize and order tasks effectively; to employ a systematic approach to achieving objectives; to make appropriate use of limited resources.

- **Judgment.** To discern what is appropriate, practical, and realistic in a given situation; to weigh relative merits of competing demands.

- **Resourcefulness.** To formulate creative alternatives or solutions to resolve problems; to show flexibility in response to unanticipated circumstances.

- **Initiative and Leadership.** To recognize and assume responsibility for work that needs to be done; to persist in the completion of a task; to influence significant group activity, direction, or opinion; to motivate others to participate in the activity one is leading.

- **Experience and Motivation.** To demonstrate knowledge, skills, or other attributes gained from previous experience of relevance to the Foreign Service.

- **Working with Others.** To interact in a constructive, cooperative, and harmonious manner; to work effectively as a team player; to establish positive relationships and gain the confidence of others; to use humor as appropriate.

- **Composure.** To stay calm, poised, and effective in stressful or difficult situations; to think on one's feet, adjusting quickly to changing situations; to maintain self-control.

- **Quantitative Analysis.** To identify, compile, analyze, and draw correct conclusions from pertinent data; to recognize patterns or trends in numerical data; and perform simple mathematical operations.

- **Objectivity and Integrity.** To be fair and honest; to avoid deceit, favoritism, and discrimination; to present issues frankly and fully, without injecting subjective bias; to work without letting personal bias prejudice actions.

- **Cultural Adaptability.** To work and communicate effectively and harmoniously with persons of other cultures, value systems, political beliefs, and economic circumstances; to recognize and respect differences in new and different cultural environments.

Candidates are evaluated solely against these criteria by four assessors who observe the performance of candidates in a variety of situations designed to enable the candidates to demonstrate the requisite skills. The assessors are Foreign Service Officers from various career tracks with a wide variety of experience in the geographic and functional Bureaus of the Department. Assessors receive training from professional consultants on how to conduct assessments in an objective manner in which the candidate's performance is observed and where the candidate's score correlates to an established performance standard.

Normally, a candidate must participate in the assessment process within 12 months of passing the written examination. However, if the candidate is outside the United States

NOTE

The Oral Assessment is not an adversarial process. Candidates do not compete against one another but instead are judged on their capacity to demonstrate the skills and abilities necessary to be an effective Foreign Service Officer.

for part or all of the 12-month period following the written examination, the candidacy may be extended upon authorization of the Board of Examiners. In such cases, the candidacy will be terminated if the candidate does not take the assessment within three months of returning to the United States.

Candidates who are invited to the Oral Assessment must complete and bring to the Oral Assessment the DS-1950 application form and their Statement of Interest. Those who do not bring these documents with them will not be assessed. There are no other documents required at this time. Candidates who ultimately receive a conditional offer of employment will be given additional required documents during the employment phase of their candidacy.

Oral Assessment Day Schedule

This section describes the Oral Assessment day as it has been conducted during the last several years. However, nothing in government is immutable, and the Board of Examiners for the Foreign Service is currently revising its assessment day procedures. The specific exercises, questions, and timing will be different for your assessment. However, the goal of the assessment to identify those candidates with the skills and characteristics that make for success in the Foreign Service will remain the same. Careful attention to the criteria for evaluating candidates and to our advice for handling each stage of the oral assessment will stand you in excellent stead.

Candidates must report to their assigned Assessment Center at 7:00 a.m. on their scheduled day. The assessment may end as late as 6:00 p.m. for successful candidates. The letter or e-mail message that advises candidates that they have passed the Foreign Service Written Exam also advises candidates what documents they need to bring to the Assessment Center. This list of documents can be downloaded at www.careers.state.gov/fs/employmentforms.html. In addition to the listed documents, candidates are also asked to bring the social security numbers of family members who might be traveling with them overseas. This will help the medical clearance process. Provisions for candidates with disabilities will be made available at each Assessment Center but must be arranged with the U.S. Department of State's Board of Examiners in advance. Keep in mind that this is an evaluation, not a job interview. The receptionist will give you information on how the day is organized, pass out individual schedules, and so on. An assessor will welcome the candidates and brief them on the conduct of the various component examinations and exercises.

Assessment Day Sites

The oral assessment is given in Washington, D.C., and also in several major cities throughout the U.S. For the testing cycle beginning in August 2004 and continuing into late Spring or early Summer 2005, other assessment sites include Seattle, San Francisco, Atlanta, and Chicago. The assessment calendar depends upon the location. In Washington, D.C., it usually runs from March to September. In other locations, the opening and closing dates will differ from city to city. You are responsible for your own travel expenses.

How Should You Dress?

Select clothes that approximate the dress code of the profession you wish to enter. You would not interview for a professional position with a corporation or law firm clad in sneakers, T-shirt, and blue jeans. Likewise, you should not present yourself for the Oral Assessment in such casual attire. Men need not feel obliged to wear a three-piece, pinstripe suit. A sport jacket, tie, and slacks will do nicely for those who prefer a less formal look. Women may "dress for success" if they wish, in a conservative tailored suit, but they shouldn't hesitate to wear a less formal outfit: a dress or a blazer and skirt combination if they like it better. Candidates who like to dress in elegant clothes should by all means wear them for the assessment day, although this alone will not earn them a competitive advantage over their less elegant counterparts. Assessors know that most candidates are young and that few of them are rich. So just dress sensibly; beyond that, don't worry about your clothes.

How Should You Conduct Yourself before the Assessors?

This question comes up mainly in relation to the Oral Assessment, the only exercise which involves lengthy face-to-face interaction with the assessors. A manner of relaxed and pleasant courtesy will serve you best. The assessor is not your adversary. He or she has no trick questions to ask, no oral traps to set for you. Such tactics would be self—defeating; the assessor's purpose is to put you as much at ease as possible and to see how well you can perform free of crippling stage fright or similar emotional impediments. Assessors find good performances much more entertaining than bad ones. Granted, they will ask you some difficult questions; that is their role. But it is human nature to admire a deft response and to feel some discomfort at a clumsy one. You may find it hard to believe, but the assessors would rather see you pass than fail.

Can You Prepare for the Oral Assessment?

Candidates can most certainly prepare for the Oral Assessment, yet most candidates make little or no effort at advance preparation, according to experienced assessors. These assessors report surprise at how little most candidates know of the factual and theoretical material directly relevant to the profession for which they are being examined. With the kind of sustained effort that most successful students apply to their college semester finals, many otherwise blank spaces on the exam can be filled.

Quite a number of candidates convey an impression of competence and lively intelligence, yet they somehow fail to demonstrate their potential convincingly by their actual performance during the assessment day. This can be attributed to lack of any organized preparatory effort.

Here are a few suggested "dos and don'ts" for conducting yourself during your Oral Assessment:

- Don't give information about your personal background. This state of ignorance helps assessors to avoid bias in either direction. Candidates who use any pretext during the oral examination or elsewhere to insert some comments about their distinguished educational, social, or professional background are more likely to hurt than to help themselves.

- Do ask for clarification if you don't understand a question, but don't ask for it so often that you have little time left for your answer.

- Do keep your composure even if you know you have botched an answer. You'll have plenty of chances to recoup. In fact, if you remain confident and unperturbed, the assessors will likely admire your poise under pressure and you may gain as many points under the stability and adjustment dimension as your poor answer cost you under perspective and breadth of knowledge.

- If you are completely stumped by a particular question, don't hesitate to acknowledge your ignorance and to ask for another question from the same general knowledge area (economics, politics, etc.).

- Don't fight the question; answer it. If you think it is a bad question, disguise your sentiments and get on with the answer.

Oral Assessment Exercises

1. THE GROUP EXERCISE

Preparation Phase

For the first exercise of the day, candidates are brought together in a group of three to six to comprise an Embassy task force charged with allocating resources to competing projects in their host country. Candidates are given information concerning the individual project each is asked to present, as well as a package of common background materials consisting of the following:

- Memorandum from a senior U.S. Embassy official in one of various mythical countries appointing the candidate to a task force to consider proposals for use of scarce resources

- The U.S. Country Plan and Objectives

- Lists of senior U.S. Embassy and host government officials

- A map of the country and background notes

Candidates are given 30 minutes to read and absorb these materials; they may take notes. When the 30-minute preparation time is over, four assessors join the group and take seats in the corners of the room. At this point in the assessment, the assessors know nothing about the candidates. The assessors do not participate; they only observe the group exercise. Candidates are briefed on the ground rules and are invited to begin their individual project presentations in any order they choose; however, they are cautioned that projects are not to be compared or evaluated in the presentation phase. Each candidate has six minutes to present his or her project to the others, covering all relevant facets of the project, including both negative and positive points, U.S. interests, and required resources. Time may be left at the end of the presentation for questions from other candidates.

Discussion Phase

After the last presentation is made, the lead examiner informs the group that it is now entering the discussion phase of the exercise, the stage in which the candidates must reach a consensus on project selection and allocation of their limited resources.

In this phase, candidates discuss and debate the merits and/or drawbacks of the various projects in order to make recommendations to the Ambassador. Toward that end, the group negotiates and debates pros and cons with the goal of reaching, within the time allotted (20–25 minutes—depending on group size), a consensus on which projects should be supported and at what level.

The group exercise measures oral communication, objectivity and integrity, ability to work with others, information integration and analysis, planning, judgment, initiative, leadership, and composure. Strong candidates are those who keep in mind the objective of the exercise: to help the Ambassador decide how best to allocate limited U.S. Government resources among a number of worthy projects. They have the ability to integrate information not just about their own projects but also about projects presented by their colleagues. They may suggest original ideas and solutions. A good leader can draw out others and help move the group to consensus.

Active participation is essential to successful performance. Examiners cannot judge qualities they cannot see. Even if a candidate presents a clear project, lack of involvement in the discussion phase can make the difference when the scores are determined.

2. THE STRUCTURED INTERVIEW

All candidates participate individually in a Structured Interview conducted by two assessors. For this portion of the Oral Assessment, assessors will have reviewed the candidates' DS-1950 (Application for Employment), Statement of Interest, and stated career track preference. Candidates are expected to respond to questions based on their personal background, experience, and motivation.

This portion of the assessment consists of three testing modules lasting a total of approximately one hour.

Experience and Motivation Interview Phase

In this portion of the assessment, the candidate should convey to the examiners a clear and precise picture of him- or herself, including personality traits, and his or her understanding of the Foreign Service. The candidate's work experience and motivation to join the Foreign Service as well as cross-cultural skills are considered. Assessors will evaluate a candidate's potential to serve successfully as a Foreign Service Officer, including in the selected career track, by discussing what the candidate has done with the opportunities presented to this point in his or her life. Candidates must be succinct and persuasive in responding to the examiner's questions. Candidates should have previously informed themselves about the Foreign Service in general, and also about the work related to the career track they have selected.

Hypothetical Scenarios Phase

The second assessment module in the Structured Interview consists of a series of hypothetical scenarios designed to test the candidate's situational judgment.

Assessors will give the candidate a brief scenario to read that provides information about the country and the candidate's position in the embassy, setting the scene for the hypothetical situation. Assessors' questions test the candidate's interpersonal skills, problem-solving abilities, initiative, objectivity, judgment, planning and organizing skills, composure, and cultural adaptability. Although the problems presented in this exercise are hypothetical, they are closely related to real-life situations regularly encountered by Foreign Service Officers overseas. Candidates are advised, however, that, while the problems occur in a Foreign Service setting, candidates are not expected to know how an Embassy operates or to be familiar with government rules and regulations. They are asked to fashion a solution that employs good judgment and common sense.

The hypothetical scenarios challenge candidates to think quickly. Assessors look for a candidate who can organize for action, take responsibility, and respond to new situations creatively and effectively. While there is no single right or correct answer, a strong candidate will demonstrate mature thinking, recognize alternative approaches, and consider both the long- and short-term consequences of responses.

Past Behavior Interview Phase

In the final segment of the Structured Interview, the assessors ask the candidate a series of questions, to which the candidate should respond with examples from his or her own experience. The questions are designed to assess a range of dimensions determined through a documented job analysis to be key to successful performance as a Foreign Service Officer.

3. CASE MANAGEMENT

The third part of the oral assessment is the 90-minute Case Management Exercise. The purpose of this segment is to evaluate the candidate's management skills, interpersonal skills, and quantitative ability. Writing concise, correct, and persuasive English is also important in this exercise. This exercise is indicative of the candidate's ability to integrate and analyze information, to interpret quantitative data, and to display sound judgment. The candidate will be asked to incorporate data and other statistical information in the analysis and recommended solutions.

The candidate is given a memo describing the tasks to complete and a variety of information about the central issue, including a summary of the major issues (from the candidate's supervisor), an organizational chart, e-mail messages from a host of different perspectives at different levels in the Embassy, and details about the past performance of the staff. A calculator is not needed in reviewing the quantitative data, but these data must be incorporated in the analysis and recommendations.

The candidate may want to spend 30 minutes reading and analyzing the material, 45 minutes writing the required memo, and 15 minutes reviewing and revising.

Scoring the Exercises

Assessors observe the candidate's performance closely, taking notes during the testing module. At the end of each exercise, assessors individually enter their scores into a computer. The average of the exercise scores determines a candidate's overall score. The Oral Assessment cut-off score to continue a candidacy is 5.25 out of a possible 7. For the current cycle, each exercise and each component of each exercise has equal weight. The Group Exercise, Structured Interview, and Case Management Study each count for one third of the total grade. Within the Structured Interview, the Experience and Motivation, Hypothetical, and Past Behavior modules are equally weighted. Overall scoring is on a scale from 1 to 7, with 1 representing poor performance and 7 representing an outstanding performance.

After the assessors complete the integration of their scores, candidates are notified whether they have been successful in reaching the cut-off score. Along with their final overall score, candidates receive an indication as to whether they reached or exceeded the cut-off score on any of the three major components of the exam.

Exit Interviews

Unsuccessful candidates are informed of their results in a private interview with two assessors. At this point, the candidate is given an opportunity to ask questions about the assessment process and future exams. Assessors are not permitted to provide specific feedback or critiques of the candidate's performance. This prevents any undue advantage to those who take the exam more than once.

What's Next?

Successful candidates are given a briefing on the next steps in the Foreign Service hiring process, including information on the security background investigation, language bonus point system, veterans' preference points, the medical examination, and final suitability review. Candidates are also given the opportunity to ask questions about Foreign Service life. A Diplomatic Security background interview may be initiated on the day of the assessment for candidates whose passing score qualifies for an immediate conditional offer. Immediate Conditional Offers (ICO) will be made to the following candidates:

NOTE

In the first half of 2004, roughly one out of five candidates passed the Oral Assessment.

1. Political candidates who achieve a minimum score of 5.6

2. Economic, Public Diplomacy, and Consular candidates who achieve a minimum score of 5.5

3. Management candidates who achieve a score of 5.25

Political, Economic, Public Diplomacy, and Consular candidates who pass the exam (passing score remains 5.25) but do not qualify for an ICO will be put on a list of eligible hires. Candidates can remain on this list for up to 24 months.

Background Investigation

Applicants who are successful in the Oral Assessment will be asked to submit forms for a security clearance required for appointment to the Foreign Service. The clearance process considers such factors as registration for the Selective Service; failure to repay a U.S. Government-guaranteed student loans; past problems with credit or bankruptcy; failure to meet tax obligations; unsatisfactory employment records; violations of the law; drug or alcohol abuse; a criminal record; extensive travel, education, residence, and/or employment overseas; dual citizenship; foreign contacts; immediate family or relatives who are not citizens of the United States and/or a foreign-born spouse; or a less than honorable discharge from the armed forces. The Department of State conducts background investigations on each candidate to determine eligibility for security clearance. Investigations include interviews with current and previous contacts, supervisors, and coworkers. Candidates who do not receive security clearances are ineligible for appointment. Potential candidates who have any serious issues that could prevent them from receiving their clearance should give some thought to the likelihood of their being found ineligible before starting this process. These investigations are conducted by the Department of State in cooperation with other federal, state, and local agencies.

List of Eligible Hires

The names of candidates who are successful at the Oral Assessment are placed on a list of eligible candidates, based on the career track they chose and the scores they received during the oral assessment. A candidate's rank may be raised by claiming veterans' preference and/or a demonstrated proficiency in a foreign language as determined by the Department through a telephonic assessment. Extra points are given to candidates who pass language tests in Critical Needs languages. As of October 2004, these are Arabic, Chinese (Cantonese and Standard/Mandarin), Indic languages (Urdu, Hindi, Nepali, Bengali, Punjabi), Iranian languages (Farsi/Persian, Dari, Tajiki, Pashto), Korean, Russian, and Turkic languages (Azerbaijani, Kazakh, Kyrgyz, Turkish, Turkmen, Uzbek). This list is subject to change at any time depending upon the State Department's needs.

Those who receive an Immediate Conditional Offer of employment because of additional points received through the Critical Needs Language program are expected to serve at a post where that specific language can be used in their first 4–5 years with the State Department. If during the background investigation process it is determined that the candidate cannot be assigned to such a post, then the extra points received for the Critical Needs Language will be withdrawn.

Personal Interview

The last step in the application process is the personal interview. Keep in mind that what you wear is important. Take special care to look businesslike and professional. You must not appear to be too casual, and certainly not sloppy. Overdressing is also inappropriate. A neat dress or skirted suit is fine for women; men should wear shirt and tie with suit or slacks and a jacket. Do pay attention to your grooming.

Interviews take up an interviewer's time. When you are called for an interview, you are under serious consideration. There may still be competition for the job, someone else may be more suited than you, but you are qualified and your skills and background have appealed to someone in the hiring office. The interview may be aimed at getting information about:

- **Your knowledge.** The interviewer wants to know what you know about the area in which you applied to work. For instance, if you are applying to work as an interviewer to determine eligibility, what do you know about the eligibility process? You may also be asked questions probing your knowledge of the agency for which you are interviewing. Do you care enough to have educated yourself about the functions and role of the agency, whether it's child welfare, pollution control, or international trade?

- **Your judgment.** You may be faced with hypothetical situations, job-related or in interpersonal relations, and asked, "What would you do if . . . ?" questions. Think carefully before answering. You must be decisive but diplomatic. There are no "right answers." The interviewer is aware that you are being put on the spot. How well you can handle this type of question is an indication of your flexibility and maturity. As a Foreign Service Officer, for example, your judgment is always called into play.

- **Your personality.** You will have to be trained and supervised. You will have to work with others. What is your attitude? How will you fit in? The interviewer will be trying to make judgments in these areas on the basis of general conversation with you and from your responses to specific lines of questioning. Be pleasant, polite, and open with your answers, but do not volunteer a great deal of extra information. Stick to the subjects introduced by the interviewer. Answer fully, but resist the urge to ramble on.

- **Your attitude toward work conditions.** These are practical concerns: If the job will require frequent travel for extended periods, how do you feel about it? What is your family's attitude? If you will be very unhappy about the travel, you may leave the job and your training will have been a waste of the taxpayers' money. The interviewer also wants to know how you will react to overtime or irregular shifts.

Remember, working for the government is working for the people. Government revenues come from taxes. The hiring officers have a responsibility to put the right people into the right jobs to spend taxpayers' money most effectively. And, as a government employee, you have a responsibility to give the people (including yourself) their money's worth.

Other steps along the hiring route may be a medical examination, physical performance testing, and psychological interviewing. If there is a written test, these steps do not occur until the written tests are scored and ranked. Steps that require the time of one examiner with one applicant are taken only when there is reasonable expectation of hiring.

Selection of Candidates

Selection

The background of candidates successful in the assessment is investigated thoroughly to determine suitability for appointment to the Foreign Service. To initiate this investigation after notification of successful performance in the assessment, certain forms must be completed as soon as possible.

Once the background investigation forms are received, authorization for a comprehensive medical examination is provided to candidates and their dependents. Medical clearances for full overseas duty are required for all candidates and their dependents.

Candidates must submit the forms necessary for their background investigation and obtain all medical clearances within six months after notification of successful performance in the assessment. Candidates must also submit university transcripts and a 1,000-word autobiography within this same period. If these requirements are not fulfilled within six months, the candidacy is typically terminated.

Medical Clearance

Worldwide availability is determined, in addition to the candidate's affirmed willingness to serve anywhere, by the medical clearance process. Before appointment to the Foreign Service, a candidate's medical history and comprehensive physical examination must be thoroughly evaluated to determine fitness to serve at any State Department post worldwide. Many of these posts are located in areas that are remote and/or offer extremely limited medical support. Therefore, each candidate must meet medical fitness standards that are, of necessity, more rigorous than those of most other professions and that may exclude from employment candidates who have medical conditions that they manage successfully in their current environment.

Prior to any final offer of employment, the candidate must undergo a thorough medical examination and be cleared for unlimited assignment worldwide by the Department's

Office of Medical Services. Candidates who fail to receive an unlimited medical clearance will be ineligible for appointment to the Foreign Service. All medical clearance determinations are based on an individual assessment of the needs of each candidate in light of his or her particular medical history and condition.

All potential candidates, especially those with known medical conditions, should be aware of the possibility that they may not be granted an unlimited medical clearance if the Office of Medical Services determines that their condition requires monitoring or follow-up care that would not be available at Foreign Service posts, that service in a particular area would pose a significant medical risk, and/or that adequate medical care would not be available for them at all posts should life-threatening symptoms manifest or should the known medical condition require specialist or health care provider intervention. Some characteristics of the most isolated and limited posts include:

- Medically underserved in terms of inadequate medical resources—both medical and/or nursing staff and/or physical resources
- Unsanitary due to no public health infrastructure resulting in no potable water or sewage system
- Ridden with infectious and communicable diseases
- Isolated with no reliable electricity or lines of communication (e.g., transportation links, telecommunications services, postal and delivery systems, etc.)
- Dangerous and insecure
- Stressful
- Polluted environmentally via dust, dirt, and other air contaminants

After receiving a conditional offer of employment, each candidate is provided with instructions for the examining physician(s), which outline the Department of State's precise requirements. Candidates living within a fifty-mile radius of Washington, D.C., must have the medical exam performed by the Office of Medical Services' Exam Clinic.

While the candidate must be medically cleared for worldwide duty, the Department of State does not consider the medical condition of eligible family members for pre-employment purposes. However, the Department does require medical clearances for family members before they can travel overseas at U.S. Government expense to accompany an employee on assignment. The consequence of this policy is that employees with family members with limited medical clearances may be assigned to posts where those family members could not accompany them. We strongly advise candidates to consider this situation as they pursue employment with the State Department, especially those with a family member whose medical condition(s) might ultimately limit their clearance.

When requested by the candidate, the Director General of the Foreign Service, or designee, will review the case of any candidate who has been determined not to be worldwide available. This review will determine whether or not it is in the best interests of the Service to appoint the candidate despite not being worldwide available. Waivers of the worldwide availability requirement are rare, however.

Worldwide availability is both an affirmed willingness to serve anywhere in the world and a matter of being medically qualified to do so. Both the willingness and being medically qualified are essential requirements for appointment to the Foreign Service. Regardless of who administers the medical clearance exam, the Department's Office of Medical Services determines whether or not a candidate is medically eligible for assignment to all Department of State posts worldwide.

While a candidate may effectively manage a chronic health condition or limitation within the United States or in specific areas outside of the U.S., the Office of Medical Services might well determine that the same individual is not eligible for a worldwide ("Class One") medical clearance. Such clearances may only be issued to candidates whom the Office of Medical Services deems able to serve at the most isolated and restricted overseas posts.

Such a post could feature extreme isolation in terms of limitations on reliable air service in and out of the country, unreliable Internet and telecommunications connections, and/or unreliable postal and delivery systems. Any of these limited services can have a severe adverse impact in terms of both bringing in required medical services and/or supplies, and/or permitting timely medical evacuations. Other infrastructure at such a post might also be inadequate. There might be a poor or negligible public health system, poor sanitation, unreliable electricity, and a lack of potable water. There might also be infectious and communicable diseases, such as malaria, dengue fever, typhoid, tuberculosis, rabies, encephalitis, and gastrointestinal diseases. There might be no health unit at the post and next to no local medical facilities. The emergency room, for example, might be completely inadequate, without ventilators, defibrillators, or X-ray capabilities. There are often no blood bank or medical supplies or medications available locally. Because of political instability, security could be a concern.

Candidates should be aware that these posts are not few in number nor confined to a specific geographic region. Also, there are numerous other posts—in Asia and Europe, for example—where conditions appear similar to that of the U.S. but that also feature some of these prohibitive characteristics.

As a result of these characteristics of a post, the stress level among employees might be very high. Given these concerns, the Department of State would only assign employees with unrestricted medical clearances to such posts, and is unable to hire new employees without such clearances.

Final Review

Upon completion of the background investigation, a Final Review Panel will review the completed file to determine the candidate's suitability for employment with the Foreign Service.

The attainment of U.S. foreign policy objectives depends substantially on the confidence of the public (both American and foreign) in the individuals selected to serve in the Foreign Service. The Department of State, therefore, requires the highest standards of conduct by employees of the Foreign Service, including an especially high degree of integrity, reliability, and prudence. Given the representational nature of employment in the Service, employees must observe standards at all times. The purpose of the Final Review is to determine, from the candidate's total record, whether the candidate is indeed suitable to represent the United States.

In evaluating suitability, the Final Review Panel takes into consideration the following factors:

- Misconduct in prior employment, including marginal performance or inability to interact effectively with others
- Criminal, dishonest, or disgraceful conduct
- Misrepresentation, including deception or fraud, in the application process
- Repeated or habitual use to excess of intoxicating beverages affecting the ability to perform the duties and responsibilities of the employee's position
- Trafficking in or abuse of narcotics or controlled substances
- Reasonable doubt as to loyalty to the U.S. Government
- Conduct that clearly shows poor judgment and/or lack of discretion which may reasonably affect an individual or the agency's ability to carry out its responsibilities or mission
- Financial irresponsibility, including a history of not meeting financial obligations or an inability to satisfy debts

The most common grounds for a finding of unsuitability are a recent history of drug or alcohol abuse and delinquency in repaying debt or other evidence of financial irresponsibility. Candidates whose file indicates such issues are unlikely to be found suitable for the Foreign Service. Potential candidates should give some thought to these suitability factors and the likelihood of obtaining a positive decision from the Final Review Panel before starting the application process.

The names of those candidates who successfully complete the entire examination and selection process and have obtained medical clearance for full overseas duty are placed on rank-order registers in the functional cones in which they have been judged qualified. Each register lists qualified candidates in the order of their combined scores in the various phases of the examination and assessment process. When classes of new FSO

NOTE

The Final Review Panel has the authority to terminate a candidacy at this stage.

NOTE

It is important to note that simply by being listed on one or more registers, a candidate is not assured an offer of employment.

Career Candidates are scheduled, candidates are invited to join them in the order of their competitive rank in the functional cones then being filled.

The overall number of FSO Career Candidates hired each year, as well as the number hired from any particular register, varies with the needs of the Foreign Service. Candidates remain eligible for appointment for 18 months from the date their names are placed on a register. Time spent in civilian government service abroad (to a maximum of two years of such service), including Peace Corps volunteer service, or in required active regular or reserve military service, are not counted as part of the 18-month eligibility period. Candidates who are spouses accompanying employees serving in civilian government service abroad or in required military service may also be entitled to similar extensions of their eligibility for appointment.

Some candidates who are already on the FSO registers have found it to their advantage to take the written examination and assessment process again in an effort to improve their relative standing on the registers. No limit is imposed on the number of times a candidate may compete.

These descriptions of the FSO examination procedures are intended to give an indication of the types of challenges each candidate will face. The procedures described in this book are those in effect at the time of publication. Because of the long lead-time between publication and the conduct of the various phases of the examination, some changes may be unavoidable due to the needs of the Foreign Service and the revision of examination techniques and materials.

Appointment

Candidates who succeed in the examination and selection process are given probationary appointments as Foreign Service Officer Career Candidates for a period of four years. Appointments are made at the FS-6 through FS-4 levels, depending on the appointee's previous education and work experience. Career Candidates failing to perform satisfactorily may be terminated at any time during the four-year probationary period. Successful Career Candidates can be expected to be commissioned as Foreign Service Officers by the fourth year of their probationary appointment, following approval by the Commissioning and Tenure Board.

Promotions earned during the probationary period are based on satisfactory performance. Promotions occur after 12 months at the FS-6 level and after 18 months at the FS-5 level. Language probation will not delay these first promotions; however, no Career Candidates can be commissioned as permanent officers or promoted beyond FS-4 until language probation is lifted.

All Career Candidate appointments must be made before the individual's 60th birthday. The maximum age for entry into the Foreign Service is based on such factors as eligibility for retirement benefits, assignment requirements, and the mandatory retirement age of 65.

INITIAL TRAINING AND ASSIGNMENTS

Before accepting employment with the Foreign Service, officers must agree to be available for worldwide assignment. Service needs, individual skills and specialization, and personal preferences are all factors in selection of initial and subsequent assignments. The changing needs of foreign policy and departmental responsibilities make it difficult to predict individual career patterns. However, all Department of State Career Candidates should expect to spend a minimum of one year—more typically, two or more years—performing consular work during their first two tours of duty. During this period, the department will also attempt to offer some working experience in other functional fields. After the first few assignments in a variety of geographical and functional fields, specialization at mid-career in one functional field, and sometimes in a single geographical area, is normal.

Upon entering the Foreign Service, all Career Candidates receive several weeks of basic orientation at the Department of State's Foreign Service Institute. An officer may expect up to seven months of subsequent training prior to the first overseas assignment. Since most of this training involves language instruction, entering officers who already have professional competence in a foreign language may have a significantly shorter period in Washington, D.C., before leaving on their first overseas assignment. Other training may include area studies and functional courses to prepare an officer for the first overseas assignment.

CAREER STATUS AND DEVELOPMENT

Once tenured, officers continue in the career functional field to which they were originally assigned unless they choose to apply and are accepted for a change of career function. In the middle grades—Classes 3 through 1—officers concentrate on their functional specialty, but most serve in occasional out-of-function assignments to broaden their experience and to prepare for senior management responsibility. In preparation for mid-level service, career officers are assigned to a five-month training course on foreign affairs operations and management and elective courses to broaden professional knowledge. In addition, officers may serve tours with other federal agencies or may be selected for assignments to units of state and local government or public institutions, to work with the U.S. Congress as Congressional Fellows, to universities, to the Department of Defense's War Colleges, or to the Department of State's Executive Seminar in National and International Affairs.

After achieving career status, officers must compete for promotions. Each officer is rated by a supervisor at least once a year, and such performance evaluations are considered annually by specially appointed promotion boards. Any who fail to meet competitive standards are subject to termination or early retirement. All officers are subject to possible retirement or termination for exceeding established limits on time-in-class without a promotion.

Officers may advance beyond Class 1 by applying for promotion into the Senior Foreign Service. If selected, they generally are assigned to program direction and managerial responsibilities, including—for a relative few—service as ambassadors. Small numbers of distinguished Senior Foreign Service Officers are promoted to Career Minister or receive the highest rank of honor, Career Ambassador.

In all fairness to potential candidates and the Foreign Service, and with due regard for the risk of discouraging some applicants, potential candidates must be aware of the discipline and sacrifices the career demands, as well as the nature of the rewards and benefits. It is highly unlikely that the Foreign Service will ever employ more than a small fraction of those who apply, and the competition, as keen as it is for entry, does not abate appreciably throughout the career. Promotions can be few and difficult to come by in some ranks and functional specialties and at certain times. Applicants with a sincere abiding interest in foreign affairs and public service are encouraged to apply and begin the examination process, but they are advised not to pin all of their career hopes on acceptance into the Foreign Service nor, if they are accepted, to measure their success and self-esteem by rapid advancement through the career ranks to the relatively few top positions.

COMPENSATION AND BENEFITS

New entry-level officers are appointed at Classes 6, 5, or 4, depending on their qualifications, experience, and salary record. Appointment at entry-level FS-5 normally requires a master's degree. Appointment at entry-level FS-4 normally requires a master's degree and 18 months of experience in a field closely related to the Foreign Service and in a position equivalent to at least the FS-5 level.

Salary Determination for Foreign Service Officers

The Board of Examiners and the staff of the Office of Recruitment, Examination, and Employment (HR/REE) determine a Foreign Service Officer Career Candidate's entry salary. In accordance with 22 C.F.R. 11.1(g)(iii) and 3 FAM 2216.2-7, the Board of Examiners finds that there is a need in the Foreign Service for candidates with the special experience and skills listed in the FP-5 and FP-4 education and/or experience section. Salaries are set through a two-part process.

1. Determine grade and step based on education and/or experience.

Education and/or Experience	Grade/Step
Bachelor's degree and no professional experience, or no college degree and six or fewer years' professional experience	FP-6/Step 5 ($36,929)

Candidates with a Bachelor's degree receive one additional step for each year of professional experience. For example, a candidate with a Bachelor's degree plus five years of professional experience receives FP-6, Step 10 ($42,811).

Candidates without a college degree but with more than six years of professional experience receive one additional step for each year of professional experience above six years. For example, a candidate without a college degree with 11 years of professional experience receives FP-6, Step 10 ($42,811).

Education and/or Experience	Grade/Step
Master's degree or law degree (J.D.) or Bachelor's degree and minimum of six years' professional experience, or no college degree and minimum of twelve years' professional experience	FP-5/Step 5 ($41,310)

Candidates with a master's degree or a law degree (J.D.) receive one additional step for each year of professional experience. For example, a candidate with a master's or law degree (J.D.) with five years of professional experience receives FP-5, Step 10 ($46,449).

Candidates with a bachelor's degree receive one additional step for each year of professional experience above six years. For example, a bachelor's degree plus 10 years of professional experience receives FP-5, Step 9 ($45,096).

Candidates without a college degree receive one additional step for each year of professional experience above 12 years. For example, a candidate without a degree with 17 years of experience receives FP-5, Step 10 ($47,889).

Education and/or Experience	Grade/Step
Doctorate and no professional experience, or master's or law degree (J.D.) and minimum of six years' professional experience, or bachelor's degree and minimum of 12 years' professional experience, or no college degree and minimum of 18 years' professional experience	FP-4/Step 5 ($50,981)

2. Attempt to match salary for those who lose money in joining the Foreign Service.

Once grade and step are determined, based on education and experience listed in Part 1, the candidate's current salary is examined to see if he or she will lose money by joining the Foreign Service. If so, the starting salary should be raised to the step in the grade for which the candidate is qualified that is closest to the current salary. If the current salary falls between two steps, the higher of the two steps is the starting salary. If the current salary is too high to be matched in the class for which qualified, Step 14 of that class is the starting salary.

Federal civilian employees currently receiving DC locality pay will be allowed to include DC locality pay as part of their current salary. Federal civilian employees who do not currently receive DC locality pay will not be allowed to include locality pay as part of their current salary. Current salary is defined as salary earned for at least 90 days prior to appointment as a Foreign Service Career Candidate. Candidates must submit proof of the current salary; for example: a copy of 90 days' worth of earnings statements; SF-50 Notification of Personnel Action (for federal civilian employees only); a statement on letterhead from the Human Resources Office of their most recent employer; or other appropriate documentation.

For those in the private sector, current salary also means that there must not have been a break in service of more than 45 calendar days between the candidate's most recent employment and appointment as a Foreign Service Career Candidate. For federal civilian employees, there must not have been a break in service of more than three calendar days between their civilian employment and appointment to the Foreign Service (in accordance with government-wide regulations).

Benefits

The government bears the expense of the travel of employees and their families to Washington, D.C., for appointment; for any subsequent temporary duty assignments to Washington; and to and from posts of assignment abroad.

Basic salaries of Foreign Service personnel serving overseas may be supplemented by:

- Shipment of automobile and personal effects to and from posts abroad (automobiles cannot be shipped within the United States at government expense)
- Government-provided quarters or housing allowances
- Government-provided furniture and storage of personal furniture, or shipment of personal furniture
- Home leave, including travel expenses, and hospitalization benefits

The following benefits are provided when appropriate:

- Education allowance
- Education travel for dependent children
- Temporary lodging allowance
- Separate maintenance allowance
- Cost-of-living allowance
- Hardship post salary supplements
- Danger pay
- Travel for children of separated parents

INFORMATION FOR FAMILY MEMBERS

A Foreign Service career deeply involves not only the employee but also the entire family. The Departments of State and Commerce recognize that members of a Foreign Service family essentially are private individuals. However, the diplomatic community and people of the country of assignment often view the entire family as representatives of the United States.

Foreign Service life affects family members in many ways. Education of children and health care are both special factors to be considered. The quality of overseas education is uneven, and providing continuity of subjects and of instructional methods is difficult. Testing and college counseling are often inadequate. In brief, parents tend to take much greater responsibility for a child's schooling than in the United States. As for medical facilities, they too are uneven. Some posts have no resident American doctor or nurse. It may be necessary to travel by air to reach an acceptable hospital.

Married applicants whose spouses seek their own careers should carefully weigh the implications of joining a highly mobile service in which worldwide availability is required. Approximately 60 percent of a person's Foreign Service career may be spent abroad; in both Washington, D.C., and overseas, the Foreign Service spouse is at a career disadvantage. Prospective employers often are reluctant to hire a spouse for a limited period of time. It is difficult to maintain professional contacts and to keep up-to-date in a given field. Some spouses are able to work, but local regulations and circumstances typically limit opportunities severely and salaries may be considerably reduced. However, continued efforts to improve employment prospects are under way.

On the other hand, close involvement in other societies and cultures provides unique opportunities for spouses with varied interests, transferable skills, and portable professions. Involvement in community life abroad and the opportunity to take part in representing the United States are voluntary, but many families find that such activities broaden their contact with the citizens and culture of the country of assignment. A Foreign Service existence can be undeniably rewarding; however, applicants have to decide how flexible they and their families are willing to be in matters of schooling, medical care, and employment for spouses. Child-care facilities vary greatly overseas.

When a husband and wife are both members of the Foreign Service, the Departments of State and Commerce make every reasonable effort to assign them to the same post without placing other employees at a disadvantage. While tandem assignments can usually be arranged, couples must be prepared to accept the possibility that they may, during their careers, have to accept separate assignments or leave without pay for one spouse.

Reading all the applications and weeding out the unqualified ones takes time. Weighing education and experience factors takes time. Administering and scoring of exams takes time. Interviews, medical exams, and physical performance tests take time. Verifying references takes time. And, finally, the vacancies must occur, and the government agency must have the funds to fill the vacancies. But when you finally do get that job, you will have a good income, many benefits, and job security.

NOTE

In the interest of personal safety at some locations, some restrictions in lifestyle may occur.

TIP

Additional information on Foreign Service family life abroad, including schools, educational benefits, health-care and medical facilities, and job opportunities, can be found by contacting the Family Liaison Office at www.state.gov/m/dghr/flo or by phone at 202-647-1076.

Diagnostic Test

OVERVIEW

- **Preparing to take the diagnostic test**
- **Diagnostic test**
- **Answer Key and Explanation**
- **Biographical questionnaire**

Before you begin the practice tests in this book, it is important to know your strengths and weaknesses and the areas you need improvement in. If you are confident in your ability to answer the knowledge questions, it would be a mistake to dedicate hours practicing them. Taking the Diagnostic Test in this chapter will help you determine which sections you'll need to devote additional study time to.

PREPARING TO TAKE THE DIAGNOSTIC TEST

If possible, take the test in one sitting. This will give you an idea of how long the sections are and how long it will take you to complete each section.

First, assemble all the things you will need to take the test. These include:

- Number 2 pencils
- The answer sheet

chapter 4

DIAGNOSTIC TEST ANSWER SHEET

Knowledge Questions

1. Ⓐ Ⓑ Ⓒ Ⓓ	11. Ⓐ Ⓑ Ⓒ Ⓓ	21. Ⓐ Ⓑ Ⓒ Ⓓ
2. Ⓐ Ⓑ Ⓒ Ⓓ	12. Ⓐ Ⓑ Ⓒ Ⓓ	22. Ⓐ Ⓑ Ⓒ Ⓓ
3. Ⓐ Ⓑ Ⓒ Ⓓ	13. Ⓐ Ⓑ Ⓒ Ⓓ	23. Ⓐ Ⓑ Ⓒ Ⓓ
4. Ⓐ Ⓑ Ⓒ Ⓓ	14. Ⓐ Ⓑ Ⓒ Ⓓ	24. Ⓐ Ⓑ Ⓒ Ⓓ
5. Ⓐ Ⓑ Ⓒ Ⓓ	15. Ⓐ Ⓑ Ⓒ Ⓓ	25. Ⓐ Ⓑ Ⓒ Ⓓ
6. Ⓐ Ⓑ Ⓒ Ⓓ	16. Ⓐ Ⓑ Ⓒ Ⓓ	26. Ⓐ Ⓑ Ⓒ Ⓓ
7. Ⓐ Ⓑ Ⓒ Ⓓ	17. Ⓐ Ⓑ Ⓒ Ⓓ	
8. Ⓐ Ⓑ Ⓒ Ⓓ	18. Ⓐ Ⓑ Ⓒ Ⓓ	
9. Ⓐ Ⓑ Ⓒ Ⓓ	19. Ⓐ Ⓑ Ⓒ Ⓓ	
10. Ⓐ Ⓑ Ⓒ Ⓓ	20. Ⓐ Ⓑ Ⓒ Ⓓ	

English Expression

1. Ⓐ Ⓑ Ⓒ Ⓓ Ⓔ	11. Ⓐ Ⓑ Ⓒ Ⓓ Ⓔ	21. Ⓐ Ⓑ Ⓒ Ⓓ Ⓔ
2. Ⓐ Ⓑ Ⓒ Ⓓ Ⓔ	12. Ⓐ Ⓑ Ⓒ Ⓓ Ⓔ	22. Ⓐ Ⓑ Ⓒ Ⓓ Ⓔ
3. Ⓐ Ⓑ Ⓒ Ⓓ Ⓔ	13. Ⓐ Ⓑ Ⓒ Ⓓ Ⓔ	23. Ⓐ Ⓑ Ⓒ Ⓓ Ⓔ
4. Ⓐ Ⓑ Ⓒ Ⓓ Ⓔ	14. Ⓐ Ⓑ Ⓒ Ⓓ Ⓔ	
5. Ⓐ Ⓑ Ⓒ Ⓓ Ⓔ	15. Ⓐ Ⓑ Ⓒ Ⓓ Ⓔ	
6. Ⓐ Ⓑ Ⓒ Ⓓ Ⓔ	16. Ⓐ Ⓑ Ⓒ Ⓓ Ⓔ	
7. Ⓐ Ⓑ Ⓒ Ⓓ Ⓔ	17. Ⓐ Ⓑ Ⓒ Ⓓ Ⓔ	
8. Ⓐ Ⓑ Ⓒ Ⓓ Ⓔ	18. Ⓐ Ⓑ Ⓒ Ⓓ Ⓔ	
9. Ⓐ Ⓑ Ⓒ Ⓓ Ⓔ	19. Ⓐ Ⓑ Ⓒ Ⓓ Ⓔ	
10. Ⓐ Ⓑ Ⓒ Ⓓ Ⓔ	20. Ⓐ Ⓑ Ⓒ Ⓓ Ⓔ	

KNOWLEDGE QUESTIONS

Directions: Each of the questions or incomplete statements below is followed by four possible answers. Select the best answer for each question and then blacken the corresponding space on the answer sheet. Some sets of questions are presented with material such as reading passages, plans, graphs, tables, etc. Answers to such questions may require interpretation of the material and/or outside knowledge relevant to its content.

KNOWLEDGE AREA: THE HISTORICAL ANTECEDENTS OF INTERNATIONAL AFFAIRS (E.G., ISLAM, COLONIALISM, INDUSTRIAL REVOLUTION) TO AID UNDERSTANDING OF FOREIGN GOVERNMENTS AND SOCIETIES.

1. All of the following are necessary attributes of a nation-state EXCEPT

    (A) occupation of a definite territory.

    (B) an organized government.

    (C) predominant use of a single language.

    (D) possession of internal and external sovereignty.

2. Many of the developing nations that achieved independence after 1945 have become noted for their chronic instability. Which of the following factors generally contributes LEAST to this instability?

    (A) The rise of political factionalism

    (B) The large numbers of unassimilated ethnic and/or religious minorities

    (C) The artificiality of national boundaries drawn by former colonial rulers

    (D) The continued use of administrative systems inherited from colonial powers

KNOWLEDGE AREA: WORLD GEOGRAPHY (E.G., LOCATION OF COUNTRIES, SIGNIFICANT PHYSICAL FEATURES, DISTRIBUTION OF KEY NATURAL RESOURCES, GEOGRAPHY-BASED NATIONAL RIVALRIES AND ALLIANCES) IN ORDER TO UNDERSTAND THE GEOGRAPHIC CONTEXT OF FOREIGN RELATIONS AND U.S. FOREIGN POLICY.

QUESTIONS 3 AND 4 REFER TO THE FOLLOWING MAP:

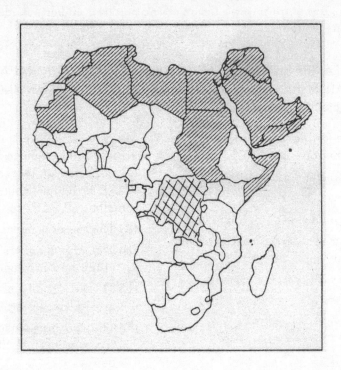

3. The cross-hatched country is a leading exporter of which of the following primary products?

(A) Bauxite

(B) Textile products

(C) Tin

(D) Diamonds

4. The shaded area on the map above identifies, as of the mid-1970s, members of which of the following organizations?

(A) The Organization of Petroleum Exporting Countries (OPEC)

(B) The Arab League

(C) The Central Treaty Organization (LENTO)

(D) The Organization of African Unity (OAU)

KNOWLEDGE AREA: MAJOR EVENTS, INSTITUTIONS, AND MOVEMENTS IN THE HISTORY OF THE UNITED STATES (E.G., SLAVERY, CONSTITUTIONAL CONVENTION, CIVIL WAR, GREAT DEPRESSION, CIVIL RIGHTS MOVEMENT) TO FACILITATE UNDERSTANDING OF THE U.S. SYSTEM OF GOVERNMENT.

5. The Scopes Trial of 1925 took on national significance because it
   (A) marked the first time that a U.S. court ruled that the theory of evolution was correct.
   (B) led to the first federal appropriation of aid for scientific research.
   (C) symbolically pitted the new scientific outlook against the religious outlook of the Fundamentalists.
   (D) was William Jennings Bryan's last major attempt to attract national attention in an attempt to capture the Democratic Presidential nomination.

6. The precipitous decline of the New World's indigenous population in the first century after its initial contact with Europeans was largely due to
   (A) disease.
   (B) enslavement.
   (C) warfare.
   (D) famine.

KNOWLEDGE AREA: HISTORY OF U.S. INTELLECTUAL, ARTISTIC, AND CULTURAL LIFE (E.G., LITERATURE, SOCIAL PHILOSOPHY, PERFORMING ARTS, SPORTS, VISUAL ARTS) IN ORDER TO INTERPRET U.S. CULTURAL LIFE FOR FOREIGN NATIONALS.

7. Who said, "In the future, everyone will be famous for at least 15 minutes"?
   (A) Mike Wallace
   (B) Andy Warhol
   (C) Barbara Walters
   (D) Marshall McLuhan

8. Milton Babbitt, John Harrison, Gunther Schuller, and John Cage are BEST known as
   (A) conductors of symphonic orchestras.
   (B) ballet choreographers.
   (C) playwrights.
   (D) contemporary composers.

diagnostic test

KNOWLEDGE AREA: SOCIAL, POLITICAL, AND ECONOMIC TRENDS IN THE UNITED STATES (E.G., WOMEN AND MINORITY ROLES, DEMOGRAPHIC SHIFTS, PATTERNS OF IMMIGRATION, INFORMATION AGE, BIOMEDICINE).

9. All of the following circumstances have contributed to the current emphasis on protecting the U.S. environment from toxic wastes EXCEPT

   (A) Safe places to store toxic wastes in the United States have become scarce.

   (B) Research has increased knowledge of the toxicity of many widely used chemicals.

   (C) The amount of wastes of all kinds has grown.

   (D) Deregulation has made it easier for the public to purchase and use toxic substances.

10. In some areas of the United States, the presence of Southeast Asian refugees has produced considerable tension for which of the following reasons?

   I. Fear of their impact on welfare rolls

   II. Anti-Asian racism

   III. Resentment of their entrepreneurial competition

   IV. Perceptions of them as clannish

   (A) I only

   (B) III only

   (C) I and II only

   (D) I, II, III, IV

KNOWLEDGE AREA: CONTEMPORARY CULTURAL TRENDS IN THE UNITED STATES (E.G., FILM, MUSIC, SPORTS, MAGAZINES, NEWSPAPERS, CLOTHING, AND LIFESTYLES).

11. Which of the following columnists is known for the conservative tone of his or her work?

   (A) Russell Baker

   (B) Carl Rowan

   (C) Meg Greenfield

   (D) George Will

12. To the argument that television gives a truer account of what happens in a courtroom than does any other news medium, all of the following objections may reasonably be advanced EXCEPT

   (A) The television director, by choosing the image on which the camera focuses, engages in a process of selection just as a newspaper reporter or an editor does.

   (B) A pictorial medium has difficulty in dealing with abstract ideas, such as points of law, which are often the most important part of a court proceeding.

   (C) Television inevitably becomes an "actor" in the courtroom proceedings and thereby changes the event as it records it.

   (D) Television reporters, because they must concentrate on the technical and theatrical aspects of electronic journalism, have little time to master the complexities of a court case.

KNOWLEDGE AREA: U.S. POLITICAL PROCESS AND ITS IMPACT ON POLICY (E.G., ROLE OF SPECIAL INTEREST GROUPS, THE MEDIA, POLITICAL PARTIES).

13. In the United States, campaigns for major public offices are increasingly being controlled by

    (A) political action committees.

    (B) media consultants.

    (C) candidates' press agents.

    (D) local political party chairpersons.

14. Which of the following is the major reason that it is easy to block a bill in Congress but difficult to enact one?

    (A) Well-organized opposing political parties in Congress

    (B) The decentralized committee structure of Congress

    (C) The influence of pork-barrel politics on congressional voting

    (D) Institutional conflict between Congress and the president

KNOWLEDGE AREA: U.S. CONSTITUTION AND THE STRUCTURE OF THE U.S. GOVERNMENT (E.G., SEPARATION OF POWERS, FUNCTIONS OF CABINET DEPARTMENTS, LAWMAKING, FEDERALISM, APPROPRIATION PROCESS).

15. Two key precepts of the Constitution that were not present in the Articles of Confederation are to

    (A) buffer the government from the immediate impact of popular impulse and extend the vote to all.

    (B) promote the power of individual states over that of the federal government and keep the branches of the federal government separate but linked.

    (C) keep the president closely tied to the will of the majority and promote the power of individual states over that of the federal government.

    (D) buffer the government from the immediate impact of popular impulse and keep the branches of the federal government separate but linked.

16. Which of the following statements is true about executive privilege?

    (A) It allows the president to withhold certain information from Congress and the courts.

    (B) It protects members of the executive branch from prosecution for any acts committed in the course of performing their jobs.

    (C) It is the concept that underlies the president's use of a pocket veto during a session of Congress.

    (D) It protects the members of the Cabinet when the president faces impeachment proceedings.

KNOWLEDGE AREA: U.S. ECONOMIC SYSTEMS, ITS INSTITUTIONS, AND PHILOSOPHICAL PRINCIPLES, TO AID IN INTERPRETING U.S. POLICIES AND ACTIONS TO FOREIGN NATIONALS.

17. If the Federal Reserve were to adopt an accommodative policy and then decrease the discount rate and buy government securities in the open market, it would most likely be responding to

   (A) rising interest rates due to an increase in the money supply.

   (B) rising interest rates due to a decrease in the money supply.

   (C) falling interest rates due to an increase in the money supply.

   (D) falling interest rates due to a decrease in the money supply.

18. In the United States, the last twenty-five years of the nineteenth century were characterized by several violent conflicts between capital and labor, which by 1900 resulted in

   (A) the use of federal court injunctions to jail strikers without a jury trial.

   (B) the intensive participation of the American Federation of Labor (AFL) in politics.

   (C) the unionization of the vast majority of factory workers.

   (D) general acceptance of the closed shop by employers.

KNOWLEDGE AREA: U.S. EDUCATIONAL SYSTEM (E.G., PUBLIC VERSUS PRIVATE INSTITUTIONS, SCHOLARSHIPS).

19. All of the following were objectives of the common, or public, school movement of 1840–1860 EXCEPT

   (A) primary school education for all white Americans, regardless of sex.

   (B) a professionally trained teaching force.

   (C) establishment of a uniform national curriculum.

   (D) introduction of a new pedagogy based on the idea that children were capable of infinite improvement.

20. In the United States, at which of the following levels of education are there more privately than publicly controlled schools?

   I. Elementary

   II. Secondary

   III. Postsecondary

   (A) III only

   (B) I and II only

   (C) II and III only

   (D) I, II, and III

KNOWLEDGE AREA: FOREIGN POLITICAL SYSTEMS (E.G., PARLIAMENTARY, FEDERAL, DICTATORSHIP, ONE PARTY).

21. A major difference between U.S. political parties and political parties in European parliamentary systems is that

   (A) European parties are less ideologically rigid.

   (B) U.S. parties have stronger local organizations.

   (C) European parties exercise more discipline over their elected representatives in the legislature.

   (D) U.S. parties better represent special interests.

22. A distinguishing feature of the parliamentary form of government is that

   (A) Parliament is the sole repository of legitimacy and may not delegate governmental authority to regional or local units.

   (B) no final action may be taken on a bill until all members of Parliament have had an opportunity to speak either for or against it.

   (C) members of the government are not allowed to take part in parliamentary debates that involve appropriations.

   (D) Parliament has the power to call for an election or require the Prime Minister to resign.

KNOWLEDGE AREA: BASIC PRINCIPLES OF ECONOMICS (E.G., SUPPLY AND DEMAND, MONEY SUPPLY, INTERNATIONAL TRADE, COMPARATIVE ECONOMIC SYSTEMS).

QUESTION 23 REFERS TO THE FOLLOWING GRAPH:

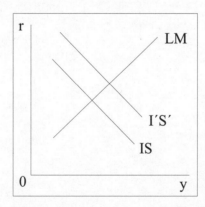

23. In the graph above, the shift of the IS curve to the new position, I′S′, illustrates the Keynesian proposition that increases in both gross national product (GNP) and interest rates could result from increases in

   (A) the money supply.

   (B) the demand for money.

   (C) government spending.

   (D) taxes.

24. A "dirty float" system is one in which

   (A) exchange rates are permitted to fluctuate freely.

   (B) governments act to influence the exchange value of their own currencies.

   (C) assets of foreign banks are undervalued.

   (D) exchange rates are determined by an automatic gold standard.

KNOWLEDGE AREA: MAJOR CONTEMPORARY INTERNATIONAL ECONOMIC AND COMMERCIAL ISSUES (E.G., UNEMPLOYMENT, INFLATION, TRADE DEFICIT, THIRD-WORLD DEBT) IN ORDER TO UNDERSTAND THE IMPACT OF ECONOMIC CONDITIONS ON A FOREIGN COUNTRY AND ON U.S. PROGRAMS AND POLICY INTEREST.

25. To conform with the chronological sequence most commonly followed by U.S. manufacturers that are launching international operations, the activities below should be undertaken in which of the following sequences?

I.   Establish a foreign sales branch

II. Initiate overseas assembly of parts manufactured in the United States

III. Begin full-scale manufacturing overseas

IV. Export U.S. goods through a foreign distributor

(A) I, II, III, IV

(B) I, IV, III, II

(C) III, IV, II, I

(D) IV, I, II, III

26. All of the following statements concerning dumping in international trade are correct EXCEPT

(A) It is defined as selling at less than fair value.

(B) It forms the basis for a claim in the World Court.

(C) It constitutes an unfair trade practice under GATT.

(D) It is subject to U.S. law.

ENGLISH EXPRESSION

Directions: The following sentences contain problems in grammar, usage, diction (choice of words), and idiom. Some sentences are correct. No sentence contains more than one error.

You will find that the error, if there is one, is underlined and lettered. Assume that all other elements of the sentence are correct and cannot be changed. In choosing answers, follow the requirements of standard written English. If there is an error, select the one underlined part that must be changed in order to make the sentence correct, and fill in the corresponding oval on the answer sheet. If there is no error, mark answer space (E).

Example

Q He spoke <u>bluntly</u> and <u>angrily</u> to <u>we</u>
          A   B   C

<u>spectators</u>. <u>No error</u>
   D   E

A **The correct answer is (C).** He spoke bluntly and angrily to *us* spectators. Since the pronoun is the object of the preposition to, the objective case must be used.

Q She <u>works</u> <u>every day</u> <u>so that she</u> would
     A   B   C

become <u>financially</u> independent in her
         D

old age. <u>No error</u>
        E

A **The correct answer is (A).** She *worked* every day so that she would become financially independent in her old age. The verb *would become* is in the past tense; therefore, the verb in the main clause must be in the past tense.

1. Paul Klee <u>awaited</u> many long years
              A

<u>to receive</u> the recognition <u>due him</u> <u>as</u> a
   B   C   D

painter. <u>No error</u>
      E

2. Acting in skits or plays

<u>have frequently proved</u> of great benefit to
         A

mentally ill patients, <u>perhaps because</u>
                  B

<u>such activity</u> allows them to act out
        C

<u>their own</u> inner conflicts. <u>No error</u>
   D   E

3. <u>According to</u> the theory, some types of
   A

human behavior <u>once considered</u> the
             B

result of great psychological disturbance

<u>is in reality</u> caused by a chemical imbalance
   C

<u>within</u> the body. <u>No error</u>
   D   E

4. The author's novels <u>may seem</u>
                     A

   <u>somewhat old</u> and musty, but <u>their</u> form
      B   C

   <u>survives</u> in modern popular novels.
    D

   <u>No error</u>
    E

5. No sooner <u>had</u> the Great Fire burned
              A

   <u>itself out</u> <u>than</u> plans were <u>laid</u> for the
     B   C   D

   rebuilding of the city. <u>No error</u>
                     E

6. The candidate directed <u>her appeal</u> to the
                       A

   young once <u>realizing that</u> <u>she could not win</u>
            B   C

   <u>without their votes</u>. <u>No error</u>
      D   E

7. <u>Because of the increasing</u> popularity of
            A

   our national parks, the park service must

   <u>deal with the almost insolvable</u> problem
              B

   of <u>how you can let</u> every visitor
         C

   <u>in and still keep</u> the wilderness intact.
       D

   <u>No error</u>
    E

8. Herschel's catalogs of stars, <u>first published</u>
                       A

   in <u>the late</u> eighteenth century, <u>did much</u>
      B   C

   to progress astronomy. <u>No error</u>
       D   E

Directions: In each of the following sentences, some part or all of the sentence is underlined. Below each sentence you will find five ways of rephrasing the underlined part. Select the answer that produces the most effective sentence, one that is clear and exact without awkwardness or ambiguity, and fill in the corresponding oval on your answer sheet. In choosing answers, follow the requirements of standard written English. Choose the answer that best expresses the meaning of the original sentence. Choice (A) is always the same as the underlined part. Choose choice (A) if you think the original sentence needs no revision.

Example

Q Laura Ingalls Wilder published her first book and she was sixty-five years old then.

- **(A)** and she was sixty-five years old then
- **(B)** when she was sixty-five years old
- **(C)** at age sixty-five years old
- **(D)** upon reaching sixty-five years
- **(E)** at the time when she was sixty-five

A **The correct answer is (B).** Laura Ingalls Wilder published her first book *when she was sixty-five years old*. All of the other choices are unnecessarily wordy.

9. Finally, public and legal pressures forced the auto manufacturers to abandon racing, and they would thus then develop more rapidly pollution controls and safety devices.

- **(A)** racing, and they would thus then develop more rapidly
- **(B)** racing and exchange it for more rapid development of
- **(C)** racing, and thus they would favor the more rapid development of
- **(D)** racing to be developing more rapidly
- **(E)** racing in favor of more rapid development of

10. Almost all folk singers have several ballads from the Child collection in their repertoires, whether they know it or not.

- **(A)** whether they know it or not
- **(B)** whether or not they know anything about it
- **(C)** whether knowing it or not
- **(D)** whether with their knowledge or without
- **(E)** whether knowingly or unknowingly

11. Because extremely low-frequency radio waves can penetrate deep water, much research has, as a result, been devoted to their potential use in underwater communications.

- **(A)** much research has, as a result, been devoted to their potential use in underwater communications
- **(B)** much research on their potential use in underwater communications has resulted
- **(C)** it has resulted in the devotion of much research to their potential use in underwater communications
- **(D)** devotion of much research to using them in underwater communications has taken place
- **(E)** much research has been devoted to their potential use in underwater communications

12. <u>They have been sent to help people of developing countries, and much useful work has been done by members of the Peace Corps.</u>

    (A) They have been sent to help people of developing countries, and much useful work has been done by members of the Peace Corps.

    (B) Members of the Peace Corps have been sent to help people of developing countries and much useful work has been done.

    (C) They have been sent to help people of developing countries, and members of the Peace Corps have done much useful work.

    (D) Sent to help people of developing countries, members of the Peace Corps have done much useful work.

    (E) Having been sent to help people of developing countries, much useful work has been done by members of the Peace Corps.

13. Horseshoe crabs are not crabs at all; <u>its nearest living relative is the spider</u>.

    (A) its nearest living relative is the spider

    (B) their nearest living relatives are the spiders

    (C) the nearest living relatives are the spider

    (D) their nearest living relative is spiders

    (E) its nearest living relatives are spiders

14. Drops of water acting like prisms refract <u>sunlight, which process causes</u> rainbows.

    (A) sunlight, which process causes

    (B) sunlight, and it causes

    (C) sunlight, which is the cause of

    (D) sunlight and thus cause

    (E) sunlight and this, therefore, causes

Directions: In each of the following questions you are given a complete sentence to be rephrased according to the directions that follow it. You should rephrase the sentence mentally to save time, although you may make notes in your test book if you wish.

Below each sentence and its directions are listed words or phrases that may occur in your revised sentence. When you have thought out a good sentence, look in the choices (A) through (E) for the word or entire phrase that is included in your revised sentence, and fill in the corresponding oval on the answer sheet. The word or phrase you choose should be the most accurate and most nearly complete of all the choices given, and should be part of a sentence that meets the requirements of standard written English.

Of course, a number of different sentences can be obtained if the sentence is revised according to the directions, and not all of these possibilities can be included in only five choices. If you should find that you have thought of a sentence that contains none of the words or phrases listed in the choices, you should attempt to rephrase the sentence again so that it includes a word or phrase that is listed.

Although the directions may at times require you to change the relationship between parts of the sentence or to make slight changes in meaning in other ways, make only those changes that the directions require. Keep the meaning the same or as nearly the same as the directions permit. If you think that more than one good sentence can be made according to the directions, select the sentence that is most exact, effective, and natural in phrasing and construction.

Example

Q Coming to the city as a young man, he found a job as a newspaper reporter.

Substitute <u>He came</u> for <u>Coming</u>.

(A) and so he found
(B) and found
(C) and there he found
(D) and then finding
(E) and had found

A Your rephrased sentence will probably read: "He came to the city as a young man and found a job as a newspaper reporter." This sentence contains the correct part *and found* that is given in answer choice (B). A sentence that used one of the alternate phrases would change the meaning or intention of the original sentence, would be a poorly written sentence, or would be less effective than another possible revision.

15. Root feeding is necessary for the survival of many old trees.

Begin with <u>Many old trees need</u>.

(A) for their surviving
(B) so they survive
(C) to survive
(D) in surviving
(E) as a survival measure

16. Only wealthy people can afford the luxury of hiring architects to design their homes.

Begin with <u>Hiring an architect</u>.

(A) and only
(B) therefore only
(C) luxury that only
(D) luxury; only
(E) something that only

17. The term "institutionalized racism" was coined by Stokely Carmichael and Charles V. Hamilton in their book *Black Power*.

Begin with <u>In their book</u>.
(A) has been coined
(B) they coined
(C) coined
(D) is coined
(E) was coined

18. The disturbance to the ecology of the area that the wastes from the new mill could create was mentioned in the article; however, greater emphasis was placed on the contributions that the mill could make to the economic development of the area.

Begin with <u>The article placed less</u>.
(A) rather than on the contributions
(B) than on the disturbance
(C) instead of the disturbance
(D) than on the contributions
(E) than on the ecology

19. The most extensive changes in the English language have come about through contact with different cultures, rather than through gradual changes in meaning.

Substitute <u>about, not through</u> for <u>about through</u>.
(A) but by contact
(B) but through contact
(C) rather by contact
(D) rather than by contact
(E) although through contact

20. Though, for the most part, German shepherds are intelligent and well-behaved, they often make difficult pets because of their tendency to recognize only one master.

Begin with <u>The tendency</u>.
(A) it is often difficult for them
(B) for difficulty in their
(C) them often have difficulty with
(D) them difficult for
(E) them difficult

Directions: In each of the following questions you are given four sentences and a question that asks for the best sequence to make a clear, sensible paragraph. Choose the option that reflects the best ordering of the sentences for a clear, sensible paragraph.

21. I. Women are responsible for much of this wealth.
    II. Phillis Wheatley, the poet, was one of the earliest to write of her life.
    III. Since the eighteenth century, African-American women have been writing the stories of their lives.
    IV. Although most readers have heard of the lives of Booker T. Washington, Malcolm X, and Richard Wright, they are generally ignorant of the wealth of African-American autobiographies.

Which of the following presents the best sequence of the sentences above to make a clear, sensible paragraph?
    (A) I, III, II, IV
    (B) II, III, IV, I
    (C) III, I, II, IV
    (D) III, II, I, IV
    (E) IV, I, III, II

22. I. However, after Tito's death, the various ethnic, linguistic, and religious groups in Yugoslavia began to assert their independence.
    II. Yugoslavia was formed as a federation of disparate states after the Second World War.
    III. The charismatic domination of Marshal Tito was the major force that bound this federation.
    IV. In the last decade of the twentieth century, the unity of Yugoslavia remains uncertain.

Which of the following presents the best sequence of the sentences above to make a clear, sensible paragraph?
    (A) I, IV, III, II
    (B) II, I, III, IV
    (C) II, III, I, IV
    (D) IV, II, I, III
    (E) IV, III, II, I

23. I. No single group has been able to rest easy in its hegemony, however, because one or more of the other groups was always ready to dispute the first group's right to rule.
    II. The Middle East's relatively dense population, its scarcity of water and arable land, and its location at a crossroads between the East, West, North, and South have all contributed to this conflict.
    III. Throughout recorded history, the Middle East has been an area of strife between peoples of different ethnic and religious backgrounds.
    IV. Persians, Kurds, Arabs, Jews, Turks, Christians, and Shiite and Sunni Muslims have all struggled to gain, hold, or regain power over the territory in the Middle East.

Which of the following presents the best sequence of the sentences above to make a clear, sensible paragraph?
    (A) I, II, III, IV
    (B) II, III, I, IV
    (C) III, I, IV, II
    (D) III, II, IV, I
    (E) IV, II, III, I

ANSWER KEY AND EXPLANATIONS

Knowledge Questions

1.	C	7.	B	13.	B	19.	C	25.	D
2.	D	8.	D	14.	B	20.	A	26.	B
3.	C	9.	D	15.	D	21.	C		
4.	B	10.	D	16.	A	22.	D		
5.	C	11.	D	17.	A	23.	C		
6.	A	12.	D	18.	A	24.	B		

1. **The correct answer is (C).** Many nation-states have a wide diversity of official languages. As an example, we could look to India. Hindi is the national language, but is spoken by only 30% of the population. At the same time, there are 14 official languages.

2. **The correct answer is (D).** Each of the first three choices lends itself to either internal or external political hostilities. These hostilities can range from civil wars to border skirmishes. In most of these nations, the administrative systems inherited from colonial powers serve as the stabilizing factor.

3. **The correct answer is (D).** The country indicated on the map is the Democratic Republic of the Congo. Its chief exports include diamonds, copper, cobalt, coffee, and crude oil. Since 1994, diamonds have been the country's leading export, following a decline in the production of copper (once the leading mineral product in terms of value). The country produces much of the world's small industrial diamonds.

4. **The correct answer is (B).** The countries indicated on the map are members of the Arab League, officially known as the League of Arab States. Membership consists of the following nations: Algeria, Bahrain, Comoros, Djibouti, Egypt, Iraq, Jordan, Kuwait, Lebanon, Libya, Mauritania, Morocco, Oman, Palestine, Qatar, Saudi Arabia, Somalia, Sudan, Syria, Tunisia, United Arab Emirates, and Yeman.

5. **The correct answer is (C).** The Scopes Trial pitted the Modernists (represented by Clarence Darrow) against the Fundamentalists (represented by William Jennings Bryan). Bryan's political career had come to an end 10 years earlier and the court found John Scopes guilty of teaching evolution, which was against Tennessee state law.

6. **The correct answer is (A).** Disease was the number-one killer of Native Americans. Over the centuries, Europeans had built up natural immunities to such diseases as smallpox, typhus, and measles. Native Americans, having no immunity to such diseases, were decimated when they came into contact with these diseases.

7. **The correct answer is (B).** This quote comes from entries on Thursday, July 27, 1978, and Thursday, June 2, 1983, in *The Andy Warhol Diaries.*

8. **The correct answer is (D).** Milton Babbitt, John Harrison, Gunther Schuller, and John Cage are all contemporary composers. This is the only characteristic listed that is shared by all four individuals.

9. **The correct answer is (D).** Current regulations have made it more difficult for the public to purchase and use toxic substances. This is the exact opposite of what is stated in choice (D).

10. **The correct answer is (D).** This is the best possible choice because all four statements are true. Some people fear that the status of Southeast Asian refugees will automatically make them welfare recipients. In addition, nativism has led to anti-Asian racism since the nineteenth century. The entrepreneurial work ethic of many Asians has led to success, which is resented by some, and, whether by choice or circumstance, many immigrants tend to reside in localized communities, which leads some people to perceive them as being clannish.

11. **The correct answer is (D).** George Will is a conservative political writer and commentator for the *Chicago Sun-Times*. Russell Baker is best known as a political satirist, Carl Rowan for his work with Civil Rights, and Meg Greenfield as an editor/writer.

12. **The correct answer is (D).** The first three choices are all factual statements that can reasonably be advanced as arguments against the statement. The fourth choice would not be acceptable because reporters from all mediums would have the same difficulty in mastering the complexities of the court case.

13. **The correct answer is (B).** Candidates today are being advertised to the voter. With the advent of "spin," which has become so important in political campaigns, media consultants can make or break a candidate. They can positively portray him/her on TV with phrases, info, looks, etc., that will appeal to the voters. Most voters do not study the issues. They hear a "spin" and decide whether they like or dislike a candidate.

14. **The correct answer is (B).** The fact that a bill can be sent to one of many committees can doom it to failure. The Committee chairpeople can sit on a bill, never bring it before a committee, or send it to subcommittees that will study it to death or report unfavorably on it.

Also, once in committee, many add-ons, or pork barrel legislation, can be attached to the original bill, such as things a committee chairman may want for his district, things other majority members of the committee may want for their district, etc. Without their support, the original bill may be killed.

15. **The correct answer is (D).** Two key precepts of the Constitution were to buffer the government from the immediate impact of popular impulse via representative government, and to keep the branches of the federal government separate but linked via a system of checks and balances. Neither document attempted to extend the vote to all; promoting the power of individual states over that of the federal government was a key precept of the Articles of Confederation, not the Constitution.

16. **The correct answer is (A).** Executive privilege exempts an executive from disclosing information that is necessary to maintain highly important governmental operations or domestic decision-making or policy-making. In 1974, the court ruled in *United States vs. Nixon* that the president could not withhold evidence needed in a criminal trial. This meant that the idea of executive privilege was not unlimited.

17. **The correct answer is (A).** The Federal Reserve decreases the discount rate when attempting to counter rising interest rates. By purchasing government securities in the open market, the Federal Reserve is able to increase the money supply.

18. **The correct answer is (A).** A prime example of the use of federal court injunctions to jail strikers without a jury trial was the injunction that was granted during the Pullman Strike, which forbade any interference with the mail or restraint of interstate commerce. This injunction, upheld by the Supreme Court,

was used to jail Eugene V. Debs for six months.

19. **The correct answer is (C).** For the time period given, the responsibility for education was still within the domain of the individual states. It would not be until the 1950s that the Federal government would use the "elastic clause" to assume partial control of the education system for reasons of national security.

20. **The correct answer is (A).** According to the *Digest of Education Statistics, 2000,* privately controlled elementary schools account for 25% of all elementary schools, privately controlled secondary schools account for 14% of all secondary schools, and privately controlled postsecondary schools account for 80% of all postsecondary schools.

21. **The correct answer is (C).** The political parties in the United States are very decentralized and devoid of the rigid discipline and hierarchy found in most European political parties.

22. **The correct answer is (D).** In a parliamentary government, the government only stays in power as long as Parliament supports it. If the ruling party loses on an important issue or there is a vote of no confidence, the prime minister can be required to resign. At that point, the leader of the opposition party is asked to form a new government or elections are held to determine which party shall have majority control of the government.

23. **The correct answer is (C).** The elevated shift of the IS curve to the new position, I′S′, illustrates the Keynesian proposition that increases in both gross national product (GNP) and interest rates could result from increases in government spending.

24. **The correct answer is (B).** In a "dirty float" system, a centralized bank intervenes to smooth economic crises by fluctuating the exchange rate, which directly influences the value of its country's currency. Exchange rates are allowed to fluctuate freely in a "clean float" system.

25. **The correct answer is (D).** The correct sequence would be to export U.S. goods through a foreign distributor to verify demand. If demand exists, then you would establish a foreign sales branch. The next step would be to initiate overseas assembly of parts manufactured in the United States to lower production costs, then begin full-scale manufacturing overseas.

26. **The correct answer is (B).** The statements presented in (A), (C), and (D) are all factually correct. Dumping in international trade would not in and of itself form a basis for a claim in the World Court (International Court of Justice).

English Expression

1.	A	6.	B	11.	E	16.	C	21.	E
2.	A	7.	C	12.	D	17.	C	22.	C
3.	C	8.	D	13.	B	18.	D	23.	D
4.	E	9.	E	14.	D	19.	B		
5.	E	10.	A	15.	C	20.	E		

1. **The correct answer is (A).** Paul Klee *waited* many long years to receive the recognition due him as a painter. "Awaited" means expected. Since the sentence says the recognition was received, the use of "awaited" is a diction error.

2. **The correct answer is (A).** Acting in skits or plays *has frequently proved* of great benefit to mentally ill patients, perhaps because such activity allows them to act out their own inner conflicts. "Acting" is the subject of the verb; thus the singular verb form is required. "In skits or plays" is a prepositional phrase, and the subject of a verb cannot be a prepositional phrase.

3. **The correct answer is (C).** According to the theory, some types of human behavior once considered the result of great psychological disturbance *are in reality* caused by a chemical imbalance within the body. "Types" is the subject of the verb; therefore, "are" is required.

4. **The correct answer is (E).** No error.

5. **The correct answer is (E).** No error.

6. **The correct answer is (B).** The candidate directed her appeal to the young people once *she realized that* she could not win without their votes. The verb in the main clause is in the past tense; the modifying clause must also use past tense.

7. **The correct answer is (C).** Because of the increasing popularity of our national parks, the park service must deal with the almost unsolvable problem of *how to let* every visitor in and still keep the wilderness intact. Use of the second person pronoun "you" is not appropriate in the sentence's context.

8. **The correct answer is (D).** Herschel's catalog of stars, first published in the late eighteenth century, did much *to increase interest in* astronomy. Other possibilities: *to promote* astronomy; *to increase the knowledge of* astronomy. "Progress" is an intransitive verb, which cannot be followed by an object.

9. **The correct answer is (E).** Finally, public and legal pressures forced the auto manufacturers to abandon *racing in favor of more rapid development of* pollution controls and safety devices. This answer most clearly conveys the meaning of the original sentence.

10. **The correct answer is (A).** Almost all folk singers have several ballads from the Child collection in their repertoires, *whether they know it or not.* Answer choices (C), (D), and (E) are unnecessarily wordy. Answer choice (B) uses a participle instead of a verb.

11. **The correct answer is (E).** Because extremely low-frequency radio waves can penetrate deep water, *much research has been devoted to their potential use in underwater communication.* Answer choices (A) and (C) are wordy; answer choices (B) and (E) use the passive voice.

12. **The correct answer is (D).** *Sent to help people of developing countries, members of the Peace Corps have done much useful work.* This choice conveys the meaning of the sentence most clearly and concisely.

13. The correct answer is (B). Horseshoe crabs are not crabs at all; *their nearest living relatives are the spiders*. This is the only choice that does not have an error in pronoun/antecedent or subject/verb agreement.

14. The correct answer is (D). Drops of water acting like prisms refract *sunlight and thus cause* rainbows. Choice (A) is wordy; choice (B) has no antecedent for the pronoun "it"; choices (C) and (E) add unnecessary words.

15. The correct answer is (C). Many old trees need root feeding *to survive*. This is the most concise expression of the meaning of the sentence.

16. The correct answer is (C). Hiring an architect is a *luxury that only* wealthy people can afford. The other choices slightly change the meaning of the original sentence.

17. The correct answer is (C). In their book *Black Power*, Stokely Carmichael and Charles V. Hamilton *coined* the term "institutionalized racism." This is the only correct verb form for this sentence.

18. The correct answer is (D). The article placed less emphasis on the disturbance of the ecology of the area *than on the contributions* that the mill could make to the economic development of the area. The other choices change the meaning of the original sentence.

19. The correct answer is (B). The most extensive changes in the English language have come about not through gradual changes in meaning, *but through contact* with different cultures. This wording preserves the meaning of the original sentence and maintains parallel construction.

20. The correct answer is (E). The tendency of German shepherds to recognize only one master makes *them difficult* pets, even though they are, for the most part, intelligent and well-behaved. The other choices would create awkward constructions in the new sentence.

21. The correct answer is (E). IV, I, III, II. Sentence IV introduces the subject: the "wealth" of African-American autobiographies. Sentence I refers to "this wealth." Sentence III provides a more focused statement than sentence II about women's role in this writing, and sentence II provides an example of an African-American woman writer.

22. The correct answer is (C). II, III, I, IV. Sentence II is the most general statement and thus is appropriate for the beginning of a paragraph. Sentence III refers to "this federation," mentioned in sentence II. Sentence I presents a contrast with the previous statements, indicated by "However," and sentence IV provides the effect of sentence I.

23. The correct answer is (D). III, II, IV, I. Sentence III is the most general statement. Sentence II refers to "this conflict," which is a paraphrase of the "strife" mentioned in sentence I. Sentence IV gives examples of the parties in conflict, and sentence I concludes the paragraph by providing a reason that the conflicts continue.

BIOGRAPHICAL QUESTIONNAIRE

The Foreign Service does not distribute official sample questions for this part of the written test. However, the model questions below are illustrative and typical.

Directions: Read each question and circle the answer that best reflects the correct answer.

1. My favorite subject in high school was
   (A) math.
   (B) English.
   (C) physical education.
   (D) social studies.
   (E) science.

2. My GPA upon graduation from high school (on a 4.0 scale) was
   (A) lower than 2.51.
   (B) 2.51 to 2.80.
   (C) 2.81 to 3.25.
   (D) 3.26 to 3.60.
   (E) higher than 3.60.

3. In my second year of high school, I was absent
   (A) never.
   (B) not more than 3 days.
   (C) 4 to 10 days.
   (D) more often than 10 days.
   (E) Do not recall

4. My best grades in high school were in
   (A) art.
   (B) math.
   (C) English.
   (D) social studies.
   (E) music.

5. While in high school, I participated in
   (A) one sport.
   (B) two sports and one other extracurricular activity.
   (C) three non-athletic extracurricular activities.
   (D) no extracurricular activities.
   (E) None of the above

6. During my senior year in high school, I held a paying job
   (A) 0 hours a week.
   (B) 1 to 5 hours a week.
   (C) 6 to 10 hours a week.
   (D) 11 to 16 hours a week.
   (E) more than 16 hours a week.

7. The number of semesters in which I failed a course in high school was
   (A) none.
   (B) one.
   (C) two or three.
   (D) four or five.
   (E) more than five.

8. In high school, I did volunteer work
   (A) more than 10 hours a week.
   (B) 5 to 10 hours a week on a regular basis.
   (C) sporadically.
   (D) seldom.
   (E) not at all.

9. My general area of concentration in college was
   (A) performing arts.
   (B) humanities.
   (C) social sciences.
   (D) business.
   (E) None of the above

10. At graduation from college, my age was
    (A) under 20.
    (B) 20.
    (C) 21 to 24.
    (D) 25 to 29.
    (E) 30 or over.

11. My standing in my graduating class was in the
    (A) bottom third.
    (B) middle third.
    (C) top third.
    (D) top quarter.
    (E) top 10 percent.

12. In college, I was elected to a major office in a class, club, or organization
    (A) more than six times.
    (B) four or five times.
    (C) two or three times.
    (D) once.
    (E) never.

13. In comparison to my peers, I cut classes
    (A) much less often than most.
    (B) somewhat less often than most.
    (C) just about the same as most.
    (D) somewhat more often than most.
    (E) much more often than most.

14. The campus activities in which I participated most were
    (A) social service.
    (B) political.
    (C) literary.
    (D) Did not participate in campus activities
    (E) Did not participate in any of these activities

15. My name appeared on the Dean's list
    (A) never.
    (B) once or twice.
    (C) in three or more terms.
    (D) in more terms than it did not appear.
    (E) Do not remember

16. The volunteer work I did while in college was predominantly
    (A) health-care related.
    (B) religious.
    (C) political.
    (D) educational.
    (E) Did not volunteer

17. While a college student, I spent most of my summers
    (A) in summer school.
    (B) earning money.
    (C) traveling.
    (D) in service activities.
    (E) resting.

18. My college education was financed
    (A) entirely by my parents.
    (B) by my parents and my own earnings.
    (C) by scholarships, loans, and my own earnings.
    (D) by my parents and loans.
    (E) by a combination of sources not listed above.

19. In the college classroom, I was considered
    (A) a listener.
    (B) an occasional contributor.
    (C) an average participant.
    (D) a frequent contributor.
    (E) a leader.

20. The person on campus whom I most admired was
    (A) another student.
    (B) an athletic coach.
    (C) a teacher.
    (D) an administrator.
    (E) a journalist.

21. Of the skills I developed at college, the one I value most is
    (A) foreign language ability.
    (B) oral expression.
    (C) writing skills.
    (D) facility with computers.
    (E) analytical skills.

22. I made my greatest mark in college through my
    (A) athletic prowess.
    (B) success in performing arts.
    (C) academic success.
    (D) partying reputation.
    (E) conciliatory skill with my peers.

23. My cumulative GPA (on a 4.0 scale) in courses in my major was
    (A) lower than 3.0.
    (B) 3.0 to 3.25.
    (C) 3.26 to 3.50.
    (D) 3.51 to 3.75.
    (E) higher than 3.75.

24. While in college, I
    (A) worked full-time and was a part-time student.
    (B) worked 20 hours a week and was a full-time student.
    (C) worked 20 hours a week and was a part-time student.
    (D) was a full-time student working more than 10 but less than 20 hours a week.
    (E) was a full-time student.

25. In the past six months, I have been late to work (or school)
    (A) never.
    (B) only one time.
    (C) very seldom.
    (D) more than five times.
    (E) I don't recall.

26. My supervisors (or teachers) would be most likely to describe me as
    (A) competent.
    (B) gifted.
    (C) intelligent.
    (D) fast-working.
    (E) detail-oriented.

27. My peers would probably describe me as
    (A) analytical.
    (B) glib.
    (C) organized.
    (D) funny.
    (E) helpful.

28. According to my supervisors (or teachers), my greatest asset is my
    (A) ability to communicate orally.
    (B) written expression.
    (C) ability to motivate others.
    (D) organization of time.
    (E) friendly personality.

29. In the past two years, I have applied for
    (A) no jobs other than this one.
    (B) one other job.
    (C) two to four other jobs.
    (D) five to eight other jobs.
    (E) more than eight jobs.

30. In the past year, I read strictly for pleasure
    (A) no books.
    (B) one book.
    (C) two books.
    (D) three to six books.
    (E) more than six books.

31. When I read for pleasure, I read mostly
    (A) history.
    (B) fiction.
    (C) poetry.
    (D) biography.
    (E) current events.

32. My peers would say of me that when they ask me a question, I am
    (A) helpful.
    (B) brusque.
    (C) condescending.
    (D) generous.
    (E) patient.

33. My supervisors (or teachers) would say that my area of least competence is
    (A) analytical ability.
    (B) written communication.
    (C) attention to detail.
    (D) public speaking.
    (E) self-control.

34. In the past two years, the number of full-time jobs (35 hours or more) I have held is

(A) none.

(B) one.

(C) two or three.

(D) four.

(E) five or more.

35. Compared to my peers, my supervisors (or teachers) would rank my dependability

(A) much better than average.

(B) somewhat better than average.

(C) about average.

(D) somewhat less than average.

(E) much less than average.

36. In my opinion, the most important of the following attributes in an employee is

(A) discretion.

(B) loyalty.

(C) open-mindedness.

(D) courtesy.

(E) competence.

37. My peers would say that the word that describes me least is

(A) sociable.

(B) reserved.

(C) impatient.

(D) judgmental.

(E) independent.

38. My supervisors (or teachers) would say that I react to criticism with

(A) a defensive attitude.

(B) quick capitulation.

(C) anger.

(D) interest.

(E) shame.

39. My attendance record over the past year has been

(A) not as good as I would like it to be.

(B) not as good as my supervisors (or teachers) would like it to be.

(C) a source of embarrassment.

(D) satisfactory.

(E) a source of pride.

40. My peers would say that when I feel challenged, my reaction is one of

(A) determination.

(B) energy.

(C) defiance.

(D) caution.

(E) compromise.

There are no "right" answers to these questions, so there is no answer key.

It goes without saying that you cannot learn the subject matter of the Foreign Service Officer Exam in an all-night cram session or even a week of such sessions. Your success on the Knowledge portion of the exam is based on a lifetime of learning, reading, discussing, and thinking. Some brushing up on the principles of punctuation, grammar, and English usage will raise your score on the English Expression questions.

PART II

PRACTICE TESTS

Preface to the Practice Tests

The three practice tests in this book make up one of the most important parts of your preparation. Use them as benchmarks as you work through the other chapters in this book. The practice tests give you a great opportunity to gauge your progress and focus your study in the key areas, including:

- Knowledge and understanding of the institutions and concepts that are fundamental to the development of the United States and other countries
- Knowledge of subjects basic to the functions of the Foreign Service
- Skill in written English expression

The third part of the written exam—the Biographical Questionnaire—measures your experience, skills, and achievements in school, employment, and other activities. The questionnaire does not penalize candidates who have not gone to college, have no previous work experience, are young or old, or have other varied patterns of education and experience, but credits candidates for what they have achieved relative to the opportunities they have had. The only way to prepare for the test is to gather statistical records from your school career and recall what you have achieved in your post-student years.

When you take the practice tests under real-time conditions, you will gain confidence that you are prepared for the real thing. Take them under timed conditions, and you'll experience just how it feels to take the actual exam. As you finish each exam, check your answers against the answer key and read the explanation for each question you missed.

Taking these tests will improve your familiarity with the American Foreign Service Officer Exam and reduce your number of careless errors. To get the most out of these practice tests, you should do everything you can to simulate actual test-taking conditions.

chapter 5

PRACTICE TEST 1 ANSWER SHEET

Knowledge Questions

1. Ⓐ Ⓑ Ⓒ Ⓓ   21. Ⓐ Ⓑ Ⓒ Ⓓ   41. Ⓐ Ⓑ Ⓒ Ⓓ   61. Ⓐ Ⓑ Ⓒ Ⓓ
2. Ⓐ Ⓑ Ⓒ Ⓓ   22. Ⓐ Ⓑ Ⓒ Ⓓ   42. Ⓐ Ⓑ Ⓒ Ⓓ   62. Ⓐ Ⓑ Ⓒ Ⓓ
3. Ⓐ Ⓑ Ⓒ Ⓓ   23. Ⓐ Ⓑ Ⓒ Ⓓ   43. Ⓐ Ⓑ Ⓒ Ⓓ   63. Ⓐ Ⓑ Ⓒ Ⓓ
4. Ⓐ Ⓑ Ⓒ Ⓓ   24. Ⓐ Ⓑ Ⓒ Ⓓ   44. Ⓐ Ⓑ Ⓒ Ⓓ   64. Ⓐ Ⓑ Ⓒ Ⓓ
5. Ⓐ Ⓑ Ⓒ Ⓓ   25. Ⓐ Ⓑ Ⓒ Ⓓ   45. Ⓐ Ⓑ Ⓒ Ⓓ   65. Ⓐ Ⓑ Ⓒ Ⓓ
6. Ⓐ Ⓑ Ⓒ Ⓓ   26. Ⓐ Ⓑ Ⓒ Ⓓ   46. Ⓐ Ⓑ Ⓒ Ⓓ   66. Ⓐ Ⓑ Ⓒ Ⓓ
7. Ⓐ Ⓑ Ⓒ Ⓓ   27. Ⓐ Ⓑ Ⓒ Ⓓ   47. Ⓐ Ⓑ Ⓒ Ⓓ   67. Ⓐ Ⓑ Ⓒ Ⓓ
8. Ⓐ Ⓑ Ⓒ Ⓓ   28. Ⓐ Ⓑ Ⓒ Ⓓ   48. Ⓐ Ⓑ Ⓒ Ⓓ   68. Ⓐ Ⓑ Ⓒ Ⓓ
9. Ⓐ Ⓑ Ⓒ Ⓓ   29. Ⓐ Ⓑ Ⓒ Ⓓ   49. Ⓐ Ⓑ Ⓒ Ⓓ   69. Ⓐ Ⓑ Ⓒ Ⓓ
10. Ⓐ Ⓑ Ⓒ Ⓓ   30. Ⓐ Ⓑ Ⓒ Ⓓ   50. Ⓐ Ⓑ Ⓒ Ⓓ   70. Ⓐ Ⓑ Ⓒ Ⓓ
11. Ⓐ Ⓑ Ⓒ Ⓓ   31. Ⓐ Ⓑ Ⓒ Ⓓ   51. Ⓐ Ⓑ Ⓒ Ⓓ
12. Ⓐ Ⓑ Ⓒ Ⓓ   32. Ⓐ Ⓑ Ⓒ Ⓓ   52. Ⓐ Ⓑ Ⓒ Ⓓ
13. Ⓐ Ⓑ Ⓒ Ⓓ   33. Ⓐ Ⓑ Ⓒ Ⓓ   53. Ⓐ Ⓑ Ⓒ Ⓓ
14. Ⓐ Ⓑ Ⓒ Ⓓ   34. Ⓐ Ⓑ Ⓒ Ⓓ   54. Ⓐ Ⓑ Ⓒ Ⓓ
15. Ⓐ Ⓑ Ⓒ Ⓓ   35. Ⓐ Ⓑ Ⓒ Ⓓ   55. Ⓐ Ⓑ Ⓒ Ⓓ
16. Ⓐ Ⓑ Ⓒ Ⓓ   36. Ⓐ Ⓑ Ⓒ Ⓓ   56. Ⓐ Ⓑ Ⓒ Ⓓ
17. Ⓐ Ⓑ Ⓒ Ⓓ   37. Ⓐ Ⓑ Ⓒ Ⓓ   57. Ⓐ Ⓑ Ⓒ Ⓓ
18. Ⓐ Ⓑ Ⓒ Ⓓ   38. Ⓐ Ⓑ Ⓒ Ⓓ   58. Ⓐ Ⓑ Ⓒ Ⓓ
19. Ⓐ Ⓑ Ⓒ Ⓓ   39. Ⓐ Ⓑ Ⓒ Ⓓ   59. Ⓐ Ⓑ Ⓒ Ⓓ
20. Ⓐ Ⓑ Ⓒ Ⓓ   40. Ⓐ Ⓑ Ⓒ Ⓓ   60. Ⓐ Ⓑ Ⓒ Ⓓ

English Expression

1. Ⓐ Ⓑ Ⓒ Ⓓ Ⓔ	31. Ⓐ Ⓑ Ⓒ Ⓓ Ⓔ	61. Ⓐ Ⓑ Ⓒ Ⓓ Ⓔ	91. Ⓐ Ⓑ Ⓒ Ⓓ Ⓔ
2. Ⓐ Ⓑ Ⓒ Ⓓ Ⓔ	32. Ⓐ Ⓑ Ⓒ Ⓓ Ⓔ	62. Ⓐ Ⓑ Ⓒ Ⓓ Ⓔ	92. Ⓐ Ⓑ Ⓒ Ⓓ Ⓔ
3. Ⓐ Ⓑ Ⓒ Ⓓ Ⓔ	33. Ⓐ Ⓑ Ⓒ Ⓓ Ⓔ	63. Ⓐ Ⓑ Ⓒ Ⓓ Ⓔ	93. Ⓐ Ⓑ Ⓒ Ⓓ Ⓔ
4. Ⓐ Ⓑ Ⓒ Ⓓ Ⓔ	34. Ⓐ Ⓑ Ⓒ Ⓓ Ⓔ	64. Ⓐ Ⓑ Ⓒ Ⓓ Ⓔ	94. Ⓐ Ⓑ Ⓒ Ⓓ Ⓔ
5. Ⓐ Ⓑ Ⓒ Ⓓ Ⓔ	35. Ⓐ Ⓑ Ⓒ Ⓓ Ⓔ	65. Ⓐ Ⓑ Ⓒ Ⓓ Ⓔ	95. Ⓐ Ⓑ Ⓒ Ⓓ Ⓔ
6. Ⓐ Ⓑ Ⓒ Ⓓ Ⓔ	36. Ⓐ Ⓑ Ⓒ Ⓓ Ⓔ	66. Ⓐ Ⓑ Ⓒ Ⓓ Ⓔ	96. Ⓐ Ⓑ Ⓒ Ⓓ Ⓔ
7. Ⓐ Ⓑ Ⓒ Ⓓ Ⓔ	37. Ⓐ Ⓑ Ⓒ Ⓓ Ⓔ	67. Ⓐ Ⓑ Ⓒ Ⓓ Ⓔ	97. Ⓐ Ⓑ Ⓒ Ⓓ Ⓔ
8. Ⓐ Ⓑ Ⓒ Ⓓ Ⓔ	38. Ⓐ Ⓑ Ⓒ Ⓓ Ⓔ	68. Ⓐ Ⓑ Ⓒ Ⓓ Ⓔ	98. Ⓐ Ⓑ Ⓒ Ⓓ Ⓔ
9. Ⓐ Ⓑ Ⓒ Ⓓ Ⓔ	39. Ⓐ Ⓑ Ⓒ Ⓓ Ⓔ	69. Ⓐ Ⓑ Ⓒ Ⓓ Ⓔ	99. Ⓐ Ⓑ Ⓒ Ⓓ Ⓔ
10. Ⓐ Ⓑ Ⓒ Ⓓ Ⓔ	40. Ⓐ Ⓑ Ⓒ Ⓓ Ⓔ	70. Ⓐ Ⓑ Ⓒ Ⓓ Ⓔ	100. Ⓐ Ⓑ Ⓒ Ⓓ Ⓔ
11. Ⓐ Ⓑ Ⓒ Ⓓ Ⓔ	41. Ⓐ Ⓑ Ⓒ Ⓓ Ⓔ	71. Ⓐ Ⓑ Ⓒ Ⓓ Ⓔ	101. Ⓐ Ⓑ Ⓒ Ⓓ Ⓔ
12. Ⓐ Ⓑ Ⓒ Ⓓ Ⓔ	42. Ⓐ Ⓑ Ⓒ Ⓓ Ⓔ	72. Ⓐ Ⓑ Ⓒ Ⓓ Ⓔ	102. Ⓐ Ⓑ Ⓒ Ⓓ Ⓔ
13. Ⓐ Ⓑ Ⓒ Ⓓ Ⓔ	43. Ⓐ Ⓑ Ⓒ Ⓓ Ⓔ	73. Ⓐ Ⓑ Ⓒ Ⓓ Ⓔ	103. Ⓐ Ⓑ Ⓒ Ⓓ Ⓔ
14. Ⓐ Ⓑ Ⓒ Ⓓ Ⓔ	44. Ⓐ Ⓑ Ⓒ Ⓓ Ⓔ	74. Ⓐ Ⓑ Ⓒ Ⓓ Ⓔ	104. Ⓐ Ⓑ Ⓒ Ⓓ Ⓔ
15. Ⓐ Ⓑ Ⓒ Ⓓ Ⓔ	45. Ⓐ Ⓑ Ⓒ Ⓓ Ⓔ	75. Ⓐ Ⓑ Ⓒ Ⓓ Ⓔ	105. Ⓐ Ⓑ Ⓒ Ⓓ Ⓔ
16. Ⓐ Ⓑ Ⓒ Ⓓ Ⓔ	46. Ⓐ Ⓑ Ⓒ Ⓓ Ⓔ	76. Ⓐ Ⓑ Ⓒ Ⓓ Ⓔ	106. Ⓐ Ⓑ Ⓒ Ⓓ Ⓔ
17. Ⓐ Ⓑ Ⓒ Ⓓ Ⓔ	47. Ⓐ Ⓑ Ⓒ Ⓓ Ⓔ	77. Ⓐ Ⓑ Ⓒ Ⓓ Ⓔ	107. Ⓐ Ⓑ Ⓒ Ⓓ Ⓔ
18. Ⓐ Ⓑ Ⓒ Ⓓ Ⓔ	48. Ⓐ Ⓑ Ⓒ Ⓓ Ⓔ	78. Ⓐ Ⓑ Ⓒ Ⓓ Ⓔ	108. Ⓐ Ⓑ Ⓒ Ⓓ Ⓔ
19. Ⓐ Ⓑ Ⓒ Ⓓ Ⓔ	49. Ⓐ Ⓑ Ⓒ Ⓓ Ⓔ	79. Ⓐ Ⓑ Ⓒ Ⓓ Ⓔ	109. Ⓐ Ⓑ Ⓒ Ⓓ Ⓔ
20. Ⓐ Ⓑ Ⓒ Ⓓ Ⓔ	50. Ⓐ Ⓑ Ⓒ Ⓓ Ⓔ	80. Ⓐ Ⓑ Ⓒ Ⓓ Ⓔ	110. Ⓐ Ⓑ Ⓒ Ⓓ Ⓔ
21. Ⓐ Ⓑ Ⓒ Ⓓ Ⓔ	51. Ⓐ Ⓑ Ⓒ Ⓓ Ⓔ	81. Ⓐ Ⓑ Ⓒ Ⓓ Ⓔ	
22. Ⓐ Ⓑ Ⓒ Ⓓ Ⓔ	52. Ⓐ Ⓑ Ⓒ Ⓓ Ⓔ	82. Ⓐ Ⓑ Ⓒ Ⓓ Ⓔ	
23. Ⓐ Ⓑ Ⓒ Ⓓ Ⓔ	53. Ⓐ Ⓑ Ⓒ Ⓓ Ⓔ	83. Ⓐ Ⓑ Ⓒ Ⓓ Ⓔ	
24. Ⓐ Ⓑ Ⓒ Ⓓ Ⓔ	54. Ⓐ Ⓑ Ⓒ Ⓓ Ⓔ	84. Ⓐ Ⓑ Ⓒ Ⓓ Ⓔ	
25. Ⓐ Ⓑ Ⓒ Ⓓ Ⓔ	55. Ⓐ Ⓑ Ⓒ Ⓓ Ⓔ	85. Ⓐ Ⓑ Ⓒ Ⓓ Ⓔ	
26. Ⓐ Ⓑ Ⓒ Ⓓ Ⓔ	56. Ⓐ Ⓑ Ⓒ Ⓓ Ⓔ	86. Ⓐ Ⓑ Ⓒ Ⓓ Ⓔ	
27. Ⓐ Ⓑ Ⓒ Ⓓ Ⓔ	57. Ⓐ Ⓑ Ⓒ Ⓓ Ⓔ	87. Ⓐ Ⓑ Ⓒ Ⓓ Ⓔ	
28. Ⓐ Ⓑ Ⓒ Ⓓ Ⓔ	58. Ⓐ Ⓑ Ⓒ Ⓓ Ⓔ	88. Ⓐ Ⓑ Ⓒ Ⓓ Ⓔ	
29. Ⓐ Ⓑ Ⓒ Ⓓ Ⓔ	59. Ⓐ Ⓑ Ⓒ Ⓓ Ⓔ	89. Ⓐ Ⓑ Ⓒ Ⓓ Ⓔ	
30. Ⓐ Ⓑ Ⓒ Ⓓ Ⓔ	60. Ⓐ Ⓑ Ⓒ Ⓓ Ⓔ	90. Ⓐ Ⓑ Ⓒ Ⓓ Ⓔ	

KNOWLEDGE QUESTIONS

70 Questions • 2 Hours

> **Directions:** Each of the questions or incomplete statements below is followed by four possible answers. Select the best answer for each question and then blacken the corresponding space on the answer sheet. Some sets of questions are presented with material such as reading passages, plans, graphs, tables, etc. Answers to such questions may require interpretation of the material and/or outside knowledge relevant to its content.

1. Organization structure deals with the relationship between functions and the personnel performing these functions. It is usually advisable to think first of functions, then of the individuals performing these functions. Most implicit in this approach is the recognition that

   (A) conditions outside the organization may necessitate changes in the organization structure.

   (B) functions need not always be coordinated for an organization to effectively carry out its objectives.

   (C) functions tend to change with time while the interests and abilities of personnel are usually permanent.

   (D) personnel emphasis often results in unusual combinations of duties that are difficult to manage.

QUESTIONS 2 TO 4 ARE BASED ON THE FOLLOWING CHOICES:

   (A) Specific tariffs

   (B) Ad valorem tariffs

   (C) Compound tariffs (specific or ad valorem, whichever is lower)

   (D) Quotas

2. If both domestic prices and the prices of imports fall, they tend to be more protective than before.

3. When import prices rise, they give greater protection than before.

4. They do not provide an incentive for exporting countries to decrease their prices.

5. Which pairs an important person in history with an idea or belief he supported?

   (A) Karl Marx—All history is determined by political struggles among governing elites.

   (B) John Maynard Keynes—The best way for government to fight an economic depression is to limit government spending.

   (C) Karl von Clausewitz—Warfare and politics are separate, unrelated spheres of activity.

   (D) Martin Luther King Jr.—Nonviolent protest can promote social and political change.

6. Who would feel an adverse effect of inflation most immediately?

   (A) An investor in enterprises involving real estate

   (B) A retired individual living on an insurance annuity

   (C) An individual who has most of his capital invested in common stock

   (D) A member of a union that has an escalator clause in its contract with management

7. Which of the following did NOT happen in the aftermath of the 1990–1991 Gulf War?

   (A) The Iraqi leader was removed from power.

   (B) Economic sanctions were imposed upon Iraq.

   (C) Two no-fly zones were established inside of Iraq.

   (D) The United States periodically bombed targets inside Iraq.

8. A U.S. citizen is arrested in Germany for possession of heroin. Which of the following situations is he most likely to face?

   (A) He will be released as soon as the fact that he is not a citizen of Germany is verified.

   (B) He will be imprisoned for the maximum period allowed by German law for this offense without judicial process because he is not a citizen of Germany.

   (C) He will be released to the custody of the U.S. consular officer for prosecution under U.S. law.

   (D) He will be prosecuted under the laws of Germany and will be sentenced accordingly.

9. Chinese residents of Southeast Asian countries often are regarded with suspicion and hostility by the indigenous population. Arrange the following explanations for this phenomenon in decreasing order of significance.

   I.   Most Southeast Asian countries were invaded by China at some point in their pre-colonial history.

   II. Southeast Asians often are suspicious of Chinese clannishness and tendency to preserve a separate cultural identity.

   III. Many Southeast Asians remember and resent the Chinese role as economic middleman during the colonial era.

   IV. The Chinese frequently are wealthy and control a disproportionately large share of the local economy.

   (A) II, I, IV, III

   (B) III, IV, I, II

   (C) IV, II, III, I

   (D) IV, I, III, II

10. It is estimated that prices will rise by 5 percent during the coming year. Interest on the current outstanding debt for the coming year may be expected to

(A) depend on new capital programs.

(B) increase by about 5 percent.

(C) increase by more than 5 percent because of the generally more rapid increase in construction costs.

(D) remain unchanged.

11. The War Powers Act of 1973 states that

(A) the president has the power to send combat troops overseas without consulting Congress.

(B) the president can unilaterally declare war through an executive order.

(C) Congress can require the president to bring combat troops home after 60 days.

(D) Congress can prevent the president from sending combat troops overseas through a two-thirds vote of each house.

12. All of the following statements express policies of the U.S. government during the Cold War EXCEPT

(A) "Our policy with regard to Europe is not to interfere with her internal concerns but to consider each European government de facto as the legitimate government and to cultivate friendly relations with it."

(B) "If we find it impossible to enlist Soviet cooperation in the solution of world problems, we should be prepared to join with the British and other Western countries in an attempt to build up a world of our own."

(C) "The role of this country should consist of friendly aid in the drafting of a European economic program to get Europe on its feet and to provide financial support for such a program so far as it may be practical for us to do so."

(D) "The United States seeks no territorial expansion or selfish advantage and has no plans for aggression against any other state, large or small, but is committed to the mutual security of non-Communist nations in Europe."

13. After World War II, all of the following nations were divided between communist and non-Communist spheres of influence EXCEPT

(A) Korea.

(B) Germany.

(C) Japan.

(D) Vietnam.

QUESTIONS 14 TO 16 ARE BASED ON THE FOLLOWING DIAGRAM SHOWING A FIRM'S COST AND REVENUE:

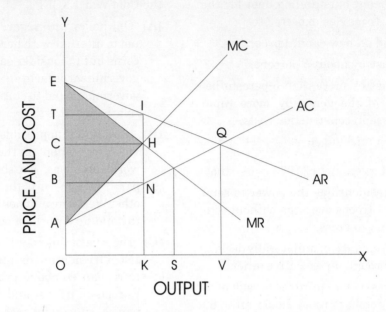

Curves:
MC = Marginal Cost
MR = Marginal Revenue
AC = Average Cost
AR = Average Revenue

14. The most profitable output for the firm to produce is

(A) OS.

(B) OV.

(C) OK.

(D) OA.

15. The amount of profits will be shown by

(A) INQ.

(B) TICH.

(C) ACH.

(D) either AEH or BTIN.

16. If the government levied a tax per unit of output, the price per unit for the firm would

(A) rise by the amount of the tax.

(B) rise by more than the amount of the tax.

(C) rise by less than the amount of the tax.

(D) remain the same.

17. Which of the following is a TRUE statement regarding UN peacekeeping efforts?

    (A) The frequency and number of peacekeeping missions have declined during the last decade.

    (B) Most peacekeeping troops have been supplied by smaller or non-aligned nations.

    (C) American troops have become a common part of UN peacekeeping missions.

    (D) In nearly all cases, UN peacekeeping missions have been able to establish a "permanent" peace.

18. All of the following are specifically found in the U.S. Constitution EXCEPT

    (A) the establishment of the Electoral College.

    (B) a prohibition against bills of attainder.

    (C) a statement creating national political parties.

    (D) a provision that establishes an "Acting President."

19. "A man who lived from 1865 to 1945 would have witnessed developments that in European history occupied several centuries: absolute monarchy, constitutional monarchy, liberalism, imperialist expansion, military dictatorship, totalitarian fascism, foreign occupation." The above description BEST fits

    (A) India.

    (B) China.

    (C) Japan.

    (D) Egypt.

20. The 1997 Kyoto Treaty dealt with the international issue of

    (A) nuclear proliferation.

    (B) overpopulation.

    (C) global warming.

    (D) human rights and world immigration flows.

21. The increased use of executive agreements by U.S. presidents has

    (A) actually increased congressional influence over the foreign policy process.

    (B) reflected the increase in overseas American commitments and responsibilities.

    (C) basically meant that U.S. presidents no longer use executive orders as much as in the past.

    (D) had little impact upon congressional–presidential relationships in the area of foreign policy.

QUESTIONS 22 TO 24 ARE BASED ON THE MAP BELOW:

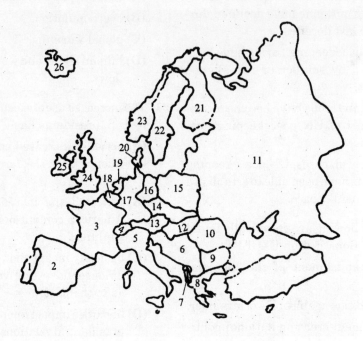

22. The country in which the United States and the former Soviet Union confronted one another both in diplomacy and in chess is

(A) 21.

(B) 26.

(C) 10.

(D) 15.

23. The country that immediately comes to mind in connection with the word *appeasement* is

(A) 4.

(B) 12.

(C) 13.

(D) 14.

24. Two countries that maintained their neutrality throughout both World Wars are

(A) 4 and 22.

(B) 12 and 25.

(C) 22 and 23.

(D) 4 and 18.

25. "I believe it must be the policy of the United States to support free peoples who are resisting attempted subjugation by armed minorities or by outside pressures . . ." is a statement taken from the famous 1947 proclamation known as the

(A) Marshall Plan.

(B) Baruch Plan.

(C) Eisenhower Doctrine.

(D) Truman Doctrine.

26. "The political system of the allied powers is essentially different from that of America. We should consider any attempt on their part to extend their system to any portion of this hemisphere as dangerous to our peace and safety." This statement is representative of the ideas expressed in

    (A) the Freeport Doctrine.
    (B) Manifest Destiny.
    (C) the Constitution of the Confederacy.
    (D) the Monroe Doctrine.

27. All of the following are in general used as payment arrangements between a U.S. seller and a foreign buyer EXCEPT

    (A) bills of exchange.
    (B) open accounts.
    (C) consular invoices.
    (D) cash.

28. The WTO is an international body that is mainly concerned with

    (A) controlling the global drug trade.
    (B) allocating loans to the lesser-developed countries.
    (C) monitoring and regulating global trading relationships.
    (D) monitoring the status of human rights around the globe.

29. Which of the following neither is, nor was, concerned with economic and military aid for Europe?

    (A) GATT
    (B) Marshall Plan
    (C) NATO
    (D) OECD

30. The basic assumptions underlying the doctrines of laissez-faire and natural rights are also the basic assumptions underlying the

    (A) divine right theory and natural law.
    (B) mercantile theory and divine right theory.
    (C) social contract theory and natural law.
    (D) social contract theory and state socialism.

31. The total market value of all final goods and services produced annually within U.S. boundaries, whether by American or foreign-supplied resources, is known as the

    (A) Gross National Product.
    (B) Gross Domestic Product.
    (C) yearly trade deficit.
    (D) national budgetary surplus.

32. A "tight bipolar" structure of international power was present during which time frame?

    (A) 1919–1941
    (B) 1992–2001
    (C) 1814–1914
    (D) 1946–1991

33. An "inflationary move" by the Federal Reserve Board is BEST characterized by

    (A) raising reserve requirements.
    (B) selling federal bonds.
    (C) raising discount rates.
    (D) purchasing government securities.

34. "During the decade 1840–1850, they left their native land in large numbers because of the famine and came to the United States to settle, for the greater part, in seaboard cities." This description BEST applies to emigrants from

    (A) Germany.

    (B) Ireland.

    (C) Russia.

    (D) Italy.

35. Which of the following novels is a polemic against slavery?

    (A) *The Nigger of the Narcissus*

    (B) *The Way of All Flesh*

    (C) *Of Human Bondage*

    (D) *Uncle Tom's Cabin*

36. "Man is born free, and everywhere he is in chains" is a quotation from the writings of

    (A) Karl Marx.

    (B) Jean Jacques Rousseau.

    (C) John Locke.

    (D) François Voltaire.

37. Avoiding conflict by recruiting potential or existing leaders of the opposition is a technique known as

    (A) pre-emption.

    (B) co-optation.

    (C) isolation.

    (D) assignation.

38. An increase in consumer spending leads to a proportionally larger increase in capital expenditure. This is an example of which of the following?

    (A) Inflation

    (B) Deflation

    (C) Accelerator

    (D) Multiplier

39. Country P, through legislative enactment, defines its monetary unit in terms of sisal. Sisal is coined in limitless quantities at slight cost and is free to move into and out of the country in any quantity. In addition, all legal tender is redeemable, at no loss, in sisal coinage upon demand. The monetary standard that MOST applies to this situation is

    (A) Full Sisal Coin Standard.

    (B) Limited Sisal Bullion Standard.

    (C) Sisal Exchange Standard.

    (D) Full Sisal Control Standard.

40. A nineteenth-century naturalist, philosopher, and writer who had a profound effect on political philosophy and action in the twentieth century and the book through which this influence was imparted are

    (A) Henry David Thoreau and *Civil Disobedience.*

    (B) Charles Darwin and *Origin of the Species.*

    (C) Adam Smith and *Wealth of Nations.*

    (D) Charles M. Sheldon and *In His Steps.*

41. Often in financial statement analysis the current ratio is used. This ratio is

    (A) current assets divided by current liabilities.

    (B) current liabilities divided by current known assets.

    (C) current assets less inventory divided by current liabilities.

    (D) current assets less current liabilities divided by working capital.

QUESTIONS 42 TO 44 ARE BASED ON THE MAP BELOW:

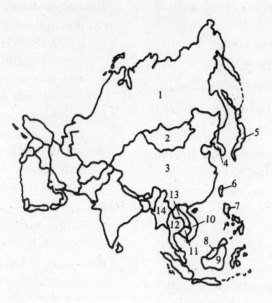

42. From among the choices offered, the ONLY country not to have been under colonial rule in modern times is

(A) 7.

(B) 9.

(C) 10.

(D) 12.

43. The countries that were once known as French Indo-China are

(A) 10, 11, and 12.

(B) 10, 11, and 13.

(C) 11, 12, and 13.

(D) 12, 13, and 14.

44. The country that is overwhelmingly Moslem, though neither controlled by Fundamentalists nor considered an Islamic state, is

(A) 2.

(B) 7.

(C) 9.

(D) 14.

45. Place the following post–World War II events by designated letter in the correct chronological order from earliest to the most recent:

A The Bay of Pigs

B The Gulf of Tonkin Resolution

C The Berlin Airlift

D The Yom Kippur War

E The invasion of Grenada

F The founding of OPEC

(A) A, E, C, D, B, F

(B) C, A, B, F, E, D

(C) C, F, A, B, D, E

(D) F, C, B, A, D, E

46. Which of the following normally occurs when a commercial bank makes a loan to a business firm?

(A) The bank's liabilities and assets increase.

(B) The bank's liabilities and assets decrease.

(C) The bank's liabilities increase and its assets decrease.

(D) The bank's liabilities decrease and its assets increase.

47. A change in the dollar–pound sterling exchange ratio from 3:1 to 4:1 is BEST described as

   (A) depreciation of the pound.

   (B) devaluation of the dollar.

   (C) depreciation of the two currencies.

   (D) depreciation of the dollar relative to the pound.

48. The cabinet department that has the smallest annual budget is

   (A) Commerce.

   (B) Justice.

   (C) State.

   (D) Defense.

49. Sometimes "the impossible" can only be accomplished by the most "improbable" person. Thus, only a leader with well-established credentials as a hardliner can get away with making overtures to "the other side." Of the following, which visit does NOT fit into this category?

   (A) The visit of Nixon to China

   (B) The visit of John Paul II to the Temple in Rome

   (C) The visit of Willy Brandt to the United States

   (D) The visit of Sadat to Jerusalem

50. The responsibility for specific types of decisions generally is BEST delegated to

   (A) the highest organizational level at which there is an individual possessing the ability, desire, impartiality, and access to relevant information needed to make these decisions.

   (B) the lowest organizational level at which there is an individual possessing the ability, desire, impartiality, and access to relevant information needed to make these decisions.

   (C) a group of executives, rather than a single executive, if these decisions deal with an emergency.

   (D) the organizational level midway between that which will have to carry out these decisions and that which will have to authorize the resources for their implementation.

51. An American student in London becomes friendly with "the wrong crowd" and soon is involved in a bungled bank robbery. The robbers are apprehended, and the American student calls the American consulate for help. The consul can offer advice and encouragement to the jailed student, but he/she CANNOT

   (A) request release of the student for trial in the United States as a U.S. citizen.

   (B) attend the trial as an observer.

   (C) communicate with the student's parents to reassure them that the student is being treated fairly.

   (D) visit the student in prison if the student is convicted.

52. The Boxers, whose name comes down in history because of their role as the aggressors in the Boxer Rebellion in China in 1900, drew that name from

    (A) their attempt to box China in from the rest of the world, in other words, their isolationism.

    (B) their attempt to box missionaries into tiny isolated enclaves.

    (C) the fact that they relied heavily on hand-to-hand combat.

    (D) the Chinese Secret Society of the Righteous and Harmonious Fists to which they belonged and in which they practiced boxing and callisthenic rituals that they believed made them impervious to bullets.

53. The Boxer Rebellion was limited to North China because

    (A) it was a rogue operation, not sanctioned by the government.

    (B) viceroys in South China refused to obey the Empress Dowager and protected their foreigners.

    (C) poverty and foreign aggression were serious problems only in North China.

    (D) missionaries had attracted few converts in South China.

54. The historical basis for the Sanctuary Movement in the U.S. Southwest is

    (A) the non-establishment clause of the First Amendment.

    (B) St. Thomas More's search for sanctuary in the cathedral.

    (C) the role of ancient Greek temples as a refuge for criminals.

    (D) the international law principle that clerics should always receive safe passage.

55. The Department of Justice has been actively prosecuting the church workers who are involved in the Sanctuary Movement because the Justice Department claims that

    (A) the Sanctuary Movement is simply abetting illegal immigration.

    (B) many of those seeking sanctuary are simply common criminals seeking to escape justice at home.

    (C) the churches and shelters do not meet standards of health and sanitation.

    (D) because of separation of church and state, the United States does not recognize the sanctity of the confessional.

56. The Iran-Contra Scandal occurred during whose presidency and involved what other nation?

    (A) Nixon—China

    (B) Reagan—Nicaragua

    (C) Carter—Russia

    (D) Kennedy—Cuba

57. In the terminology of the late 1990s, which of the following nations was NOT deemed to be a "rogue state" by American foreign policy leaders?

    (A) North Korea

    (B) Iraq

    (C) Iran

    (D) Mexico

58. Mikhail Gorbachev, the last leader of the Soviet Union, tried to reform his nation through the dual policies of *glasnost* and *perestroika*. Which of the following BEST defines those two terms, in consecutive order?

(A) Privatization and competitive political parties

(B) Openness of expression and economic restructuring

(C) Socialist realism and a full capitalist economy

(D) Educational reform and laissez-faire economics

59. Which of the following is the MOST accurate description of the European Union in the early twenty-first century?

(A) It is essentially a confederation of states with no centralized, all-European institutions.

(B) It is a true "United States of Europe" in the same sense as the United States of America.

(C) It is a common market for tariff-free trade and nothing more.

(D) It is a union of both centralized and decentralized institutions.

60. Precursors of the European Economic Community and the European Free Trade Association were the

I.   Franco-Prussian Alliance.

II. Hanseatic League.

III. Zollverein.

IV. League of Nations.

(A) I and II only

(B) II and III only

(C) II and IV only

(D) I and IV only

61. Occasionally an individual who was at one time a militant activist against the establishment spends a period in reflection and study and does a total turnabout, encouraging peaceful coexistence and positive cooperation. Such a person has the potential of changing the attitudes and behavior of large groups of followers. Two members of the black community who offered this promise after their "conversions" were/are

(A) Lew Alcindor and Kareem Abdul Jabbar.

(B) Eldridge Cleaver and Malcolm X.

(C) W.E.B. DuBois and Martin Luther King Jr.

(D) Gwendolyn Brooks and Matthew Henson.

QUESTIONS 62 AND 63 ARE BASED ON THE FOLLOWING PARAGRAPH FROM THE CONSTITUTION OF THE UNITED STATES:

Article I, Section 8, paragraph 12 of the U.S. Constitution states: "The Congress shall have Power to raise and support Armies, but no Appropriation of Money to that Use shall be for a longer Term than two Years."

62. The two-year funding restriction imposed by this article affects the Defense Department most directly in its

(A) preparation of its annual budget.

(B) guarantee of pay to members of the volunteer army.

(C) development of sophisticated new aircraft.

(D) construction of domestic missile silos.

63. The most likely reason that the framers of the Constitution worded Article I, Section 8, paragraph 12 in this way is that they

(A) did not want to commit funds they had not yet raised.

(B) believed that if they were truly defenseless, no one would attack them.

(C) did not want to give the military the power that the guarantee of long-term funding might bestow.

(D) wanted to allow each Congress to appropriate funds on the basis of its own priorities and its own philosophies.

64. It has been suggested that tax reform in Japan would ease our own balance of trade problems. U.S. economists suggest that Japan should make mortgage interest deductible, end the exemption of taxation on interest income, and expand mortgage availability at lower rates and with longer maturities. These measures should stimulate a housing boom in Japan as an alternative to the export orientation of its economy. The idea is intriguing but impractical and unlikely to occur because

(A) Japan has not asked for our advice and the United States has no business meddling in Japan's internal economics.

(B) Japan has severe restrictions on the height of buildings.

(C) conversion of industries for domestic consumption is difficult and expensive.

(D) Japan is unconcerned with our financial woes.

65. Individuals who are actively involved in righting injustices against their own people often extend their interests and activities into working for other causes. Thus, Martin Luther King Jr., who actively and eloquently worked and argued for civil rights for American blacks, also was an active participant in the movement protesting our involvement in Vietnam. Similarly, the abolitionist Frederick Douglass also took an active role in

(A) defending free immigration for famine-struck refugees from Ireland.

(B) the struggle of Massachusetts factory workers to organize for higher wages and a 10-hour work day.

(C) seeking equal rights for women by speaking at the Seneca Falls Convention of 1848.

(D) seeking better conditions for mental patients by working with Dorothea Dix.

66. Alice Walker, well-known as the author of *The Color Purple*, is most appropriately placed in a grouping with

(A) Jean Toomer and Virginia Woolf.

(B) Zora Neale Hurston and Nikki Giovanni.

(C) Shirley Chisholm and Coretta King.

(D) Flannery O'Connor and Lorraine Hansberry.

67. The U.S. Constitution, an eighteenth-century document, is still relevant to American political life in the twenty-first century, due mainly to its

(A) relative brevity and clarity.

(B) flexible language and periodic judicial interpretation.

(C) provisions that allow amendments to be added with minimal difficulty.

(D) having been totally revised in several post-1787 constitutional conventions.

68. Native Americans have been much admired for their skill at arts and crafts and at artistic design, but are seldom given adequate credit for their intellectual achievements. All of the following are Native Americans who are correctly paired with their achievements EXCEPT

(A) Sequoya—developer of the Cherokee phonetic alphabet and creator of a literate Indian nation

(B) General Eli Parker—civil engineer and draftsman of the articles of Lee's surrender at Appomattox

(C) George Catlin—author and artist

(D) Dr. Charles Eastman—physician, YMCA director, organizer of Boy Scouts and Camp Fire Girls

69. Excesses of one sort often lead to a backlash that results in excesses of another sort. Which of the following is the MOST likely result of the excessive materialism and uninhibited sexual freedom of the 1970s?

(A) The rapid spread of the disease AIDS

(B) Much highly restrictive legislation

(C) The resurgence of religious fundamentalism

(D) A rash of bankruptcies

70. A manufacturing company finds itself in financial difficulty, but wishes to weather the storm and remain in business. The first step is to reduce the budget. For the long-run survival of the company, which of the following is the LEAST desirable way to trim the budget?

(A) Cut back on research and development

(B) Defer raises across the board

(C) Omit allocations for capital improvements to plant

(D) Lay off a portion of the work force

ENGLISH EXPRESSION

110 Questions • 60 Minutes

> **Directions:** The following sentences contain problems in grammar, usage, diction (choice of words), and idiom. Some sentences are correct. No sentence contains more than one error.
>
> You will find that the error, if there is one, is underlined and lettered. Assume that all other elements of the sentence are correct and cannot be changed. In choosing answers, follow the requirements of standard written English. If there is an error, select the one underlined part that must be changed in order to make the sentence correct, and fill in the corresponding oval on the answer sheet. If there is no error, mark answer choice (E).

1. When you plan to make a major purchase,
   A
   such as an automobile,
   B
   one should analyze your financial
   C
   situation, as well as your desires, before
   making a decision. No error
   D   E

2. Even though history does not actually
   A
   repeat itself, knowledge of history can give
                      B   C
   current problems a familiar, less
                                  D
   formidable look. No error
                      E

3. The Curies had almost exhausted their
                     A
   resources, and for a time it seemed
                  B
   unlikely that they ever would find the
             C
   solvent to their financial problems.
                     D
   No error
   E

4. If the rumors are correct, Haworth
      A
   will not be convicted, for each of the officers
         B
   on the court realizes that Chatham and
   Norris may be the real culprit and that
                  C
   their testimony is not completely
   D
   trustworthy. No error
               E

5. The citizens of Washington, like Los Angeles,
                                 A
   prefer to commute by automobile, even
   though motor vehicles contribute
   nearly as many contaminants to the air
      B
   as do all other sources combined. No error
      C   D   E

6. <u>By the time Ralph Rogers completes</u> his
                        A

testimony, every major executive of our

company but Mark Jamieson <u>and I</u>
                              B

<u>will have been</u> <u>accused of</u> complicity in
      C   D

the stock swindle. <u>No error</u>
                        E

7. <u>Within six months</u> the store was operating
      A

<u>profitably and efficient</u>: shelves
          B

<u>were well stocked</u>, goods were selling
      C

rapidly, and the cash register

<u>was ringing constantly</u>. <u>No error</u>
          D   E

8. Today Shakespeare's <u>sonnets are</u> more
                            A

read than <u>Milton</u>, perhaps because
              B

Shakespeare's <u>primary</u> subject <u>is love</u>.
                  C   D

<u>No error</u>
    E

9. Any true insomniac <u>is well aware</u> of the
                            A

futility of <u>such measures as</u> drinking hot
                  B

milk, <u>regular hours, deep breathing,</u>
                  C

counting sheep, and <u>concentrating on</u>
                          D

black velvet. <u>No error</u>
                  E

10. <u>I would appreciate</u> your <u>treating</u> me <u>as if</u>
          A   B   C

I <u>was</u> your brother. <u>No error</u>
    D   E

11. Enough change toward conservatism to

secure a better balance and to accept

more <u>openly</u> the fundamentals of character
        A

and <u>their</u> mastery <u>are</u> to be commended,
        B   C

but <u>not a</u> return to the unnecessarily harsh
        D

and harmful practices of a generation ago.

<u>No error</u>
    E

12. The appearance of the beggar was

<u>in one respect</u> <u>similar to the</u> elegant gentle
      A   B

man, for the beggar, too, <u>walked</u>
                              C

<u>with dignity</u>. <u>No error</u>
      D   E

13. The interest of American industry

<u>for developing</u> <u>previously wasted</u>
      A   B

intellectual resources <u>suggests</u> that we
                            C

<u>may have reached</u> a new plateau in our
      D

economic development. <u>No error</u>
                            E

14. <u>That</u> artist must have been <u>ingenuous</u> to
      A   B

<u>find uses</u> for recycled auto parts in <u>her</u>
      C   D

sculptures. <u>No error</u>
                  E

15. She was <u>promoted</u> because she had made
A

<u>less</u> errors <u>than</u> the other <u>secretary.</u>
B   C   D

<u>No error</u>
E

16. She <u>flouts</u> her mink coat <u>whenever</u> she
A   B

goes out with us so that <u>we'll</u> think <u>she's</u>
C   D

very wealthy. <u>No error</u>
E

17. We objected to <u>him</u> reprimanding us for
A

<u>our good</u>, especially when he said it <u>hurt</u>
B   C

him more than <u>us</u>. <u>No error</u>
D   E

18. The boy, <u>as well as</u> <u>his mother,</u>
A   B

<u>desperately</u> <u>need</u> help. <u>No error</u>
C   D   E

19. In the text, <u>the number</u> of careless errors
A

<u>indicate</u> <u>too little</u> attention
B   C

<u>to proofreading</u>. <u>No error</u>
D   E

20. <u>It's</u> certain that <u>between you and I</u> we can
A   B

discover a <u>practical</u> solution to this
C

<u>complex problem</u>. <u>No error</u>
D   E

21. He <u>proved</u> to his own <u>satisfaction</u> that he
A   B

was <u>as shrewd as</u>, if not <u>shrewder than,</u>
C   D

she. <u>No error</u>
E

22. The <u>award</u> should go to the pupil <u>who</u> we
A   B

think the <u>parents</u> had <u>intended</u> it for.
C   D

<u>No error</u>
E

23. If you <u>saw</u> the <u>number</u> of pancakes he
A   B

<u>consumed</u> at breakfast this morning, you
C

<u>would have understood</u> why he is so
D

overweight. <u>No error</u>
E

24. <u>Because of</u> a shortage of <u>critical parts</u>, the
A   B

company was not <u>capable to</u> supplying
C

the demand for <u>its product</u>. <u>No error</u>
D   E

25. <u>Neither</u> the Brontë sisters <u>nor</u> their
A   B

brother Branwell <u>are</u> remembered as
C

<u>healthy</u> or happy. <u>No error</u>
D   E

26. When my <u>commanding</u> officer first
A

<u>looked up</u> from his desk, he <u>took</u>
B   C

Lieutenant Baxter to be <u>I</u>. <u>No error</u>
D   E

27. It is <u>difficult</u> if not impossible <u>to predict</u>
A   B

the <u>affects</u> of the <u>proposed</u> legislation.
C   D

<u>No error</u>
E

28. The <u>mayor</u> <u>expressed</u> concood concern about the
        A   B

large <u>amount</u> of people injured at street
       C

<u>crossings</u>. <u>No error</u>
   D   E

29. "<u>Leave</u> us <u>face</u> the fact that <u>we're</u> in
     A   B   C

<u>trouble</u>!" he shouted. <u>No error</u>
  D   E

30. <u>Due to his being late</u> frequently, his
        A

employer <u>found</u> it necessary <u>to reprimand</u>
           B   C

<u>him</u>. <u>No error</u>
 D   E

31. I know that you <u>will enjoy</u> <u>receiving</u>
              A   B

flowers that <u>smell</u> so <u>sweetly</u>. <u>No error</u>
        C   D   E

32. He is <u>at least</u> ten years <u>older</u> <u>then</u> <u>she</u> is.
      A   B C D

<u>No error</u>
 E

33. I <u>found</u> one of <u>them</u> books that <u>tells</u> you
   A   B   C

how to build a <u>model</u> airplane. <u>No error</u>
           D   E

34. <u>Drawing</u> up the plan <u>promised</u> <u>to be</u> a
   A   B   C

<u>year's</u> work. <u>No error</u>
  D   E

35. There are <u>less</u> derelicts in the
        A

<u>downtown area</u> since the <u>crumbling</u>
    B   C

building was <u>razed</u>. <u>No error</u>
        D   E

Directions: In each of the following sentences, some part or all of the sentence is underlined. Below each sentence you will find five ways of rephrasing the underlined part. Select the answer that produces the most effective sentence, one that is clear and exact without awkwardness or ambiguity, and fill in the corresponding oval on your answer sheet. In choosing answers, follow the requirements of standard written English. Choose the answer that best expresses the meaning of the original sentence. Choice (A) is always the same as the underlined part. Choose choice (A) if you think the original sentence needs no revision.

36. The tribe of warriors believed that boys and girls should be <u>reared separate, and, as soon as he was weaned, the boys were taken from their mothers</u>.

    (A) reared separate, and, as soon as he was weaned, the boys were taken from their mothers

    (B) reared separate, and, as soon as he was weaned, a boy was taken from his mother

    (C) reared separately, and, as soon as he was weaned, the boys were taken from their mothers

    (D) reared separately, and, as soon as a boy was weaned, they were taken from their mothers

    (E) reared separately, and, as soon as a boy was weaned, he was taken from his mother

37. <u>Despite Vesta being only the third largest, it is by far the brightest of the known asteroids.</u>

    (A) Despite Vesta being only the third largest, it is by far the brightest of the known asteroids.

    (B) Vesta, though only the third largest asteroid, is by far the brightest of the known ones.

    (C) Being only the third largest, yet Vesta is by far the brightest of the known asteroids.

    (D) Vesta, though only the third largest of the known asteroids, is by far the brightest.

    (E) Vesta is only the third largest of the asteroids, it being, however, the brightest one.

38. As a result of the discovery of the Dead Sea Scrolls, our understanding of the roots of Christianity <u>has had to be revised considerably</u>.

    (A) has had to be revised considerably

    (B) have had to be revised considerably

    (C) has had to undergo revision to a considerable degree

    (D) have had to be subjected to considerable revision

    (E) has had to be revised in a considerable way

39. The jury was instructed to be <u>disinterested while</u> deliberating.

(A) disinterested while

(B) uinterested while

(C) disinterested of

(D) uninterested in

(E) uninterested to

40. <u>Such of his stories as was original were accepted.</u>

(A) Such of his stories as was original were accepted.

(B) Such of his stories as were original was accepted.

(C) Such of his stories as were original were accepted.

(D) Such of his stories as were original were excepted.

(E) His stories such as were original were excepted.

41. The jackets are so similar <u>its hard to tell mine from yours</u>.

(A) its hard to tell mine from yours

(B) it's hard to tell mine from your's

(C) its' hard to tell mine from yours'

(D) it's hard to tell mine from yours

(E) its hard to tell which is mine and which one is yours

42. Do you think that Alice has shown <u>more progress than any girl in the class</u>?

(A) more progress than any girl in the class

(B) greater progress than any girl in the class

(C) more progress than any girl in the class has shown

(D) more progress than any other girl in the class

(E) more progress from that shown by any girl in the class

43. Although she was unable to attend the concert, she insisted <u>on me going</u>.

(A) on me going

(B) on I going

(C) for me to go

(D) upon me going

(E) on my going

44. <u>Everyone, including Anne and Helen, was there</u> in time for the ceremony.

(A) Everyone, including Anne and Helen, was there

(B) Everyone including Anne and Helen, was there

(C) Everyone, including Anne and Helen, were there

(D) Everyone including Anne, and Helen, was there

(E) Everyone including Anne and Helen was there

45. She had eaten lunch <u>late, that's why</u> she had no appetite for dinner.

(A) late, that's why

(B) late, that is the reason why

(C) late; that's why

(D) late, the reason being that

(E) late that's why

46. My brother and I look so much alike that the professor <u>supposed me to be him</u>.

(A) supposed me to be him

(B) supposed me to be he

(C) supposed I to be him

(D) supposed I to be he

(E) thought me to be he

47. With a sigh of relief, <u>she set the completed report on the desk; then she herself laid down</u> and fell asleep.

    (A) she set the completed report on the desk; then she herself laid down

    (B) she sat the completed report on the desk; then she herself laid down

    (C) she sat the completed report on the desk; then she herself lay down

    (D) she set the completed report desk; then she herself lay down

    (E) she set the completed report desk; then herself she laid down

48. Is the climate of Italy <u>somewhat like Florida</u>?

    (A) somewhat like Florida

    (B) somewhat similar to Florida

    (C) somewhat like that of Florida

    (D) something like Florida

    (E) similar to Florida

49. <u>Everyone except Ruth and I know her.</u>

    (A) Everyone except Ruth and I know her.

    (B) Everyone except Ruth and I knows her.

    (C) Everyone besides Ruth and me knows her.

    (D) Everyone knows her except Ruth and I.

    (E) Everyone knows her except Ruth and me.

50. <u>As a child, my mother encouraged me to learn to play the piano.</u>

    (A) As a child, my mother encouraged me to learn to play the piano.

    (B) My mother encourage me to learn to play the piano as a child.

    (C) When I was a child, my mother encouraged me to learn to play the piano.

    (D) As a child, by my mother I was encouraged to learn to play the piano.

    (E) I was encouraged to learn to play the piano childishly by my mother.

51. The reason I want to have dinner with him is <u>because I enjoy his company</u>.

    (A) because I enjoy his company

    (B) that I enjoy his company

    (C) because I have enjoyment in his company

    (D) on account of I enjoy his company

    (E) because I shall enjoy his company

52. <u>The usher won't leave us come</u> into the auditorium once the lecture has begun.

    (A) The usher won't leave us come

    (B) The usher won't let us come

    (C) The usher refuses to leave us come

    (D) The usher won't leave us enter

    (E) The usher won't allow that we come

53. <u>Let's you and me settle the matter between ourselves.</u>

    (A) Let's you and me settle the matter between ourselves.

    (B) Let's I and you settle the matter between ourselves.

    (C) Let's both of us settle the matter among ourselves.

    (D) Let's me and you settle the matter between ourselves.

    (E) Let you and me settle the matter among ourselves.

54. The Potsdam Conference of 1945 was the final wartime conference of <u>World War II, which was held in a Berlin suburb and attended</u> by Joseph Stalin, Harry Truman, and Clement Atlee.

(A) World War II, which was held in a Berlin suburb and attended

(B) World War II, and was held in a Berlin suburb and was attended

(C) World War II; was held in a Berlin suburb and it was attended

(D) World War II. It was held in a Berlin suburb and was attended

(E) World War II, and it was held in a Berlin suburb and attended

55. The work can be a challenging and exciting <u>experience, which demands</u> a degree of flexibility, adaptability, and self-sufficiency.

(A) experience, which demands

(B) experience. It demands

(C) experience, demanding

(D) experience; which demands

(E) experience and demands

Directions: In each of the following questions you are given a complete sentence to be rephrased according to the directions that follow it. You should rephrase the sentence mentally to save time, although you may make notes in your test book if you wish.

Below each sentence and its directions are listed words or phrases that may occur in your revised sentence. When you have thought out a good sentence, look in the choices (A) through (E) for the word or entire phrase that is included in your revised sentence, and fill in the corresponding oval on the answer sheet. The word or phrase you choose should be the most accurate and most nearly complete of all the choices given, and should be part of a sentence that meets the requirements of standard written English.

Of course, a number of different sentences can be obtained if the sentence is revised according to the directions, and not all of these possibilities can be included in only five choices. If you should find that you have thought of a sentence that contains none of the words or phrases listed in the choices, you should attempt to rephrase the sentence again so that it includes a word or phrase that is listed.

Although the directions may at times require you to change the relationship between parts of the sentence or to make slight changes in meaning in other ways, make only those changes that the directions require. Keep the meaning the same or as nearly the same as the directions permit. If you think that more than one good sentence can be made according to the directions, select the sentence that is most exact, effective, and natural in phrasing and construction.

56. The archaeologists could only mark out the burial site, for then winter came.

Begin with <u>Winter came before</u>.

(A) could do nothing more
(B) could not do anything
(C) could only do
(D) could do something
(E) could do anything more

57. The white reader often receives some insight into the reasons why black men are angry from descriptions by a black writer of the injustice they encounter in a white society.

Begin with <u>A black writer often gives</u>.

(A) when describing
(B) by describing
(C) he has described
(D) in the descriptions
(E) because of describing

58. The agreement between the university officials and the dissident students provides for student representation on every university committee and on the board of trustees.

Substitute <u>provides that</u> for <u>provides for</u>.

(A) be
(B) are
(C) would have
(D) would be
(E) is to be

59. A tap on the door having interrupted her musings, she decided to finish washing her hair.

Begin the sentence with <u>Since a tap on the door</u>.

(A) had interrupted

(B) occurred to interpret

(C) broke up

(D) interrupted

(E) was interrupting

60. The novel is complicated; it is full of sub-plots.

Change the semicolon to <u>because</u>.

(A) it is filled with

(B) there is in it

(C) it is stuffed with

(D) we find in it

(E) it has many

61. Returning as a mature person to the town of his birth, he was greeted by those who had shunned him as a boy.

Begin the sentence with <u>When he returned</u>.

(A) to the town where he was born

(B) to his birthplace town

(C) to the town where he was given birth

(D) to his birth town

(E) to the place of his birth

62. The delegation to the convention selected by the committee included several new members: Mr. Garcia, Ms. Kim, and me.

Begin with <u>The committee selected</u>.

(A) members, Mr. Garcia, Ms. Kim, and me.

(B) members, Mr. Garcia, Ms. Kim, and I.

(C) members—Mr. Garcia, Ms. Kim, and me.

(D) members including Mr. Garcia, Ms. Kim, and me.

63. The gate opened and the two men emerged.

Change <u>The gate</u> to <u>As soon as the gate</u>.

(A) , here the two men emerged.

(B) , we found that the two men emerged.

(C) , the two men had emerged.

(D) , only the two men emerged.

(E) , the two men emerged.

64. Summer was now coming on with hasty steps, and I was aware that my day of decision was fast approaching.

Change <u>Summer was</u> to <u>Now that summer was</u>.

(A) steps, I realized

(B) steps, because

(C) steps, it dawned on me

(D) steps, at last

(E) steps, I found

65. When he had swum until his strength was exhausted, Tom threw up his arms and sank.

Begin the sentence with <u>He swam</u>.

(A) exhausted, Tom threw

(B) exhausted. Tom, however,

(C) exhausted, so Tom

(D) exhausted. Tom then

(E) exhausted while Tom

66. Differences of climate and of surroundings have, in the course of ages, caused differences of speech.

Begin the sentence with <u>Because of differences</u>.

(A) speech differences have come to pass.

(B) differences of speech have occurred.

(C) speech differences have been caused.

(D) differences of speech have remained.

(E) we come upon differences of speech.

67. The special rewards of a Foreign Service career include the pride and satisfaction of representing the United States abroad, the challenge of working in an action-oriented profession, and the opportunity for growth and change.

    Begin the sentence with <u>Foreign Service careers</u>.

    (A) include pride and satisfaction

    (B) includes such rewards

    (C) are special rewards

    (D) are rewarding for their

    (E) offer such special rewards

68. That man is a famous man in England as well as in Russia.

    Begin with <u>He is</u>.

    (A) not only of fame in England but also in Russia.

    (B) also famous in England as well as in Russia.

    (C) famous not only in England but also in Russia.

    (D) not only famous in England but also in Russia.

    (E) of a famous reputation in England as well as in Russia.

69. She likes camping and she also likes riding horses.

    Change <u>camping</u> to <u>to camp</u>.

    (A) and riding horses.

    (B) and she likes riding horses.

    (C) and she likes to ride horses.

    (D) and to ride horses.

    (E) also to ride horses.

70. The search for the lost ring was abandoned as we had been raking the beach for hours.

    Change <u>as</u> to <u>after</u>.

    (A) raking the beach

    (B) the beach had been raked

    (C) having the beach raked

    (D) the time that the beach was raked

    (E) we had raked the beach

71. Her brother at no time has been dependable and he never will be dependable.

    Begin with <u>Her brother has never</u>.

    (A) been dependable and he never will be.

    (B) tried to be dependable and never will be.

    (C) been dependable and never will be.

    (D) shown dependability and never will be.

    (E) at any time been dependable and never will be.

72. The chairman of a committee of Congress is the individual on the committee having the greatest seniority as well as being a member of the majority party.

    Begin with <u>The member of the majority party</u>.

    (A) has seniority as chairman

    (B) serves as chairman

    (C) serves as congressional chairman

    (D) will be the senior chairman

    (E) serves as party chairman

73. About eleven cents of every tax dollar is spent for interest, which constitutes the second largest item of the federal budget.

    Begin with <u>Interest</u>.

    (A) it costing about eleven cents

    (B) and spending about eleven cents

    (C) constituting about eleven cents

    (D) consuming about eleven cents

    (E) with about eleven cents

74. The Sirens were mythical creatures who sang for sailors and beguiled them toward the rocks where they were shipwrecked.

Omit <u>and</u>.

(A) sailors; beguiled them

(B) sailors, beguiled the sailors

(C) sailors, also beguiling them

(D) sailors. They beguiled them

(E) sailors, beguiling them

75. A dictator is an absolute ruler of a country. He may be a ruler who was legally elected and who has declared that an emergency necessitates his absolute rule, or he may be a ruler who has seized power by force.

Write as one sentence ending with <u>is called a dictator</u>.

(A) or one who

(B) or he may be a ruler who

(C) or one ruler who

(D) or an absolute ruler who

(E) and a ruler who

76. He was euphoric because of his recent achievement; therefore, he continued his studies.

Begin with <u>Euphoric</u>.

(A) achievement, and he

(B) achievement, so he

(C) achievement; therefore, he

(D) achieving; therefore, he

(E) achievement, he

77. Whether a play is realistic or unrealistic is dependent upon the style in which it is written.

Begin with <u>The style</u>.

(A) depends on

(B) is dependent upon

(C) is determined by

(D) determines whether

(E) will determine

78. The concepts were important not only to the Cubist painters but also to the practitioners of Dadaism.

Substitute <u>both</u> for <u>not only</u>.

(A) also

(B) as well as

(C) but

(D) too

(E) and

79. A register of all the varieties of flora and fauna of a region represents its plants and animals in the same way as a listing of all the elements of the general customs of a people represents its culture.

Begin with <u>Just as</u>.

(A) like a listing

(B) so a list

(C) therefore a list

(D) in the same way a listing

(E) while a listing

80. Because the airline had overbooked the flight, three passengers with tickets were not permitted to board.

Begin with <u>Three passengers</u>.

(A) in view of the airline having overbooked the flight.

(B) due to the airline having overbooked the flight.

(C) by the airline having overbooked the flight.

(D) although the airline had overbooked the flight.

(E) because the airline had overbooked the flight.

81. The puppies, frightened by the banging of the front door, all rolled or jumped from the sofa and scrambled back to their box.

    Begin with <u>Scrambling back to their box</u>.

    (A) the front door, had jumped and rolled

    (B) had rolled by the front door

    (C) the door, had all jumped

    (D) the front door, had all rolled

    (E) the front door, all frightened

82. Dwindling resources, another of many ecological problems said to be increasing rapidly, is exacerbated by increased consumption.

    Change <u>Dwindling resources, another of</u> to <u>Dwindling resources is one of many</u>.

    (A) rapidly, is exacerbated

    (B) is exacerbated rapidly

    (C) rapidly, but is exacerbated

    (D) rapidly, and it is exacerbated

    (E) but is rapidly exacerbated

83. Running across the lush meadow, she tossed her head back and smiled at the sun.

    Begin with <u>She tossed</u>.

    (A) sun while running

    (B) sun all the while running

    (C) while the sun

    (D) as if running

    (E) sun even while she ran

84. Considerable energy has been expended by those who criticize the present system.

    Begin with <u>Those who</u>.

    (A) had expended

    (B) had to expend

    (C) have expended

    (D) expenditure

    (E) in expenditure

85. It occurred to her as she stepped into the bright sunshine that she had forgotten her sun hat.

    Begin with <u>As she stepped</u>.

    (A) to her that

    (B) her but that

    (C) to her with

    (D) her with

    (E) to her sun hat

86. Martin Luther King Jr., a minister, was a political leader and a superb rhetorician.

    Begin with <u>Martin Luther King Jr. was not only</u>.

    (A) minister, was a

    (B) minister, political leader

    (C) minister, a political leader

    (D) minister and also

    (E) minister, but also

87. The two poets who introduced the sonnet form to English poetry were Wyatt and Surrey.

    Begin with <u>Wyatt</u>.

    (A) were two poets

    (B) were the two

    (C) were poets

    (D) was the poets

    (E) were the only

88. The boys burst into the room sniffing the air like a pack of hungry hounds.

    Begin with <u>The boys sniffed</u>.

    (A) hounds after having

    (B) hounds after had burst

    (C) hounds burst into the room

    (D) hounds the pack of boys

    (E) hounds, the boys

89. One final doubt mars this vision of paradise.

Begin with <u>This vision of paradise</u>.

(A) is not moved by

(B) is marred over by

(C) could be marred by

(D) must have been marred by

(E) is marred by

90. The business of the old men of the tribe was to teach the young men the wisdom of ancient ways devised by ancestors who had become gods.

Begin with <u>The wisdom of ancient ways</u>.

(A) gods, were taught to the old men

(B) ancestors were taught

(C) gods, was taught to the young men

(D) gods, were taught to the young men

(E) ancestors who had been taught

Directions: In each of the following questions you are given four sentences and a question that asks for the best sequence to make a clear, sensible paragraph. Choose the option that reflects the best ordering of the sentences for a clear, sensible paragraph.

---

91. I.   Nations and regions are empowered to determine for themselves the relative weights to give to equality, growth, provision of basic needs, dignity, etc., and also to be able to implement development as they have defined it.

II.   Under this definition, development is a process of empowerment, where people and, on the international level, nations, gain the power to control some of the basic factors affecting their lives.

III. One definition of underdevelopment characterizes it as vulnerability and, consequently, development as emancipation from that vulnerability.

IV.   On the personal level, development also encompasses gaining the ability to define for oneself and to implement one's own plan for mental and physical well-being.

Which of the following presents the BEST sequence of the sentences above to make a clear, sensible paragraph?

(A) I, II, III, IV

(B) III, I, II, IV

(C) III, II, I, IV

(D) IV, II, III, I

(E) I, IV, III, II

92. I.   And while American children are encouraged to be independent and assertive, Japanese children are taught that the interdependence between the self and the family or group and restraint in social interaction take precedence over personal autonomy.

II.   American children easily learn there are two personal pronouns, I and you; whereas the Japanese language does not use such words.

III. In Japan, the personal referent depends on the relationship of the speaker and listener, defining the self in terms of a specific social interaction.

IV.   These differences illustrate the contrast between the egocentric and the sociocentric views of the self.

Which of the following presents the BEST sequence of the sentences above to make a clear, sensible paragraph?

(A) I, III, IV, II

(B) I, II, IV, III

(C) II, III, I, IV

(D) II, IV, III, I

(E) IV, II, III, I

93. I. Sometimes young people make the mistake of picking a job just because a much-admired relative or friend likes that job.

    II. It is risky to choose an occupation just because you admire or are fond of someone who has chosen it.

    III. You may admire Joe Montana, Louis Nizer, or a good homicide detective.

    IV. But this does not mean that you can count on being successful or happy as a professional ball player, criminal lawyer, or detective.

    Which of the following presents the BEST sequence of the sentences above to make a clear, sensible paragraph?

    (A) I, II, III, IV
    (B) III, IV, I, II
    (C) I, IV, III, II
    (D) III, II, I, IV
    (E) I, III, II, IV

94. I. Sri Lanka must diversify its exports while concentrating more of its agricultural energy on the production of staple foods.

    II. Because so much land and manpower is devoted to cultivating cash crops, staple foods like rice, sugar, and flour must be imported.

    III. These three crops are oriented almost entirely toward export and do little to feed the impoverished nation.

    IV. Sri Lanka has an ever-widening trade deficit, a predominantly agricultural economy, and dependency for its foreign exchange upon three cash crops: tea, rubber, and coconuts.

    Which of the following presents the BEST sequence of the sentences above to make a clear, sensible paragraph?

    (A) I, II, III, IV
    (B) II, III, I, IV
    (C) III, II, IV, I
    (D) IV, III, I, II
    (E) IV, III, II, I

95. I. If future organizations are to be unstable, shifting coalitions, then individual skills and abilities, particularly those emphasizing innovativeness, creativity, flexibility, and the latest technological knowledge, are crucial, and individual training is most appropriate.

    II. This approach seems better designed for overcoming hierarchical barriers, for developing a degree of interpersonal relationships that make communication along the chain of command possible, and for retaining a modicum of innovation and/or flexibility.

    III. But if there is to be little change in organizational structure, then the main thrust of training should be group-oriented or organizational development.

    IV. The kind of training that an organization should emphasize depends upon the present and future structure of the organization.

    Which of the following presents the BEST sequence of the sentences above to make a clear, sensible paragraph?

    (A) I, II, III, IV
    (B) II, III, I, IV
    (C) IV, I, III, II
    (D) III, I, II, IV
    (E) IV, III, II, I

96. I.   In Tanzania, these divisions have not appeared for several reasons.

II. Many nations have emerged from the anti-colonial struggle with one strong ruling party.

III. In most of these nations, soon after independence, the support for and/or unity of this party rapidly diminished as divisions arose between interest groups that had supported independence.

IV. Struggles were often between tribes or were between the wealthy western-educated elite and the rest of society.

Which of the following presents the BEST sequence of the sentences above to make a clear, sensible paragraph?

(A) I, II, III, IV
(B) II, I, IV, III
(C) II, I, III, IV
(D) II, III, IV, I
(E) III, IV, II, I

97. I.   An Italian at the close of the war might well have said: "We have poured out more blood and treasure to gain southern Tyrol and a few coast towns on the Adriatic than we did in all the wars for national liberty and union during the nineteenth century."

II. But many Italians felt that the war had cost Italy more than had been gained.

III. "Perhaps a stronger government might have won for us richer spoils of victory."

IV. Italy supposedly was more fortunate than its former allies, Germany and Austria-Hungary, because it was on the winning side when World War I ended.

Which of the following presents the BEST sequence of the sentences above to make a clear, sensible paragraph?

(A) IV, II, I, III
(B) IV, I, II, III
(C) IV, III, I, II
(D) I, II, III, IV
(E) I, III, IV, II

98.
  I. These moving portions of the Earth's crust are the plates on which continents are carried.
  II. Two hundred kilometers below the crust of the Earth, rocks are so hot that they are molten.
  III. The metallic core of the Earth beneath these rocks is even hotter.
  IV. This heat causes slow currents in the layers above the core the layers to rise and drag the basalt floor of the ocean with them.

Which of the following presents the BEST sequence of the sentences above to make a clear, sensible paragraph?

  (A) II, I, III, IV
  (B) II, III, IV, I
  (C) III, II, IV, I
  (D) III, I, II, IV
  (E) IV, II, III, I

99.
  I. It is only with respect to those laws which offend fundamental values of human life that moral defense of civil disobedience can be rationally supported.
  II. However, disobedience of laws not the subject of dissent, but merely used to dramatize dissent, is regarded as morally as well as legally unacceptable.
  III. Civil disobedience is by definition a violation of the law.
  IV. The theory of civil disobedience recognizes that its actions, regardless of their justification, must be punished.

Which of the following presents the BEST sequence of the sentences above to make a clear, sensible paragraph?

  (A) II, I, IV, III
  (B) I, II, III, IV
  (C) III, IV, II, I
  (D) III, II, I, IV
  (E) IV, III, II, I

100.
  I. Revolutions have tended to result in authoritarian regimes.
  II. However, when the masses rioted and staged a violent revolution, the new government ended up being extremely authoritarian.
  III. In fact, in European history since 1789, the more involved the people became in a change of governments, the more likely the new government was to be an authoritarian one.
  IV. When the change in government was controlled by the middle class, a relatively peaceful coup d'etat took place and a regime no more authoritarian than the one before it came into power.

Which of the following presents the BEST sequence of the sentences above to make a clear, sensible paragraph?

  (A) I, IV, III, II
  (B) I, III, IV, II
  (C) IV, I, III, II
  (D) I, II, IV, III
  (E) III, IV, I, II

101. I. The proponents of the evolutionary theory adamantly insist that special creation be excluded from any possible consideration as an explanation for origins on the basis that it does not qualify as a scientific theory.

II. On the other hand, they would view as unthinkable the consideration of evolution as anything less than pure science.

III. These considerations alone convince most people that molecules-to-man evolution has actually occurred.

IV. Almost all science books and school texts present evolution as an established fact.

Which of the following presents the BEST sequence of the sentences above to make a clear, sensible paragraph?

(A) I, II, III, IV
(B) I, II, IV, III
(C) III, IV, I, II
(D) IV, III, I, II
(E) IV, III, II, I

102. I. The State today is in more danger from suppression than from violence, because, in the end, suppression leads to violence.

II. Whoever pleads for justice helps to keep the peace; and whoever tramples upon the plea for justice, temperately made in the name of peace, only outrages peace and kills something fine in the heart of man that was put there when we received our humanity.

III. When that is killed, brute meets brute on each side of the line.

IV. Violence is the child of suppression.

Which of the following presents the BEST sequence of the sentences above to make a clear, sensible paragraph?

(A) I, IV, III, II
(B) II, I, III, IV
(C) I, IV, II, III
(D) II, IV, I, III
(E) IV, I, III, II

103. I. In a living organism, the rate of assimilation of cosmic radiation and the rate of disintegration of radiocarbon are in precise equilibrium.

    II. Radiocarbon dating, the process by which the age of long-preserved organic remains is determined, is derived from this knowledge.

    III. At death, however, assimilation ceases and disintegration proceeds at the known immutable rate.

    IV. The rate of disintegration of radioactive bodies is independent of the nature of the chemical compound in which the radioactive body resides and of the temperature, pressure, and other physical characteristics of its environment.

    Which of the following presents the BEST sequence of the sentences above to make a clear, sensible paragraph?

    (A) I, III, IV, II

    (B) I, II, III, IV

    (C) II, I, IV, III

    (D) IV, III, I, II

    (E) IV, III, II, I

104. I. Today China remains one of the great cultures of the world, while the Mayan culture has all but disappeared.

    II. The culture of China two thousand years ago was somewhat similar to that of the ancient Mayas.

    III. Both cultures had made great advances in medicine and religion, and both had highly developed social and political structures.

    IV. Yet, during those twenty centuries, the geographical conditions around which these cultures developed have not shown much change.

    Which of the following presents the BEST sequence of the sentences above to make a clear, sensible paragraph?

    (A) I, II, III, IV

    (B) I, II, IV, III

    (C) II, I, III, IV

    (D) II, III, IV, I

    (E) II, III, I, IV

105. I. The target is wrong, for in attacking the tests, critics divert attention from the fault that lies with ill-informed or incompetent users.

II. The standardized educational or psychological tests that are widely used to aid in selecting, classifying, assigning, or promoting students, employees, and military personnel have been the target of recent attacks.

III. Whether the results will be valuable, meaningless, or even misleading depends partly upon the tool itself but largely upon the user.

IV. The tests themselves are merely tools, with characteristics that can be measured with reasonable precision under specified conditions.

Which of the following presents the BEST sequence of the sentences above to make a clear, sensible paragraph?

(A) I, II, III, IV
(B) I, IV, III, II
(C) II, I, III, IV
(D) IV, III, II, I
(E) IV, II, I, III

106. I. Heraclites used a metaphor to describe the flux of reality: one cannot step into the same river twice.

II. Subsequently, Plato's *Allegory of the Cave* explores both the nature of reality and epistemology, as well as considering the meaning of goodness or virtue.

III. Modern philosophy also uses figurative language; in Sartre's play "No Exit," life is allegorized as a hell from which there is no escape.

IV. The use of figurative language and allegory to explain philosophical concepts has a long tradition in western thought.

Which of the following presents the BEST sequence of the sentences above to make a clear, sensible paragraph?

(A) I, II, III, IV
(B) I, II, IV, III
(C) III, I, II, IV
(D) IV, I, II, III
(E) IV, II, I, III

107.

I. Program management is an administrative system combining planning and control techniques to guide and coordinate all of the activities that contribute to one overall program or project.

II. The concept of "program management" was first developed in order to handle some of the complex projects undertaken by the U.S. Department of Defense in the 1950s.

III. It has been used by the federal government to manage space exploration and other programs involving many contributing organizations.

IV. It is also used by state and local governments and by some large firms to provide administrative integration of work from a number of sources, be they individuals, departments, or outside companies.

Which of the following presents the BEST sequence of the sentences above to make a clear, sensible paragraph?

(A) I, II, III, IV
(B) II, I, III, IV
(C) I, III, IV, II
(D) II, III, IV, I
(E) I, III, II, IV

108.

I. In some countries, such as Botswana, Lesotho, and Swaziland, South Africa has rarely had to interfere directly in national affairs.

II. In other cases, such as in Mozambique, Zimbabwe, and Angola, governments that are more hostile to South Africa have been brought to power, and South Africa has imposed its will through force.

III. The South African government has consistently been able to keep its neighbors, if not in a state of peaceful coexistence, at least in a state of fear and dependency toward South Africa.

IV. These countries' economic dependency on South Africa and the interests of their ruling classes have brought about governments that are unlikely to threaten South Africa nor to leave South Africa's political-economic sphere of influence.

Which of the following presents the BEST sequence of the sentences above to make a clear, sensible paragraph?

(A) I, II, IV, III
(B) III, I, II, IV
(C) I, IV, III, II
(D) III, IV, I, II
(E) III, I, IV, II

109. I.   In the American legal system, the same act may result in a criminal indictment, or civil liability, or both.

II. If a defendant caused harm or wrong to another, the wronged party may seek a remedy in civil law, and the defendant can be required to compensate the plaintiff financially.

III. But the same act which resulted in civil liability can be a criminal act, resulting in the guilty defendant's punishment by fine and/or imprisonment, if the act violates a statute.

IV. A criminal defendant accused of killing someone may be found not guilty beyond a reasonable doubt, but the victim's survivors can sue in civil court for wrongful death, seeking monetary damages as compensation for their loss.

Which of the following presents the BEST sequence of the sentences above to make a clear, sensible paragraph?

(A) I, II, III, IV
(B) I, IV, II, III
(C) IV, I, III, II
(D) II, III, I, IV
(E) IV, III, I, II

110. I.   A major task imposed upon education and on the schools was that which we call Americanization.

II. No other people had ever absorbed such large and varied racial stock so rapidly or so successfully.

III. Each decade after 1840 saw from two to eight million immigrants pour into America.

IV. It was the public school that proved itself the most efficacious of all agencies of Americanization—Americanization not only of the children but, through them, of the parents as well.

Which of the following presents the BEST sequence of the sentences above to make a clear, sensible paragraph?

(A) I, III, II, IV
(B) II, III, I, IV
(C) I, II, III, IV
(D) III, IV, II, I
(E) IV, II, III, I

ANSWER KEY AND EXPLANATIONS

Knowledge Questions

1.	B	15.	D	29.	A	43.	B	57.	D
2.	A	16.	C	30.	C	44.	C	58.	B
3.	B	17.	B	31.	B	45.	C	59.	D
4.	D	18.	C	32.	D	46.	A	60.	B
5.	D	19.	C	33.	D	47.	D	61.	B
6.	B	20.	C	34.	B	48.	C	62.	C
7.	A	21.	B	35.	D	49.	C	63.	D
8.	D	22.	B	36.	B	50.	B	64.	A
9.	D	23.	D	37.	B	51.	A	65.	C
10.	D	24.	A	38.	C	52.	D	66.	B
11.	C	25.	D	39.	A	53.	B	67.	B
12.	A	26.	D	40.	A	54.	C	68.	C
13.	C	27.	C	41.	A	55.	A	69.	C
14.	C	28.	C	42.	D	56.	B	70.	A

Maps: Europe—Questions 22 to 24

1. Portugal
2. Spain
3. France
4. Switzerland
5. Italy
6. Yugoslavia (now Serbia and Montenegro)
7. Albania
8. Greece
9. Bulgaria
10. Romania
11. Soviet Union (now the Commonwealth of Independent States)
12. Hungary
13. Austria
14. Czechoslovakia (now the Czech Republic and Slovakia)
15. Poland
16. German Democratic Republic (now Germany)
17. Federal Republic of Germany (now Germany)
18. Belgium
19. Netherlands
20. Denmark
21. Finland
22. Sweden
23. Norway
24. Great Britain
25. Ireland
26. Iceland

Maps: East Asia—Questions 42 to 44

1. Soviet Union (now the Commonwealth of Independent States)
2. Mongolia
3. China
4. North and South Korea
5. Japan
6. Taiwan
7. Philippines
8. Malaysia
9. Indonesia
10. Vietnam
11. Kampuchea (Cambodia)
12. Thailand
13. Laos
14. Myanmar

1. **The correct answer is (B).** By stating that in dealing with organization structure it is "usually advisable" to think first of the functions, the implication is made that not all organizations coordinate their functions. The coordination is of the personnel performing the functions.

2. **The correct answer is (A).** Specific tariffs remain constant in price. If domestic and import prices should both fall, the specific tariff would be a higher percentage, thus making it more protective.

3. **The correct answer is (B).** Ad valorem tariffs are a fixed percentage regardless of the price of the commodity. If import prices rise so does the tariff, which makes it more protective than before.

4. **The correct answer is (D).** If an exporting country can only ship a fixed number of items due to a quota, there is no incentive to decrease prices. If the quota were to be removed, the exporting country might be inclined to decrease prices to capture a larger portion of the market.

5. **The correct answer is (D).** Martin Luther King Jr. believed in nonviolent protest as the means by which one could best promote social and political change. The other three choices all put forth a reverse view of the individual. Marx believed the struggles were between the bourgeois and proletariat, Keynes believed that to fight an economic depression you should increase government spending, and Clausewitz put forth the thesis that war is politics by any other means.

6. **The correct answer is (B).** A retired individual living on an insurance annuity has a fixed income. The second inflation starts, the value of their income depreciates. The other three choices would feel little or no immediate effect from inflation.

7. **The correct answer is (A).** On February 27, 1991, President Bush ordered a cease-fire. At that time, Saddam Hussein was left in control of Iraq. Although Kurds in the north and Shi'ite Muslims in the south attempted to overthrow Saddam, he was able to put down both rebellions.

8. **The correct answer is (D).** Generally speaking, when American citizens commit a crime in a foreign nation, they are subject to the laws of the nation in which the crime was committed. At the same time, given the fact that Germany signed the Universal Declaration of Human Rights, any other choice would be in violation of its precepts.

9. **The correct answer is (D).** Of the statements listed, the fourth statement is clearly the most significant because it deals with current conditions within Southeast Asian nations that place the Chinese in a position of power. The least significant would be the second statement. While it may lead to suspicion, it has no direct impact on the residents themselves.

answers

10. The correct answer is (D). The expected 5 percent rise in prices is a result of inflation, which will affect goods, services, and debts made only in the coming year. Interest rates on government debts are for a fixed period of time with a fixed interest rate. The interest rate for the current debt would have been established when the debt was incurred, so it would remain unchanged.

11. The correct answer is (C). The War Powers Act of 1973 places the following limits on the president's use of the military: He must report in writing to Congress within 48 hours after he sends troops into any conflict. Congress then has sixty days to declare war or provide for the continued use of the troops in other ways. If Congress fails to provide such authorization, the president must remove the troops.

12. The correct answer is (A). This statement was not a policy of the United States during the Cold War. The second statement describes the origins of NATO, the third statement describes the Marshall Plan, and the fourth statement describes the U.S. policy of containment.

13. The correct answer is (C). Japan was the only nation not to be divided into communist and non-communist spheres of influence. Korea was divided into North and South Korea, Vietnam into North and South Vietnam, and Germany into East and West Germany.

14. The correct answer is (C). The most profitable level of output is OK. The marginal revenue curve (MR) and the marginal cost curve (MC) intersect at point H. The intersection of MR and MC gives us the profit maximizing level (or loss minimizing) of output. At this point, the slopes of total revenue curve and total cost curve are equal. Any other level of output will reduce total profits.

15. The correct answer is (D). The amount of profits are shown by the area of BTIN or AEH. The area BTIN is based on subtracting total revenue from total cost. Average revenue (AR) is total revenue divided by output and average cost is total cost divided by output. Since AR is equal to OT and AC is equal to OB, if we multiply by output OK, then total revenue is OTIK and total cost is OBNK. The difference between total revenue and total cost is then BTIN. If, alternatively, you add up the differences between marginal revenue and marginal cost for each unit of output, you get the area AEH, which is the same as BTIN.

16. The correct answer is (C). A per-unit tax or an excise tax changes the cost curves. The cost curves rise by the amount of the tax. The new profit maximizing level of output will be lower and the price will be higher. Unless the demand curve is vertical, the price will rise by less than the tax. The burden of the tax is partially paid by the consumer (higher prices and less output) and partially paid by the firm (lower net price and lower output).

17. The correct answer is (B). While the United States remains the largest financial contributor to UN peacekeeping efforts, smaller or non-aligned nations supply the majority of the troops. The top five troop contributors are India, Nigeria, Jordan, Bangladesh, and Australia. The number of peacekeeping missions escalated in 1993, then declined from 1996 to 1999, but rose again in 2000.

18. The correct answer is (C). The Electoral College is established in Article II, Section 1.2. Bills of attainder are prohibited in Article 1, Section 9.3. An "Acting President" is established in Article II, Section 1.1. Nowhere in the Constitution is there any provision for the creation of national political parties.

19. **The correct answer is (C).** This series of events best describes the political changes within Japan during the time period given. It begins with the removal of the Tokugawa Shogun and beginning of the Meiji Restoration (1868) and ends with the American occupation of Japan at the end of World War II (1945).

20. **The correct answer is (C).** The 1997 Kyoto Treaty (Protocol) was an agreement on global warming reached by representatives from more than 150 nations. The agreement would require industrialized countries to decrease emissions of greenhouse gases.

21. **The correct answer is (B).** An executive agreement is an agreement reached by the president between the United States and a foreign country. It is less formal than a treaty so it does not need Senate ratification. The more involved the United States becomes with other countries, the larger the number of executive agreements.

22. **The correct answer is (B).** The correct choice would be Iceland (number 26 on map). Reykjavik, Iceland was the location of the 1986 summit between Reagan and Gorbachev. This is also the location of the Reykjavik International Chess Tournament.

23. **The correct answer is (D).** The correct choice would be Czechoslovakia (number 14 on map). It was the appeasement policies of England and France that let Hitler take control of Czechoslovakia (now the Czech Republic and Slovakia) prior to the outbreak of World War II.

24. **The correct answer is (A).** The two countries that were able to maintain their neutrality through both World Wars were Switzerland (number 4 on map) and Sweden (number 22 on map).

25. **The correct answer is (D).** This statement is taken from the Truman Doctrine in which President Truman requested 400 million dollars from Congress to aid Turkey and Greece in their efforts to resist Soviet ambitions in their countries.

26. **The correct answer is (D).** This statement is taken from the Monroe Doctrine in which President Monroe in effect closed the western hemisphere to any further colonization or interference by European powers.

27. **The correct answer is (C).** In 1995, the United Nations Economic Commission for Europe recommended that consular invoices be abolished. Therefore, it would not be an acceptable method of payment arrangement between a U.S. seller and a foreign buyer.

28. **The correct answer is (C).** WTO is the acronym for the World Trade Organization. It is mainly concerned with monitoring and regulating global trading relationships.

29. **The correct answer is (A).** The Marshall Plan, the North Atlantic Treaty Organization (NATO), and the Organization for Economic Cooperation and Development (OECD) all deal with economic and military aid for Europe. The General Agreement on Tariffs and Trade (GATT) is a multilateral trade agreement.

30. **The correct answer is (C).** The doctrines of laissez-faire and social contract theory are based on the same basic assumptions. The same is true of the doctrines of natural rights and natural law.

31. **The correct answer is (B).** The Gross Domestic Product (GDP) is defined as the total market value of all final goods and services produced annually within U.S. boundaries, whether by American or foreign-supplied resources.

32. **The correct answer is (D).** The years 1946 to 1991 witnessed a "tight bipolar" structure in international power as evidenced by the Cold War. It began in 1946 with Winston Churchill's "Iron Curtain" speech and ended in 1991 with the dissolution of the Warsaw Pact.

33. **The correct answer is (D).** When the Federal Reserve Board purchases government securities in the market, they add either directly or indirectly to the quantity of bank reserves. With additional reserves, the banking system can increase the quantity of loans. The result is an increase in the money supply that leads to an increase in demand for goods and services resulting in upward pressure on the rate of inflation. All the other choices could potentially reduce the quantity of bank reserves available.

34. **The correct answer is (B).** Over a million people emigrated from Ireland after the devastating potato famines of 1846 and 1848. Many of them settled in the United States along the eastern seaboard.

35. **The correct answer is (D).** *Uncle Tom's Cabin* by Harriet Beecher Stowe was instrumental in convincing many Americans in the northern part of the United States of the inherent evils of slavery.

36. **The correct answer is (B).** "Man is born free, and everywhere he is in chains. One man thinks himself the master of others, but remains more of a slave than they are." This is the opening passage to *The Social Contract* by Jean Jacques Rousseau.

37. **The correct answer is (B).** Co-optation is defined as the act of persuading or luring the opposition to join your side.

38. **The correct answer is (C).** The proportionally larger increase in capital expenditures was accelerated by the increase in consumer spending.

39. **The correct answer is (A).** Because we are dealing with the coinage of sisal and all legal tender is redeemable in that coinage, the monetary standard would best be characterized as Full Sisal Coin Standard.

40. **The correct answer is (A).** The impact of Thoreau's *Civil Disobedience* on the twentieth century has been global. This is clearly evidenced by the actions of Martin Luther King Jr. in the United States, Gandhi in India, and blacks protesting against apartheid in South Africa.

41. **The correct answer is (A).** The current ratio in financial statement analysis is used to assess the short-term liquidity or debt-paying ability of a business. The formula is current assets (C/A) divided by current liabilities (C/L).

42. **The correct answer is (D).** Thailand is the only country from the choices given that has not been under colonial rule in modern times. The Philippines were ruled by Spain until 1898 and were then under American colonial influence during the first half of the twentieth century. The Dutch controlled Indonesia until 1949. Vietnam was controlled by the French until 1954.

43. **The correct answer is (B).** The former French Indo-China was composed of the nations of Kampuchea (Cambodia), Laos, and Vietnam.

44. **The correct answer is (C).** About 90 percent of the people in Indonesia are Muslim, but their level of observance varies. It is not controlled by the Fundamentalists, and it is not an Islamic state.

45. **The correct answer is (C).** The events and dates are as follows:

Berlin Airlift: 1948–49

Founding of OPEC: 1960

Bay of Pigs: 1961

Gulf of Tonkin Resolution: 1964

Yom Kippur War: 1973

Invasion of Grenada: 1983

46. **The correct answer is (A).** When a commercial bank makes a loan to a business firm, the loan increases the bank's liabilities. At the same time, the promissory note from the business firm increases the bank's assets.

47. The correct answer is (D). If the exchange ratio of the dollar to pound sterling changes from 3:1 to 4:1, then the dollar has depreciated in value relative to the pound.

48. The correct answer is (C). The net outlays for each department for fiscal year 2000 in millions of dollars would be:

State Department: 6,849

Commerce Department: 7,931

Justice Department: 19,561

Defense Department: 281,233

49. The correct answer is (C). As mayor of West Berlin, Willy Brandt had stood fast against crises created by the Soviet Union. As a natural ally of the United States and its political ideology, he would not fit into the description of a hardliner making overtures to "the other side."

50. The correct answer is (B). It is more effective and expedient to delegate responsibility for specific types of decisions to the lowest organizational level at which there is an individual possessing the ability, desire, impartiality, and access to relevant information needed to make the decisions.

51. The correct answer is (A). As a signatory of the Universal Declaration of Human Rights, the United States is bound to the precept that all American citizens accused of a crime in a foreign nation are subject to the laws of that nation. Given this fact, the consul may not request release of the student for trial in the United States as a U.S. citizen.

52. The correct answer is (D). The Boxers derived their name from the Chinese secret society they belonged to called the Righteous and Harmonious Fists. They believed that certain boxing and callisthenic rituals made them impervious to bullets.

53. The correct answer is (B). Although officially denounced, the Boxers had the support of many in the royal court including the Empress Dowager Tzu Hsi. Viceroys in the southern provinces, fearing western reprisals, refused to support the Boxers and instead protected the foreigners in their areas.

54. The correct answer is (C). The Sanctuary Movement was established to provide a safe haven for refugees and victims of political turmoil in Central America. The historical basis of the term *sanctuary* can be traced back to the Greek practice of providing sanctuary in all temples.

55. The correct answer is (A). In 1981, the Rev. John Fife and James Corbett, among others, began smuggling Central American refugees into the United States. It was their intent to offer them sanctuary from the political chaos of their homeland. The Department of Justice indicted 16 members in 1985, 11 went to trial and 8 were convicted of alien smuggling and other charges.

56. The correct answer is (B). The Iran-Contra scandal first came to light in 1986 during President Reagan's administration. The scandal involved a violation of the Boland Amendment (1984), which banned any military aid to the contras (the forces fighting Nicaragua's Communist-dominated Sandinista government).

57. The correct answer is (D). A "rogue state" was a term designed to describe any nation that is acting aggressively towards its own people or neighboring nations. While many nations may consider the United States a "rogue state," the question here is based on U.S. interpretations of other nations. The only nation that the United States has friendly relations with from the list provided would be Mexico.

58. The correct answer is (B). *Glasnost* can be defined as the official internal policy of Russia to use candor and openness in publicizing Russian problems and weaknesses. *Perestroika* can be defined as the Russian policy of restructuring the economic, political, and social systems of the former Soviet Union.

59. **The correct answer is (D).** The European Union is an organization for the economic and political integration of Europe. Formed after World War II, it was established to forge new economic and political ties in Europe to achieve prosperity and avoid a recurrence of war. It consists of both centralized and decentralized institutions.

60. **The correct answer is (B).** The Hanseatic League was an alliance of European cities to protect their traders from plundering barons along land routes and from marauding pirates upon the seas. The Zollverein was a customs union of German states under Prussian leadership. While the other two choices are also forms of alliances, they dealt more with political alliances than economic alliances.

61. **The correct answer is (B).** Eldridge Cleaver was a leading voice of the Black Panther movement of the 1960s. Later in his life, he abandoned the radicalism of his youth to embrace Christianity and conservative causes. Malcolm X was closely associated with the Black Muslims early in his life. Later, he formed the Organization of African-American Unity, and then went on to champion Pan-Africanism.

62. **The correct answer is (C).** The development of sophisticated new aircraft is not something that can be easily accomplished in a short period of time. The planning, designing, testing, and construction of such aircraft can take several years. Given the two-year limitation, the Defense Department can only appropriate funds in a piecemeal fashion.

63. **The correct answer is (D).** The most likely reason for the wording used by the framers is that they wanted to allow each Congress to appropriate funds on the basis of its own priorities and its own philosophies. Representatives are elected on a two-year cycle. That means that the political make-up of Congress changes every two years.

64. **The correct answer is (A).** While the economy in the United States can impact Japan's economy, this plan is not likely to be adopted by the Japanese based solely on U.S. desires and input. For decades following World War II the United States mandated several political and economic policies in Japan. Only in the last few decades has Japan been able to determine its own political and economic future. They would resent any forced initiatives by the United States.

65. **The correct answer is (C).** Frederick Douglass was a strong supporter of women's right. In 1848, at Seneca Falls, he had demanded that women be allowed to vote. On the day of his death, he had attended a convention for women's suffrage.

66. **The correct answer is (B).** Nikki Giovanni is an American poet who writes about the distinctive qualities of the African-American experience. Zora Neale Hurston is an African-American author who wrote several books on black mythology, legends, and folklore. Walker, Giovanni, and Hurston all wrote about the social and cultural aspects of the Black experience.

67. **The correct answer is (B).** One of the key strengths of the U.S. Constitution is that it is a living document. Through judicial review, the amendment process, and the use of the elastic clause, the Constitution can adapt and grow based on new circumstances or needs of the nation.

68. **The correct answer is (C).** George Catlin was an author and painter. However, he was not a Native American. He was an Anglo-American who wrote about and painted pictures of Native Americans.

69. The correct answer is (C). The backlash of excess must be related but of a different type. This rules out AIDS because uninhibited sex would be a cause of the excess, not a reaction to it. There was less restrictive legislation beginning in the 1970s, not more restrictive legislation. Increases in bankruptcies would be unrelated. Religious Fundamentalism can be viewed as a reaction to excessive materialism and uninhibited sexual freedom.

70. The correct answer is (A). Choices (B), (C), and (D) will all have an immediate impact on the budget but will not negatively impact the company in the long-run. Research and development are crucial to insuring the company can meet the future needs and demands of consumers. It would therefore be the least desirable method of the options provided for trimming the budget.

answers

English Expression

1.	C	23.	A	45.	C	67.	E
2.	E	24.	C	46.	A	68.	C
3.	D	25.	C	47.	D	69.	D
4.	C	26.	D	48.	C	70.	E
5.	A	27.	C	49.	E	71.	C
6.	B	28.	C	50.	C	72.	B
7.	B	29.	A	51.	B	73.	D
8.	B	30.	A	52.	B	74.	E
9.	C	31.	D	53.	A	75.	A
10.	D	32.	C	54.	D	76.	E
11.	C	33.	B	55.	C	77.	D
12.	B	34.	E	56.	E	78.	E
13.	A	35.	A	57.	B	79.	B
14.	B	36.	E	58.	A	80.	E
15.	B	37.	D	59.	A	81.	D
16.	A	38.	A	60.	E	82.	D
17.	A	39.	A	61.	E	83.	A
18.	D	40.	C	62.	C	84.	C
19.	B	41.	D	63.	E	85.	A
20.	B	42.	D	64.	A	86.	E
21.	E	43.	E	65.	D	87.	B
22.	B	44.	A	66.	B	88.	A

89.	E
90.	C
91.	C
92.	C
93.	A
94.	E
95.	C
96.	D
97.	A
98.	B
99.	C
100.	B
101.	D
102.	C
103.	A
104.	E
105.	C
106.	D
107.	B
108.	E
109.	A
110.	A

1. **The correct answer is (C).** When you plan to make a major purchase, such as an automobile, *you* should analyze your financial situation, as well as your desires, before making a decision.

2. **The correct answer is (E).** This sentence is correct.

3. **The correct answer is (D).** The Curies had almost exhausted their resources, and for a time it seemed unlikely that they ever would find the *solution* to their financial problems.

4. **The correct answer is (C).** If the rumors are correct, Haworth will not be convicted, for each of the officers on the court realizes that Chatham and Norris may be the real *culprits* and that their testimony is not completely trustworthy.

5. **The correct answer is (A).** The citizens of Washington, like *those of* Los Angeles, prefer to commute by automobile, even though motor vehicles contribute nearly as many contaminants to the air as do all other sources combined.

6. **The correct answer is (B).** By the time Ralph Rogers completes his testimony, every major executive of our company but Mark Jamieson and *me* will have been accused of complicity in the stock swindle.

7. **The correct answer is (B).** Within six months the store was operating profitably and *efficiently*: shelves were well stocked, goods were selling rapidly, and the cash register was ringing constantly.

8. **The correct answer is (B).** Today Shakespeare's sonnets are more read than *Milton's*, perhaps because Shakespeare's primary subject is love.

9. **The correct answer is (C).** Any true insomniac is well aware of the futility of such measures as drinking hot milk, *keeping* regular hours, practicing deep breathing, counting sheep, and concentrating on black velvet.

10. **The correct answer is (D).** I would appreciate your treating me as if I *were* your brother.

11. **The correct answer is (C).** Enough change toward conservatism to secure a better balance and to accept more openly the fundamentals of character and their mastery *is* to be commended, but not a return to the unnecessarily harsh and harmful practices of a generation ago.

12. **The correct answer is (B).** The appearance of the beggar was in one respect similar to *that of* the elegant gentleman, for the beggar too, walked with dignity.

13. **The correct answer is (A).** The interest of American industry *in* developing previously wasted intellectual resources suggests that we may have reached a new plateau in our economic development.

14. **The correct answer is (B).** That artist must have been *ingenious* to find uses for recycled auto parts in her sculptures.

15. **The correct answer is (B).** She was promoted because she made *fewer* errors than the other secretary.

16. **The correct answer is (A).** She *flaunts* her mink coat whenever she goes out with us so that we'll think she's very wealthy.

17. **The correct answer is (A).** We objected to *his* reprimanding us for our good, especially when he said it hurt him more than us.

18. **The correct answer is (D).** The boy, as well as his mother, desperately *needs* help.

19. **The correct answer is (B).** In the text, the number of careless errors *indicates* too little attention to proofreading.

20. **The correct answer is (B).** It's certain that between you and *me* we can discover a practical solution to this complex problem.

21. **The correct answer is (E).** This sentence is correct.

22. **The correct answer is (B).** The award should go to the pupil *whom* we think the parents had intended it for.

23. **The correct answer is (A).** If you *had seen* the number of pancakes he consumed at breakfast this morning, you would have understood why he is so overweight.

24. **The correct answer is (C).** Because of a shortage of critical parts, the company was not *capable of* supplying the demand for its product.

25. **The correct answer is (C).** Neither the Brontë sisters nor their brother Branwell *is* remembered as healthy or happy.

26. **The correct answer is (D).** When my commanding officer first looked up from his desk, he took Lieutenant Baxter to be *me*.

27. **The correct answer is (C).** It is difficult if not impossible to predict the *effects* of the proposed legislation.

28. **The correct answer is (C).** The mayor expressed concern about the large *number* of people injured at street crossings.

29. **The correct answer is (A).** "*Let* us face the fact that we're in trouble!" he shouted.

30. **The correct answer is (A).** *Because* he was frequently late, his employer found it necessary to reprimand him.

31. **The correct answer is (D).** I know that you will enjoy receiving flowers that smell so *sweet*.

32. **The correct answer is (C).** He is at least ten years older *than* she is.

33. **The correct answer is (B).** I found one of *those* books that tells you how to build a model airplane.

34. **The correct answer is (E).** This sentence is correct.

35. **The correct answer is (A).** There are *fewer* derelicts in the downtown area since the crumbling building was razed.

36. **The correct answer is (E).** The tribe of warriors believed that boys and girls should be reared *separately*, and, as soon as *a boy* was weaned, *he* was taken from *his mother.*

37. **The correct answer is (D).** *Vesta, though only the third largest of the known asteroids, is by far the brightest.*

38. **The correct answer is (A).** As a result of the discovery of the Dead Sea Scrolls, our understanding of the roots of Christianity *has had to be revised considerably.*

39. **The correct answer is (A).** The jury was instructed to be *disinterested while* deliberating.

40. **The correct answer is (C).** Such of his stories as *were* original were accepted.

41. **The correct answer is (D).** The jackets are so similar *it's hard to tell mine from yours.*

42. **The correct answer is (D).** Do you think that Alice has shown more progress than any *other* girl in the class?

43. **The correct answer is (E).** She insisted *on my going.*

44. **The correct answer is (A).** *Everyone, including Anne and Helen, was* there in time for the ceremony.

45. **The correct answer is (C).** She had eaten lunch *late; that's why* she had no appetite for dinner.

46. **The correct answer is (A).** My brother and I look so much alike that the professor *supposed me to be him.*

47. **The correct answer is (D).** With a sigh of relief, she set the completed report on the desk; then she herself *lay* down and fell asleep.

48. **The correct answer is (C).** Is the climate of Italy somewhat like *that* of Florida?

49. **The correct answer is (E).** *Everyone knows her except Ruth and me.*

50. **The correct answer is (C).** *When I was a child, my mother encouraged me to learn to play the piano.*

51. **The correct answer is (B).** The reason I want to have dinner with him is *that I enjoy his company.*

52. **The correct answer is (B).** The usher won't *let* us come into the auditorium once the lecture has begun.

53. **The correct answer is (A).** *Let's you and me settle the matter between ourselves.*

54. **The correct answer is (D).** The Potsdam Conference of 1945 was the final wartime conference of World War II. *It* was held in a Berlin suburb and was attended by Joseph Stalin, Harry Truman, and Clement Atlee.

55. **The correct answer is (C).** The work can be a challenging and exciting experience, *demanding* a degree of flexibility, adaptability, and self-sufficiency.

56. **The correct answer is (E).** Winter came before the archaeologists *could do anything more* than mark out the burial site.

57. **The correct answer is (B).** A black writer often gives the white reader some insight into the reasons why black men are angry *by describing* the injustice blacks encounter in a white society.

58. **The correct answer is (A).** The agreement between the university officials and the dissident students provides that students *be* represented on every university committee and on the board of trustees.

59. **The correct answer is (A).** Since a tap on the door *had interrupted* her musings, she decided to finish washing her hair.

60. **The correct answer is (E).** The novel is complicated because *it has many* subplots.

61. **The correct answer is (E).** When he returned *to the place of his birth*, he was greeted by those who had shunned him as a boy.

62. **The correct answer is (C).** The committee selected a delegation to the convention including several new *members— Mr. Garcia, Ms. Kim, and me.*

63. **The correct answer is (E).** As soon as the gate opened, *the two men emerged.*

64. **The correct answer is (A).** Now that summer was coming on with hasty *steps, I realized* that my day of decision was fast approaching.

65. **The correct answer is (D).** He swam until his strength was *exhausted. Tom then* threw up his arms and sank.

66. **The correct answer is (B).** Because of differences of climate and of surroundings, in the course of ages, *differences of speech have occurred.*

67. **The correct answer is (E).** Foreign Service careers *offer such special rewards* as the pride and satisfaction of representing the United States abroad, the challenge of working in an action-oriented profession, and the opportunity for growth and change.

68. **The correct answer is (C).** He is *famous not only in England but also in Russia.*

69. **The correct answer is (D).** She likes to camp *and to ride horses.*

70. **The correct answer is (E).** The search for the lost ring was abandoned after *we had raked the beach* for hours.

71. **The correct answer is (C).** Her brother has never *been dependable and never will be.*

72. **The correct answer is (B).** The member of the majority party with the greatest seniority *serves as chairman* of a Congressional committee.

73. **The correct answer is (D).** Interest constitutes the second largest item of the federal budget *consuming about eleven cents* of every tax dollar.

74. **The correct answer is (E).** The Sirens were mythical creatures who sang for *sailors, beguiling them* towards the rocks where they were shipwrecked.

75. **The correct answer is (A).** An absolute ruler of a country who was legally elected and has declared that an emergency necessitates his absolute rule *or one who* has seized power by force is called a dictator.

76. **The correct answer is (E).** Euphoric because of his recent *achievement, he* continued his studies.

77. **The correct answer is (D).** The style in which a play is written *determines whether* it is realistic or unrealistic.

78. **The correct answer is (E).** The concepts were important both to the Cubist painters *and* the practitioners of Dadasim.

79. **The correct answer is (B).** Just as a register of all the varieties of flora and fauna of a region represents its plants and animals, *so a list* of all the elements of the general customs of a people represents its culture.

80. **The correct answer is (E).** Three passengers with tickets were not permitted to board *because the airline had overbooked the flight.*

81. **The correct answer is (D).** Scrambling back to their box, the puppies, frightened by the banging of *the front door, had all rolled* or jumped from the sofa.

82. **The correct answer is (D).** Dwindling resources is one of many ecological problems said to be increasing *rapidly, and it is exacerbated* by increased consumption.

83. **The correct answer is (A).** She tossed her head back and smiled at the *sun while running* across the lush meadow.

84. **The correct answer is (C).** Those who criticize the present system *have expended* considerable energy.

85. **The correct answer is (A).** As she stepped into the bright sunlight it occurred *to her that* she had forgotten her sunhat.

86. **The correct answer is (E).** Martin Luther King Jr. was not only a *minister, but also* a political leader and s superb rhetorician.

87. **The correct answer is (B).** Wyatt and Surrey *were the two* poets who introduced the sonnet form to English poetry.

88. **The correct answer is (A).** The boys sniffed the air like a pack of hungry *hounds after having* burst into the room.

89. **The correct answer is (E).** This vision of paradise *is marred by* one final doubt.

90. **The correct answer is (C).** The wisdom of ancient ways, devised by ancestors who had become *gods, was taught to the young men* by the old men of the tribe.

91. **The correct answer is (C).**
92. **The correct answer is (C).**
93. **The correct answer is (A).**
94. **The correct answer is (E).**
95. **The correct answer is (C).**
96. **The correct answer is (D).**
97. **The correct answer is (A).**
98. **The correct answer is (B).**
99. **The correct answer is (C).**
100. **The correct answer is (B).**
101. **The correct answer is (D).**
102. **The correct answer is (C).**
103. **The correct answer is (A).**
104. **The correct answer is (E).**
105. **The correct answer is (C).**
106. **The correct answer is (D).**
107. **The correct answer is (B).**
108. **The correct answer is (E).**
109. **The correct answer is (A).**
110. **The correct answer is (A).**

answers

PRACTICE TEST 2 ANSWER SHEET

Knowledge Questions

1. Ⓐ Ⓑ Ⓒ Ⓓ	21. Ⓐ Ⓑ Ⓒ Ⓓ	41. Ⓐ Ⓑ Ⓒ Ⓓ	61. Ⓐ Ⓑ Ⓒ Ⓓ
2. Ⓐ Ⓑ Ⓒ Ⓓ	22. Ⓐ Ⓑ Ⓒ Ⓓ	42. Ⓐ Ⓑ Ⓒ Ⓓ	62. Ⓐ Ⓑ Ⓒ Ⓓ
3. Ⓐ Ⓑ Ⓒ Ⓓ	23. Ⓐ Ⓑ Ⓒ Ⓓ	43. Ⓐ Ⓑ Ⓒ Ⓓ	63. Ⓐ Ⓑ Ⓒ Ⓓ
4. Ⓐ Ⓑ Ⓒ Ⓓ	24. Ⓐ Ⓑ Ⓒ Ⓓ	44. Ⓐ Ⓑ Ⓒ Ⓓ	64. Ⓐ Ⓑ Ⓒ Ⓓ
5. Ⓐ Ⓑ Ⓒ Ⓓ	25. Ⓐ Ⓑ Ⓒ Ⓓ	45. Ⓐ Ⓑ Ⓒ Ⓓ	65. Ⓐ Ⓑ Ⓒ Ⓓ
6. Ⓐ Ⓑ Ⓒ Ⓓ	26. Ⓐ Ⓑ Ⓒ Ⓓ	46. Ⓐ Ⓑ Ⓒ Ⓓ	66. Ⓐ Ⓑ Ⓒ Ⓓ
7. Ⓐ Ⓑ Ⓒ Ⓓ	27. Ⓐ Ⓑ Ⓒ Ⓓ	47. Ⓐ Ⓑ Ⓒ Ⓓ	67. Ⓐ Ⓑ Ⓒ Ⓓ
8. Ⓐ Ⓑ Ⓒ Ⓓ	28. Ⓐ Ⓑ Ⓒ Ⓓ	48. Ⓐ Ⓑ Ⓒ Ⓓ	68. Ⓐ Ⓑ Ⓒ Ⓓ
9. Ⓐ Ⓑ Ⓒ Ⓓ	29. Ⓐ Ⓑ Ⓒ Ⓓ	49. Ⓐ Ⓑ Ⓒ Ⓓ	69. Ⓐ Ⓑ Ⓒ Ⓓ
10. Ⓐ Ⓑ Ⓒ Ⓓ	30. Ⓐ Ⓑ Ⓒ Ⓓ	50. Ⓐ Ⓑ Ⓒ Ⓓ	70. Ⓐ Ⓑ Ⓒ Ⓓ
11. Ⓐ Ⓑ Ⓒ Ⓓ	31. Ⓐ Ⓑ Ⓒ Ⓓ	51. Ⓐ Ⓑ Ⓒ Ⓓ	
12. Ⓐ Ⓑ Ⓒ Ⓓ	32. Ⓐ Ⓑ Ⓒ Ⓓ	52. Ⓐ Ⓑ Ⓒ Ⓓ	
13. Ⓐ Ⓑ Ⓒ Ⓓ	33. Ⓐ Ⓑ Ⓒ Ⓓ	53. Ⓐ Ⓑ Ⓒ Ⓓ	
14. Ⓐ Ⓑ Ⓒ Ⓓ	34. Ⓐ Ⓑ Ⓒ Ⓓ	54. Ⓐ Ⓑ Ⓒ Ⓓ	
15. Ⓐ Ⓑ Ⓒ Ⓓ	35. Ⓐ Ⓑ Ⓒ Ⓓ	55. Ⓐ Ⓑ Ⓒ Ⓓ	
16. Ⓐ Ⓑ Ⓒ Ⓓ	36. Ⓐ Ⓑ Ⓒ Ⓓ	56. Ⓐ Ⓑ Ⓒ Ⓓ	
17. Ⓐ Ⓑ Ⓒ Ⓓ	37. Ⓐ Ⓑ Ⓒ Ⓓ	57. Ⓐ Ⓑ Ⓒ Ⓓ	
18. Ⓐ Ⓑ Ⓒ Ⓓ	38. Ⓐ Ⓑ Ⓒ Ⓓ	58. Ⓐ Ⓑ Ⓒ Ⓓ	
19. Ⓐ Ⓑ Ⓒ Ⓓ	39. Ⓐ Ⓑ Ⓒ Ⓓ	59. Ⓐ Ⓑ Ⓒ Ⓓ	
20. Ⓐ Ⓑ Ⓒ Ⓓ	40. Ⓐ Ⓑ Ⓒ Ⓓ	60. Ⓐ Ⓑ Ⓒ Ⓓ	

English Expression

1. Ⓐ Ⓑ Ⓒ Ⓓ Ⓔ	31. Ⓐ Ⓑ Ⓒ Ⓓ Ⓔ	61. Ⓐ Ⓑ Ⓒ Ⓓ Ⓔ	91. Ⓐ Ⓑ Ⓒ Ⓓ Ⓔ
2. Ⓐ Ⓑ Ⓒ Ⓓ Ⓔ	32. Ⓐ Ⓑ Ⓒ Ⓓ Ⓔ	62. Ⓐ Ⓑ Ⓒ Ⓓ Ⓔ	92. Ⓐ Ⓑ Ⓒ Ⓓ Ⓔ
3. Ⓐ Ⓑ Ⓒ Ⓓ Ⓔ	33. Ⓐ Ⓑ Ⓒ Ⓓ Ⓔ	63. Ⓐ Ⓑ Ⓒ Ⓓ Ⓔ	93. Ⓐ Ⓑ Ⓒ Ⓓ Ⓔ
4. Ⓐ Ⓑ Ⓒ Ⓓ Ⓔ	34. Ⓐ Ⓑ Ⓒ Ⓓ Ⓔ	64. Ⓐ Ⓑ Ⓒ Ⓓ Ⓔ	94. Ⓐ Ⓑ Ⓒ Ⓓ Ⓔ
5. Ⓐ Ⓑ Ⓒ Ⓓ Ⓔ	35. Ⓐ Ⓑ Ⓒ Ⓓ Ⓔ	65. Ⓐ Ⓑ Ⓒ Ⓓ Ⓔ	95. Ⓐ Ⓑ Ⓒ Ⓓ Ⓔ
6. Ⓐ Ⓑ Ⓒ Ⓓ Ⓔ	36. Ⓐ Ⓑ Ⓒ Ⓓ Ⓔ	66. Ⓐ Ⓑ Ⓒ Ⓓ Ⓔ	96. Ⓐ Ⓑ Ⓒ Ⓓ Ⓔ
7. Ⓐ Ⓑ Ⓒ Ⓓ Ⓔ	37. Ⓐ Ⓑ Ⓒ Ⓓ Ⓔ	67. Ⓐ Ⓑ Ⓒ Ⓓ Ⓔ	97. Ⓐ Ⓑ Ⓒ Ⓓ Ⓔ
8. Ⓐ Ⓑ Ⓒ Ⓓ Ⓔ	38. Ⓐ Ⓑ Ⓒ Ⓓ Ⓔ	68. Ⓐ Ⓑ Ⓒ Ⓓ Ⓔ	98. Ⓐ Ⓑ Ⓒ Ⓓ Ⓔ
9. Ⓐ Ⓑ Ⓒ Ⓓ Ⓔ	39. Ⓐ Ⓑ Ⓒ Ⓓ Ⓔ	69. Ⓐ Ⓑ Ⓒ Ⓓ Ⓔ	99. Ⓐ Ⓑ Ⓒ Ⓓ Ⓔ
10. Ⓐ Ⓑ Ⓒ Ⓓ Ⓔ	40. Ⓐ Ⓑ Ⓒ Ⓓ Ⓔ	70. Ⓐ Ⓑ Ⓒ Ⓓ Ⓔ	100. Ⓐ Ⓑ Ⓒ Ⓓ Ⓔ
11. Ⓐ Ⓑ Ⓒ Ⓓ Ⓔ	41. Ⓐ Ⓑ Ⓒ Ⓓ Ⓔ	71. Ⓐ Ⓑ Ⓒ Ⓓ Ⓔ	101. Ⓐ Ⓑ Ⓒ Ⓓ Ⓔ
12. Ⓐ Ⓑ Ⓒ Ⓓ Ⓔ	42. Ⓐ Ⓑ Ⓒ Ⓓ Ⓔ	72. Ⓐ Ⓑ Ⓒ Ⓓ Ⓔ	102. Ⓐ Ⓑ Ⓒ Ⓓ Ⓔ
13. Ⓐ Ⓑ Ⓒ Ⓓ Ⓔ	43. Ⓐ Ⓑ Ⓒ Ⓓ Ⓔ	73. Ⓐ Ⓑ Ⓒ Ⓓ Ⓔ	103. Ⓐ Ⓑ Ⓒ Ⓓ Ⓔ
14. Ⓐ Ⓑ Ⓒ Ⓓ Ⓔ	44. Ⓐ Ⓑ Ⓒ Ⓓ Ⓔ	74. Ⓐ Ⓑ Ⓒ Ⓓ Ⓔ	104. Ⓐ Ⓑ Ⓒ Ⓓ Ⓔ
15. Ⓐ Ⓑ Ⓒ Ⓓ Ⓔ	45. Ⓐ Ⓑ Ⓒ Ⓓ Ⓔ	75. Ⓐ Ⓑ Ⓒ Ⓓ Ⓔ	105. Ⓐ Ⓑ Ⓒ Ⓓ Ⓔ
16. Ⓐ Ⓑ Ⓒ Ⓓ Ⓔ	46. Ⓐ Ⓑ Ⓒ Ⓓ Ⓔ	76. Ⓐ Ⓑ Ⓒ Ⓓ Ⓔ	106. Ⓐ Ⓑ Ⓒ Ⓓ Ⓔ
17. Ⓐ Ⓑ Ⓒ Ⓓ Ⓔ	47. Ⓐ Ⓑ Ⓒ Ⓓ Ⓔ	77. Ⓐ Ⓑ Ⓒ Ⓓ Ⓔ	107. Ⓐ Ⓑ Ⓒ Ⓓ Ⓔ
18. Ⓐ Ⓑ Ⓒ Ⓓ Ⓔ	48. Ⓐ Ⓑ Ⓒ Ⓓ Ⓔ	78. Ⓐ Ⓑ Ⓒ Ⓓ Ⓔ	108. Ⓐ Ⓑ Ⓒ Ⓓ Ⓔ
19. Ⓐ Ⓑ Ⓒ Ⓓ Ⓔ	49. Ⓐ Ⓑ Ⓒ Ⓓ Ⓔ	79. Ⓐ Ⓑ Ⓒ Ⓓ Ⓔ	109. Ⓐ Ⓑ Ⓒ Ⓓ Ⓔ
20. Ⓐ Ⓑ Ⓒ Ⓓ Ⓔ	50. Ⓐ Ⓑ Ⓒ Ⓓ Ⓔ	80. Ⓐ Ⓑ Ⓒ Ⓓ Ⓔ	110. Ⓐ Ⓑ Ⓒ Ⓓ Ⓔ
21. Ⓐ Ⓑ Ⓒ Ⓓ Ⓔ	51. Ⓐ Ⓑ Ⓒ Ⓓ Ⓔ	81. Ⓐ Ⓑ Ⓒ Ⓓ Ⓔ	
22. Ⓐ Ⓑ Ⓒ Ⓓ Ⓔ	52. Ⓐ Ⓑ Ⓒ Ⓓ Ⓔ	82. Ⓐ Ⓑ Ⓒ Ⓓ Ⓔ	
23. Ⓐ Ⓑ Ⓒ Ⓓ Ⓔ	53. Ⓐ Ⓑ Ⓒ Ⓓ Ⓔ	83. Ⓐ Ⓑ Ⓒ Ⓓ Ⓔ	
24. Ⓐ Ⓑ Ⓒ Ⓓ Ⓔ	54. Ⓐ Ⓑ Ⓒ Ⓓ Ⓔ	84. Ⓐ Ⓑ Ⓒ Ⓓ Ⓔ	
25. Ⓐ Ⓑ Ⓒ Ⓓ Ⓔ	55. Ⓐ Ⓑ Ⓒ Ⓓ Ⓔ	85. Ⓐ Ⓑ Ⓒ Ⓓ Ⓔ	
26. Ⓐ Ⓑ Ⓒ Ⓓ Ⓔ	56. Ⓐ Ⓑ Ⓒ Ⓓ Ⓔ	86. Ⓐ Ⓑ Ⓒ Ⓓ Ⓔ	
27. Ⓐ Ⓑ Ⓒ Ⓓ Ⓔ	57. Ⓐ Ⓑ Ⓒ Ⓓ Ⓔ	87. Ⓐ Ⓑ Ⓒ Ⓓ Ⓔ	
28. Ⓐ Ⓑ Ⓒ Ⓓ Ⓔ	58. Ⓐ Ⓑ Ⓒ Ⓓ Ⓔ	88. Ⓐ Ⓑ Ⓒ Ⓓ Ⓔ	
29. Ⓐ Ⓑ Ⓒ Ⓓ Ⓔ	59. Ⓐ Ⓑ Ⓒ Ⓓ Ⓔ	89. Ⓐ Ⓑ Ⓒ Ⓓ Ⓔ	
30. Ⓐ Ⓑ Ⓒ Ⓓ Ⓔ	60. Ⓐ Ⓑ Ⓒ Ⓓ Ⓔ	90. Ⓐ Ⓑ Ⓒ Ⓓ Ⓔ	

70 Questions • 2 Hours

Directions: Each of the questions or incomplete statements below is followed by four possible answers. Select the best answer for each question and then blacken the corresponding space on the answer sheet. Some sets of questions are presented with material such as reading passages, plans, graphs, tables, etc. Answers to such questions may require interpretation of the material and/or outside knowledge relevant to its content.

1. The Supreme Court has ruled that no one has the right to yell fire falsely in a crowded theater. According to the Court, this would be an abuse of freedom of speech under the

   (A) preferred position doctrine.

   (B) clear and present danger doctrine.

   (C) least drastic means doctrine.

   (D) bad tendency doctrine.

2. A nation that follows the realist approach to the balance of power would do all of the following EXCEPT

   (A) form alliances.

   (B) unilaterally disarm.

   (C) agree to arms control treaties that stabilize the balance.

   (D) increase its intelligence capabilities overseas.

3. If Country K can produce Commodity A with 1 unit of input and Commodity B with 3 units of input, and Country P can produce Commodity A with 5 units of input and Commodity B with 10 units of input, it would be most likely that

   (A) Country K would produce both commodities and Country P neither.

   (B) Country P would gain from trade and Country K would not.

   (C) Country K would gain from trade and Country P would not.

   (D) each country would gain by trading with the other.

4. If each of the following groups of artists could collaborate on a work, which group would most probably create an American folk opera based upon themes drawn from the early history of the nation?

   (A) Leonard Bernstein, Jack Kerouac, and Pearl Primus

   (B) Aaron Copland, Carl Sandburg, and Agnes de Mille

   (C) Lukas Foss, Ernest Hemingway, and George Balanchine

   (D) Paul Hindemith, Henry Miller, and Anthony Tudor

5. A diplomatic pouch shares extraterritorial privileges with an embassy or consulate; that is, it is exempt from customs inspection and from local jurisdiction. This special status is granted to a diplomatic pouch to provide a government with some confidential means for transmitting confidential messages and documents. If a consular official sends diamonds to his home country in a diplomatic pouch, he is

   (A) fully within his rights and privileges.

   (B) in violation of moral law.

   (C) in violation of international law.

   (D) in violation of the laws of all countries through which the pouch must travel.

6. "His attitude is as provincial as an isolationist country's unwillingness to engage in any international trade whatever, on the ground that it will be required to buy something from outsiders which could possibly be produced by local talent, although not as well and not as cheaply." This statement is most descriptive of the attitude of the division chief in a government agency who

   (A) wishes to restrict promotions to supervisory positions in his division exclusively to employees in his division.

   (B) refuses to delegate responsible tasks to subordinates qualified to perform these tasks.

   (C) believes that informal on-the-job training of new staff members is superior to formal training methods.

   (D) frequently makes personal issues out of matters that should be handled on an impersonal basis.

QUESTIONS 7 AND 8 ARE BASED ON THE DIAGRAM BELOW:

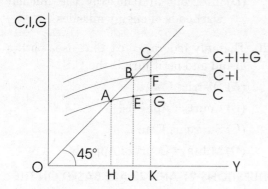

7. Equilibrium national income would be
    (A) OK.
    (B) BJ.
    (C) FK.
    (D) OJ.

8. Savings plus taxes would be
    (A) FG.
    (B) BE.
    (C) CG.
    (D) AH.

9. According to the international relations concept of "hegemonic stability," the nation that BEST performed that role for a major part of the nineteenth century was
    (A) the United States.
    (B) Germany.
    (C) Russia.
    (D) Great Britain.

10. According to the 2000 census, the fastest growing minority in the United States consisted of
    (A) African-Americans.
    (B) Asian-Americans.
    (C) Native Americans.
    (D) Hispanics.

11. The United States has declared war at some time or other against all of the following countries EXCEPT
    (A) England.
    (B) Russia.
    (C) Spain.
    (D) Italy.

12. Which of the following African nations suffered a terrible 1994 internal war between the Tutsis and Hutus, resulting in the slaughter of hundreds of thousands of people?
    (A) Nigeria
    (B) Botswana
    (C) Zaire
    (D) Rwanda

13. Between 1989 and 1999, which world event occurred earliest (first) before the other three?
    (A) The Wye River Accord involving peace in the Middle East
    (B) The United Nations' fiftieth anniversary
    (C) The Earth Summit
    (D) The Tiananmen Square massacre

14. An *amicus curiae* brief before the Supreme Court means that
    (A) an individual or organization has presented additional arguments to those presented by the party to the case.
    (B) the rule of precedent cannot apply to the case under consideration because the case currently being argued is unique in terms of issues and content.
    (C) the case now being considered by the Court has reached the Court due to the original jurisdiction clause of the Constitution.
    (D) this brief's legal validity has been accepted by both the plaintiff and defendant prior to actual oral arguments before the Court.

15. "With two films, *Z* and *State of Siege*, he has emerged as the contemporary director who has best mastered the technique of transforming odious political situations into tension-filled feature films, and he has moved the political film from a genre with sectarian appeal to one with a mass audience." The film director described above is

    (A) Costa Gavras.

    (B) Jean-Luc Godard.

    (C) Michelangelo Antonioni.

    (D) Ingmar Bergman.

16. In American education, which of the following issues or policies has generated the LEAST amount of controversy?

    (A) School vouchers

    (B) School busing

    (C) Local control over the curriculum

    (D) National, standardized high school exit exams

17. The event that initiated the voluntary participation of states in multilateral, high-level political conferences and eventually led to the formation of the League of Nations and the United Nations was

    (A) the Hague Conference.

    (B) the Congress of Vienna.

    (C) the Geneva Conference.

    (D) the Paris Peace Conference.

18. Voter turnout has declined for all of the following reasons EXCEPT

    (A) registration requirements.

    (B) residency requirements.

    (C) a paucity of political information.

    (D) a low sense of political efficacy.

19. "Star Wars," a program proposed by President Reagan, was designed to

    (A) destroy an enemy's bomber force.

    (B) detect and destroy an enemy's submarines at sea.

    (C) improve the resolution capability of U.S. "spy-in-the-sky" satellites.

    (D) intercept and destroy the nuclear warheads of enemy missiles.

20. The only federal court that uses both a grand and petit jury is the U.S.

    (A) District Court.

    (B) Court of Appeals.

    (C) Supreme Court.

    (D) Military Court of Appeals.

QUESTIONS 21 AND 22 ARE BASED ON THE FOLLOWING PRODUCTION–POSSIBILITY SCHEDULES:

For Nation A

Food	50	40	30	20	10	1
Clothing	0	6	12	18	24	30

For Nation B

Food	100	80	60	40	20	0
Clothing	0	18	36	54	72	90

21. Both schedules indicate

    (A) decreasing costs.

    (B) constant costs.

    (C) first decreasing costs, then increasing costs.

    (D) first increasing costs, then decreasing costs.

22. Nation A places a protective tariff against the textile exports of Nation B. Who is this tariff "protecting"?

    (A) The consumers of Nation A

    (B) The consumers of Nation B

    (C) The textile industry of Nation B

    (D) The textile industry of Nation A

23. Of the following, which nation has (a) had a history of political absolutism; (b) repeatedly sought a warm-water port; (c) experienced two "revolutions" early and late in the twentieth century; and (d) was one of the "poles" in a conflict-ridden bipolar global system?

    (A) Cuba
    (B) China
    (C) France
    (D) Russia

24. Which of the following assassinations was the direct cause of a major war?

    (A) Olaf Palme in Sweden
    (B) Anwar Sadat in Egypt
    (C) Archduke Francis Ferdinand in Bosnia
    (D) Mohandas Gandhi in India

25. With per capita incomes as low as they are in southern Asia, it will not be easy to raise the rate of savings and investment. These countries are caught in something like a vicious circle of poverty. Not much can be saved from low incomes; but since not much is saved and consequently invested in production equipment, income continues to remain low. It has been estimated that with population increasing at current Indian rates, a net saving of 5 percent of national income would be just about sufficient to maintain per capita incomes at their present level. Given an output–capital ratio of 1:3, the rate of population increase in India must be approximately

    (A) $\frac{1}{3}$ percent.
    (B) 1 percent.
    (C) $1\frac{2}{3}$ percent.
    (D) 3 percent.

26. The objective of the International Monetary Fund is to

    (A) underwrite loans to governments for industrial projects.
    (B) eliminate trade barriers in the form of protective tariffs.
    (C) discourage a multilateral system of international payment.
    (D) correct maladjustments in international exchange rates.

27. Which of the following has the same effect as an export on the U.S. balance of payments?

    (A) An American takes a Lufthansa flight from Boston to Frankfurt.
    (B) An American purchases preferred stock in a Korean auto manufacturing firm.
    (C) An American receives a birthday check from relatives in the Netherlands.
    (D) An American purchases goods produced in a Taiwanese plant that was built with American funds.

28. Ruth Benedict's *Chrysanthemum and the Sword* revealed the chameleon nature of which nation?

    (A) Japan
    (B) Germany
    (C) Italy
    (D) India

29. In 2001, 80 to 90 percent of America's supply of illegal cocaine originated from which nation?

    (A) Peru
    (B) Thailand
    (C) Colombia
    (D) Mexico

30. Which of the following has contributed MOST to the increase in real wages in the United States since 1900?

    (A) Rising prices

    (B) Increasing productivity

    (C) Increasing strength of labor unions

    (D) Increasing use of the corporate form of business organization

31. One reason that Soviet dictator Stalin distrusted the United States and Great Britain during World War II was the handling of the "second-front" issue. The "second front" referred to

    (A) the need for the United States and Great Britain to attack German forces in North Africa.

    (B) the need for the United States and Great Britain to invade Western Europe.

    (C) the need for the United States and Great Britain to attack Japanese-held islands in the South Pacific.

    (D) the need for American and British submarines to attack German naval forces in the Atlantic.

32. Which American president defended the decision to go to war before the Congress, by stating that the United States must fight "for the ultimate peace of the world and for the liberation of its people . . . for the rights of nations great and small and the privilege of men everywhere to choose their way of life and of obedience. The world must be made safe for democracy. Its peace must be planted upon the tested foundations of political liberty." This president was

    (A) Woodrow Wilson.

    (B) Abraham Lincoln.

    (C) Franklin D. Roosevelt.

    (D) Lyndon Johnson.

33. A contemporary political liberal in America would probably support which of the following?

    (A) Less spending on social programs by the federal government

    (B) Restricting a woman's right to an abortion in the first trimester

    (C) The abolition of the death penalty

    (D) Partial privatization of the social security system

34. All of the following were included in Woodrow Wilson's "Fourteen Points" EXCEPT

    (A) freedom of the press.

    (B) freedom of the seas.

    (C) reduction of armaments.

    (D) the establishment of a general federation of nations.

35. When President Reagan spoke of the excesses of government being pushed onto our children, he was referring specifically to

    (A) high taxes.

    (B) required cuts in aid to education.

    (C) future costs of interest payments on national debt.

    (D) the plight of the homeless.

QUESTIONS 36 TO 39 ARE BASED ON THE MAP BELOW:

36. 9 and 12 share a common

 I.   language.

 II. government.

 III. location on two continents.

 IV. state religion.

 (A) I and II only

 (B) III only

 (C) I, II, and III only

 (D) I, II, III, and IV

37. During World War II, a prominent politician in this country turned traitor and collaborated with the Nazi invaders of his country to head a puppet government. This country was

 (A) 24.

 (B) 25.

 (C) 26.

 (D) 27.

38. The name of this man, which name has now come into the language to refer specifically to a traitor/collaborator, was

 (A) Vichy.

 (B) Quisling.

 (C) Turncoat.

 (D) Maginot.

39. The area labeled 23 is

 (A) a land best known for its bucolic tranquility.

 (B) engaged in a bitter struggle for its independence from 21.

 (C) the site of a religious conflict masquerading as a political conflict.

 (D) the site of a political conflict masquerading as a religious conflict.

practice test

40. If a nation uses exchange controls to eliminate a balance-of-payments deficit, which one of the following is the nation likely to employ?

(A) Limiting its imports to the amount of its exports

(B) Lowering the nation's internal price level by passage of law

(C) Limiting its exports to the amount of its imports

(D) Increasing the value of its currency

41. John F. Kennedy once said, "A rising tide lifts all the boats." He probably did NOT mean

(A) that a fixed tax surcharge affects all citizens equally.

(B) that an improvement in the economy would be beneficial to all.

(C) that a grounded tanker will come free only once the tide comes in.

(D) that improved morale in the workplace would improve productivity.

42. All of the following high-achievers were black, EXCEPT

(A) Dr. Daniel Hale Williams, who performed open-heart surgery in Chicago in 1893.

(B) Eli Whitney, who invented the cotton gin.

(C) Garrett A. Morgan, who invented electric traffic signals.

(D) Benjamin Banneker, who laid out Washington, D.C., when the original designer, Pierre L'Enfant, had an argument with Thomas Jefferson and took the plans to France.

43. Which U.S. Supreme Court decision affirmed the right of an individual to burn the American flag under the protection of symbolic speech and the First Amendment?

(A) *Brown v. Board of Education*

(B) *Texas v. Johnson*

(C) *Roe v. Wade*

(D) *Miller v. California*

44. While in their American airport awaiting departure, the leader of a teen tour to Israel gathers the members of the tour around him and says, "If any of you has ANY drugs on your person or in your luggage—marijuana, crack, hash, or anything else—go into the restroom and flush every bit of it, no matter how little, right now." There may be a number of valid reasons for the leader of a teen tour to make this demand, but the most important reason for the leader to make the statement to this group is that

(A) teenagers who are using drugs are hard to supervise.

(B) the airport is in the United States and possession of any amount of any drugs in the United States is a crime.

(C) Israeli officials tend to deal especially harshly with American teenagers caught in any offense.

(D) Israel has extremely strict drug laws to which everyone is subject while in the State of Israel.

45. "The people are drafted into a huge army of ideological warriors. Even in peacetime, an attempt to defect for a civilian is regarded by law as high treason and is equated with the defection of a soldier to the enemy lines during a war." This reasoning is/was the rationale for

   (A) the new immigration laws in the United States.

   (B) the demilitarized zone between North and South Korea.

   (C) the Berlin Wall.

   (D) the Warsaw Ghetto.

46. If a foreign-born immigrant wishes to become a naturalized U.S. citizen, he or she must

   (A) be over the age of 18.

   (B) have resided in the U.S. for at least 1 year.

   (C) have resided in a particular state for at least 3 months.

   (D) be literate in a native language, but not necessarily English.

47. Of the following publications, all are clearly recognized as reflecting the biases of their publishers EXCEPT

   (A) *Commentary*.

   (B) *The Christian Science Monitor*.

   (C) *Insight*.

   (D) *Tile Nation*.

48. If a nation were to increase its exports substantially, which one of the following alternatives would be MOST probable?

   (A) A reduction in the nation's imports equal to the increase in its exports

   (B) A reduction in the nation's imports less the increase in its exports

   (C) An increase in the nation's imports substantially greater than the increase in exports

   (D) An increase in the nation's imports less than the increase in exports

49. The occurrence of export-biased technical change in the same nation discussed in question 48 would tend to

   (A) bring about a rise in the level of unemployment in the nation.

   (B) bring about deflation in that nation.

   (C) turn the terms of trade against the nation.

   (D) turn the terms of trade against those countries the nation trades with.

50. Over the past few years, a number of accused Nazi war criminals have been deported from the United States despite the fact that these individuals have lived here peacefully for many years and had attained U.S. citizenship. The basis for expelling these persons was that

   (A) under international law all persons must stand trial in the country in which they committed their crimes.

   (B) war criminals are not welcome here.

   (C) the countries that wished to try them threatened the United States with economic sanctions if the accused were not returned.

   (D) the individuals had lied about their criminal past when applying for immigrant visas.

An administrator with overall responsibility for all administrative operations in a large operating agency is considering organizing the agency's personnel office around either of the following two alternative concepts:

Alternative I: A corps of specialists for each branch of personnel subject matter, whose skills, counsel, or work products are coordinated only by the agency personnel officer

Alternative II: A crew of so-called "personnel generalists," who individually work with particular segments of the organization but deal with all subspecialties of the personnel function

Of the following, the one that is the biggest drawback of Alternative I, as compared with Alternative II, is that

(A) training and employee relations work call for education, interests, and talents that differ from those required for classification and compensation work.

(B) personnel office staff may develop only superficial familiarity with the specialized areas to which they have been assigned.

(C) supervisors may fail to get continuing, overall personnel advice on an integrated basis.

(D) the personnel specialists are likely to become so interested in and identified with the operating view as to particular cases that they lose their professional objectivity and become merely advocates of what some supervisor wants.

52. The Constitution of the United States

(A) places greater priority on national security than it does on the right of free expression.

(B) while recognizing the need for security places that need in a subordinate position to freedom of speech.

(C) establishes elaborate machinery for determining which speech will not damage national security.

(D) allows for self-policing and informal checks and balances in determining that which will damage national security.

53. Each branch of the government has a role in the balancing of free speech and freedom of the press with the national security. Which of the following branches is INCORRECTLY paired with a role in the process?

(A) Legislative—enacts legislation declaring specific activities to be criminal disclosure

(B) Judiciary—enjoins publication of information that the government has declared to be critical

(C) Legislative—classifies documents as to the degree of sensitivity of each

(D) Judiciary—adjudicates suits brought against the press

54. An international treaty once negotiated by the administration, ratified by Congress and signed by the president, has the force of law and is binding on future administrations. However, the United States has a congressional election every two years and a presidential election every four years. Elections can, of course, change the sentiments in Congress and in the White House. Knowing this, foreign governments

(A) do not even attempt to enter into treaties with the United States.

(B) wait until the end of a president's term to begin negotiations on treaties that they hope to enter into.

(C) contribute heavily to the campaigns of congressmembers they expect to be sympathetic to their treaties.

(D) begin negotiations as soon as possible after inauguration day.

55. An international agreement advocated by one president but rejected by his successor was the

(A) UN Convention on the Law of the Sea.

(B) Panama Canal Treaty.

(C) agreement to notify other countries immediately after a nuclear accident.

(D) League of Nations.

56. The chief responsibility for enforcing International Law lies with

(A) the International Court of Justice in the Hague.

(B) a special tribunal set up to deal with each major transgression of International Law.

(C) the courts of the aggrieved nation.

(D) each individual nation, which is responsible for its own enforcement.

57. Each of the following famous black persons is correctly paired with his or her contributions or accomplishments EXCEPT

(A) William H. Hastie—producer of spoofs at Harvard

(B) Dr. Mary McCleod Bethune—advisor to Franklin D. Roosevelt and to Harry S. Truman

(C) Gwendolyn Brooks—Pulitzer Prize-winning poet and novelist

(D) Tom Bradley—mayor of Los Angeles

TIONS 58 TO 60 ARE BASED ON THE MAP BELOW:

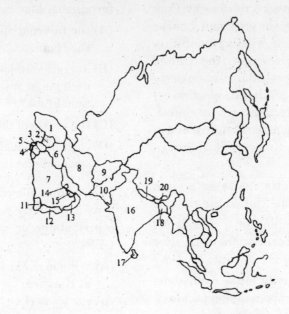

58. These two countries share a common religion and were once one. Their separation made geographical and political sense. They are

(A) 16 and 17.

(B) 10 and 18.

(C) 18 and 19.

(D) 10 and 20.

59. This nation fancies itself peacemaker and power broker of the Middle East. Through its activities, it has tried to ingratiate itself with other major powers and surrounding states (except Israel). This nation is

(A) 1.

(B) 2.

(C) 3.

(D) 14.

60. The "top of the world" is in

(A) 16.

(B) 18.

(C) 19.

(D) 20.

61. "A person charged in any State with Treason, Felony, or other Crime, who shall flee from Justice, and be found in another State, shall on Demand of the executive Authority of the State from which he fled, be delivered up, to be removed to the State having Jurisdiction of the Crime." The above quotation sums up extradition arrangements

(A) among all states under International Law.

(B) among all the member states of NATO.

(C) among states under the U.S. Constitution.

(D) under the Fugitive Slave Act.

62. The manner of avoiding deficit trading that would BEST serve the interests of the United States is

(A) isolationism and self-sufficiency.

(B) making investments abroad instead of loans.

(C) encouraging foreign investments in the United States.

(D) imposing higher tariffs to discourage imports.

63. Under international law, a nation can claim to have responded in self-defense to an armed attack when shots have been fired, when an army with guns has invaded, or when war has been declared against it on paper. Determination of identity of aggressor nation and defensive nation becomes significant

    (A) in punishing for war crimes.

    (B) in determining the status of prisoners of war.

    (C) only in the writing of histories.

    (D) after the war, in determining the status and distribution of captured territory.

64. In his book *The Souls of Black Folk*, which was published in 1903, W.E.B. DuBois urged patriotic, nonviolent activism as the route by which American blacks might best achieve civil rights and political and economic equality. He felt that Booker T. Washington's route of advancement through work and money neglected the crucial areas of dignity and manhood. W.E.B. DuBois' ideas as stated in this book probably influenced the movements and activities of

    I.   Mohandas Gandhi.

    II. Martin Luther King Jr.

    III. John L. Lewis.

    IV. Allen W. Dulles.

    (A) I only

    (B) I and II only

    (C) II and III only

    (D) III and IV only

65. One of the most important concerns of personnel administrators in a foreign outpost of any level is morale. The MOST important reason for maintaining high morale and general contentment throughout the staff is

    (A) to cover high cost of turnover.

    (B) that unhappy staffers will discourage their friends and future recruitment will be more difficult.

    (C) that happy employees are more productive.

    (D) that unhappy employees tend to be riper targets for breaches of security through carelessness or for their personal gain.

66. Article VI of the U.S. Constitution states: "The Senators and Representatives before mentioned, and the Members of the several State Legislatures, and all executive and judicial Officers, both of the United States and of the several States, shall be bound by Oath or Affirmation to support this Constitution; but no religious Test shall ever be required as a Qualification to any Office or public Trust under the United States." This article effectively

    (A) serves as a non-establishment clause.

    (B) gives freedom of religion to officeholders but denies it to the citizenry at large.

    (C) denies the exercise of religion to officeholders.

    (D) declares that the United States is an atheistic country.

67. As originally conceived in 1935, the Social Security System was to be a contributory, self-supporting system. Moneys paid in by a large force of wage earners would go into a trust fund to pay retirement, survivor, and disability benefits to a far smaller population. However, in the early 1980s, the Social Security Trust Fund found itself facing deficiencies because drafters of the Act had not considered certain contingencies in their budget projections. These included which of the following?

I.   Declining death rate

II. Inflation

III. Population cycles resulting in a smaller work force

IV. Increase in number of early retirements

(A) I and II only

(B) I and III only

(C) I, III, and IV only

(D) I, II, III, and IV

68. During the Falklands War in 1982, Argentina failed to receive support—economic, military, moral, or vocal—from the Third World countries of Asia and Africa. While economic and military support were outside the ability of most of these countries to supply, Argentina was distressed at its abandonment by these countries on the floor of the U.N. General Assembly. The most likely reason for this abandonment was that

(A) the Third World countries of Asia and Africa did not like Argentina.

(B) the countries feared reprisals from Britain.

(C) these Third World nations were trying to establish reputations as neutrals.

(D) as nations with fragile boundaries of their own they feared setting a precedent of settling territorial disputes by military means.

69. All of the following novels served to awaken black consciousness and to alert whites to the Negro condition EXCEPT

(A) *Cry, the Beloved Country.*

(B) *Roots.*

(C) *Of Human Bondage.*

(D) *Native Son.*

70. Identities of all the combatants in the Spanish Civil War were never clearly delineated, but, in the end, members of the major coalitions know who they were. Of the following alliances, the ONLY one that is certainly correct is

(A) Nationalists, Loyalists, Clergy.

(B) Anarchists, Communists, Falangists.

(C) Republicans, Monarchists, Partisans.

(D) Socialists, Anarchists, Loyalists.

ENGLISH EXPRESSION

110 Questions • 60 Minutes

> **Directions:** The following sentences contain problems in grammar, usage, diction (choice of words), and idiom. Some sentences are correct. No sentence contains more than one error.
>
> You will find that the error, if there is one, is underlined and lettered. Assume that all other elements of the sentence are correct and cannot be changed. In choosing answers, follow the requirements of standard written English. If there is an error, select the one underlined part that must be changed in order to make the sentence correct, and fill in the corresponding oval on the answer sheet. If there is no error, mark answer choice (E).

1. There are less calories in a bagel than
   A   B   C

   in a doughnut. No error
   D   E

2. The child felt very bad when his teacher
   A   B

   criticized him before the entire class.
   C   D

   No error
   E

3. He had a large amount of friends until he
   A   B   C

   lost all his money. No error
   D   E

4. Being that she was a newcomer to our
   A   B

   organization, Rose was shy. No error
   C   D   E

5. The florist asked three of us, Dan, Edward,
   A

   and I, to carry the plants down to the
   B   C   D

   loading dock. No error
   E

6. My father, along with hundreds
   A

   of other workers, have been on strike
   B   C

   since New Year's Day. No error
   D   E

7. The child dislikes green vegetables:
   A   B

   broccoli, spinach, kale, and etc. No error
   C   D   E

8. That Bill's reasoning was fallacious was
   A   B

   soon apparent to all. No error
   C   D   E

9. Neither John nor his children is likely to
   A   B   C

   attend the ceremonies. No error
   D   E

10. He will give the message to whoever opens
    A   B   C   D

    the door. No error
    E

11. The constant rise of prices and wages
    A   B

    bring about inflation. No error
    C   D   E

12. He saw <u>the same identical</u> plaid jacket
              A

    <u>on sale</u> for ten dollars <u>less</u> two weeks after
         B   C

    he <u>bought</u> it. <u>No error</u>
            D   E

13. If I <u>wasn't</u> hungry, I <u>wouldn't even</u>
           A   B

    consider <u>eating</u> that <u>peanut butter and jelly</u>
                 C   D

    sandwich. <u>No error</u>
                   E

14. It <u>was</u> not quite clear <u>whether</u> it was his
          A   B

    friend or <u>him</u> who <u>had requested</u> the
                  C   D

    favor. <u>No error</u>
               E

15. After he <u>had paid</u> the fee and <u>saw</u> the
                 A   B

    pictures, he was <u>quite</u> satisfied. <u>No error</u>
        C   D   E

16. <u>Further</u> acquaintance with the memoirs
        A

    of Elizabeth Barrett Browning and Robert

    Browning <u>enable</u> us to appreciate the
                 B

    <u>depth</u> of influence that two people of
     C

    talent can have on <u>one another</u>. <u>No error</u>
                            D   E

17. Because she <u>has always been</u> active
                    A

    <u>and with good eating habits</u>, she enjoys
             B

    <u>good health</u> and physical fitness
        C

    <u>at the age of 70</u>. <u>No error</u>
            D   E

18. <u>Having studied</u> your report carefully, I
        A

    <u>am convinced</u> that <u>neither</u> of your
        B   C

    solutions <u>are</u> correct. <u>No error</u>
                  D   E

19. If he is successful in his attempt <u>to cross</u>
                                          A

    the lake, he <u>will have swum</u> a <u>distance</u> of
                      B   C

    <u>twelve miles</u>. <u>No error</u>
        D   E

20. <u>In spite of</u> his youth, <u>no faster</u> runner
        A   B

    than <u>him</u> <u>will be found</u> on our Olympic
         C   D

    team. <u>No error</u>
              E

21. <u>Because of</u> the poor lighting, they
        A

    <u>mistakenly</u> supposed the <u>intruder</u> to be <u>I</u>.
        B   C   D

    <u>No error</u>
        E

22. <u>None</u> of the <u>diplomats</u> at the conference
        A   B

    was able either <u>to comprehend</u> or <u>solve</u>
                        C   D

    the problem. <u>No error</u>
                     E

23. It was <u>agreed</u> by a majority of the signers
               A

    of the <u>compact</u> that truth <u>as well as</u>
               B   C

    justice was to be <u>there</u> rule of life. <u>No error</u>
                          D   E

24. Everybody was <u>up</u> early on Monday
          A

    <u>because</u> our <u>local</u> store was having <u>it's</u>
     B   C   D

    annual sale. <u>No error</u>
                      E

25. A careful driver <u>watches</u> the road and
                       A

    goes <u>slowly</u> or quickly <u>depending upon</u> the
          B   C

    condition of the road, the <u>visibility</u>, and
                                    D

    the traffic. <u>No error</u>
                      E

26. What <u>affect</u> the law will have on our
           A

    <u>drivers</u> and <u>how</u> it will affect our lives
     B   C

    <u>remain</u> to be seen. <u>No error</u>
     D   E

27. If I <u>was</u> you, I <u>should be</u> careful of <u>who</u> my
          A   B   C

    friends <u>are</u>. <u>No error</u>
             D   E

28. Wilson, <u>who</u> I never thought was even
             A

    <u>in the running</u>, not only <u>won handily</u> but
     B   C

    also <u>broke</u> a record. <u>No error</u>
          D   E

29. <u>Although</u> his story had <u>aspects of truth</u>
     A   B

    about it, I <u>couldn't hardly</u> believe
                 C

    <u>what he said</u>. <u>No error</u>
     D   E

30. I would <u>have invited</u> you to <u>join me</u> at the
             A   B

    performance if you <u>told</u> me <u>that</u> you
                        C   D

    enjoy chamber music. <u>No error</u>
                              E

31. <u>You decide</u> <u>whether</u> to buy the red shirt <u>or</u>
     A   B   C

    the blue one; I like <u>the both</u> of them.
                          D

    <u>No error</u>
     E

32. A <u>torrential</u> downpour, <u>in addition</u> to long
       A   B

    stretches of road construction that made

    it necessary to slow down to fifteen miles

    an hour, <u>have</u> so delayed us that we shall
              C

    not be <u>on hand</u> for the ceremony. <u>No error</u>
            D   E

33. The soprano <u>alleged</u> <u>that</u> the dampness
                 A   B

    in the concert hall caused <u>her</u> to sing
                                C

    <u>terrible</u>. <u>No error</u>
     D   E

34. It was <u>he</u>, not <u>I</u>, who became <u>nauseous</u>
            A   B   C

    because of the <u>boat's</u> motion. <u>No error</u>
                    D   E

35. Although Richard <u>graduated</u> high school
                      A

    <u>with honors</u>, he <u>failed</u> three subjects <u>as</u> a
     B   C   D

    college freshman. <u>No error</u>
                           E

Directions: In each of the following sentences, some part or all of the sentence is underlined. Below each sentence you will find five ways of rephrasing the underlined part. Select the answer that produces the most effective sentence, one that is clear and exact without awkwardness or ambiguity, and fill in the corresponding oval on your answer sheet. In choosing answers, follow the requirements of standard written English. Choose the answer that best expresses the meaning of the original sentence. Choice (A) is always the same as the underlined part. Choose choice (A) if you think the original sentence needs no revision.

36. At first, Shakespeare's plays <u>were performed more for the roles they provided</u> the actors than for the truth of their characterizations or the beauty of their verse.

   (A) were performed more for the roles they provided
   (B) were more performed because of providing good roles for
   (C) had been performed more for the roles they could provide
   (D) had been performed more for the roles that are provided in them for
   (E) had been performed more because of the roles they provided

37. Desiring to insure the continuity of their knowledge, <u>magical lore is transmitted by the chiefs</u> to their descendants.

   (A) magical lore is transmitted by the chiefs
   (B) transmission of magical lore is made by the chiefs
   (C) the chiefs' magical lore is transmitted
   (D) the chiefs transmit magical lore
   (E) the chiefs make transmission off magical lore

38. Both diplomats have this point in common: their forte lies not so much in administrative routine or social activities <u>as much as</u> securing the greatest advantage to their country at the conference table.

   (A) as much as
   (B) as much as in
   (C) as in
   (D) but it is
   (E) but is in

39. <u>If the parent would have shown more interest</u>, her daughter would have been in college today.

   (A) If the parent would have shown more interest
   (B) If the parent had shown more interest
   (C) If the parent would have showed more interest
   (D) If the parent would have been showing more interest
   (E) Should the parent have shown more interest

40. The judge instructed the jury <u>to carefully deliberate before announcing its</u> verdict.

   (A) to carefully deliberate before announcing its
   (B) to carefully deliberate before announcing their
   (C) to deliberate carefully before announcing its
   (D) to deliberate before announcing its verdict carefully
   (E) to announce its verdict after having deliberated with great care

41. Crossing the bridge, <u>a glimpse of the islands was caught</u>.

    (A) a glimpse of the islands was caught

    (B) a glimpse: of the islands were caught

    (C) we caught a glimpse of the islands

    (D) the islands were caught a glimpse of

    (E) we caught a glimpse of the islands' view

42. This book has been <u>laying here for weeks</u>.

    (A) laying here for weeks

    (B) laying here weeks

    (C) laying down here for weeks

    (D) Being here for weeks

    (E) lying here for weeks

43. When the officer <u>will return,</u> I'll tell him you called.

    (A) will return,

    (B) will return

    (C) will have returned,

    (D) returns,

    (E) shall return,

44. <u>After he graduated school,</u> he entered the army,

    (A) After he graduated school,

    (B) After he graduated from school,

    (C) When he graduated school,

    (D) After he graduated school

    (E) As he was graduated from school,

45. A secure person is one who can make a joke even if <u>it's embarrassing to himself</u>.

    (A) it's embarrassing to himself

    (B) its embarrassing to himself

    (C) it's embarrassing to him

    (D) it shall be an embarrassment to him

    (E) embarrassing to him it will be

46. Sitting around the fire, <u>mystery stories were told by each of us</u>.

    (A) mystery stories were told by each of us

    (B) mystery stories were told by all of us

    (C) each of us told mystery stories

    (D) stories of mystery were told by each of us

    (E) mystery stories were told by us all

47. The loud noise of the subway trains and the trolley cars <u>frighten people from the country</u>.

    (A) frighten people from the country

    (B) frighten country people

    (C) frighten persons from the country

    (D) frightens country people

    (E) frighten people who come from the country

48. Inspecting the final report, <u>the director could find no fault</u> with the committee's recommendations.

    (A) the director could find no fault

    (B) the director could not find no faults

    (C) no fault could be found by the director

    (D) no fault was found by the director

    (E) the director's findings agreed

49. <u>Because of him oversleeping</u>, he arrived at work late.

    (A) Because of him oversleeping

    (B) Due to the fact that he was oversleeping

    (C) Because he overslept

    (D) Because of his oversleeping

    (E) Because that he was oversleeping

50. <u>I could not but help feel</u> that her reasons for coming here were not honest.

    (A) I could not but help feel

    (B) I could not feel

    (C) I could help feel

    (D) I could not help feel

    (E) I could feel

51. She never has and she never will do any
    work.
    (A) She never has and she never will do
        any work.
    (B) She never has and she never will do
        no work.
    (C) She never has, and she never will do
        any work.
    (D) Never has she and never will she do
        any work.
    (E) She never has done and she never will
        do any work.

52. The customized vehicle resembles a pro-
    duction sports car, but its design is more
    unique.
    (A) more unique
    (B) most unique
    (C) unique
    (D) very unusual
    (E) more stranger

53. Did you read Yeats's poem "Byzantium"?
    (A) Did you read Yeats's poem
        "Byzantium"?
    (B) Did you read Yeats's poem
        "Byzantium?"
    (C) When did you read Yeats's poem
        "Byzantium?"
    (D) Have you been reading Yeats poem
        "Byzantium"?
    (E) Did you read Yeats' poem
        "Byzantium?"

54. Security Officers perform investigative
    and protective services in the United
    States and overseas; are responsible for
    the security of U.S. facilities, operations,
    and personnel abroad; and combat crimi-
    nal, intelligence, and terrorist activities
    worldwide that might threaten American
    lives and property.
    (A) and combat criminal, intelligence, and
        terrorist activities worldwide
    (B) combating criminal, intelligence, and
        terrorist activities worldwide
    (C) and combat worldwide criminal, in-
        telligence, and terrorist activities
    (D) and they combat criminal, intelli-
        gence, and terrorist activities world-
        wide
    (E) and combat criminal, intelligence, and
        worldwide terrorist activities

55. The budget figures inferred our company
    faced financial difficulties; from this I
    implied it was not a good time to ask for a
    salary raise.
    (A) inferred our company faced financial
        difficulties; from this I implied
    (B) implied our company faced financial
        difficulties; from this I inferred
    (C) implied our company faced financial
        difficulties from this it was possible to
        infer that
    (D) implied our company faced financial
        difficulties from this I inferred
    (E) implied our company faced financial
        difficulties; from this I drew the infer-
        ence that

Directions: In each of the following questions you are given a complete sentence to be rephrased according to the directions that follow it. You should rephrase the sentence mentally to save time, although you may make notes in your test book if you wish.

Below each sentence and its directions are listed words or phrases that may occur in your revised sentence. When you have thought out a good sentence, look in the choices (A) through (E) for the word or entire phrase that is included in your revised sentence, and fill in the corresponding oval on the answer sheet. The word or phrase you choose should be the most accurate and most nearly complete of all the choices given, and should be part of a sentence that meets the requirements of standard written English.

Of course, a number of different sentences can be obtained if the sentence is revised according to the directions, and not all of these possibilities can be included in only five choices. If you should find that you have thought of a sentence that contains none of the words or phrases listed in the choices, you should attempt to rephrase the sentence again so that it includes a word or phrase that is listed.

Although the directions may at times require you to change the relationship between parts of the sentence or to make slight changes in meaning in other ways, make only those changes that the directions require. Keep the meaning the same or as nearly the same as the directions permit. If you think that more than one good sentence can be made according to the directions, select the sentence that is most exact, effective, and natural in phrasing and construction.

56. Two weeks have passed since her vacation, during which Kelly has remembered it daily.

    Begin with <u>Each day</u>.

    (A) will have passed
    (B) that have passed
    (C) that passed
    (D) were to pass
    (E) has passed

57. The reason Frank is going to Arizona is explained by the fact that he is in need of a climate that is dry.

    Change <u>is explained by the fact that</u> to <u>is that</u>.

    (A) he must have a climate which is dry
    (B) a dry climate is what he needs
    (C) a climate which is dry is what he needs
    (D) the climate is dry
    (E) he needs a dry climate

58. Perhaps by noon we shall have photographed five rabbits.

    Begin the sentence with <u>When noon arrives</u>.

    (A) we may photograph
    (B) we might have photographed
    (C) we will have photographed
    (D) we may have photographed
    (E) we photographed

59. There is a bank on which the wild thyme grows.

    Change <u>There is a bank</u> to <u>I know a bank</u>.

    (A) whereon
    (B) in which
    (C) whereby
    (D) from which
    (E) by which

60. A question was asked by the student as he was not sure he understood the assignment.

    Begin with <u>The student</u>.

    (A) asked a question on account of

    (B) asked a question because

    (C) asked a question in view of the fact that

    (D) asked a question while

    (E) asked a question although

61. If the gods wish to destroy someone, they will make him mad first.

    Begin with <u>Whomever the gods wish to destroy</u>.

    (A) they will make him mad first

    (B) they will first try to make him mad

    (C) they will first make him angry

    (D) first they make him mad

    (E) they first make mad

62. Faulkner's novels' language resembles the language of Proust's novels.

    Begin with <u>The language of Faulkner's novels</u>.

    (A) is somewhat like that of Proust

    (B) is somewhat like Proust

    (C) is somewhat like that of Proust's

    (D) is somewhat as Proust's

    (E) is somewhat like Proust's novels

63. Try to be patient considering that we can assist only one of you at a time.

    Change <u>considering that</u> to <u>since</u>.

    (A) we can assist but one of you

    (B) we can't assist but one of you

    (C) we can't only assist one of you

    (D) we can't only assist but one of you

    (E) we can't assist one of you

64. It will be two weeks tomorrow that the book will be on the shelf.

    Begin with <u>By tomorrow</u>.

    (A) the book will have lied

    (B) the book will have lain

    (C) the book will have laid

    (D) the book will be laying

    (E) the book shall have laid

65. Asia is a continent that has value equal to Africa's and has a fuller development than Africa.

    Eliminate <u>is a continent that</u>.

    (A) is as valuable as and is more fully developed

    (B) is as valuable and more fully developed

    (C) is as valued and more fully developed

    (D) is so valuable as and more fully developed

    (E) is just as valuable and more fully developed

66. Blame could not be attached to either the diplomats or our president for the fiasco.

    Begin with <u>Neither the diplomats</u>.

    (A) or our president was to blame

    (B) nor our president were to blame

    (C) or our president was to blame

    (D) nor our president was to blame

    (E) and our president were to blame

67. Rather than leaving the party, you should introduce yourself to the other guests.

    Begin with <u>Instead of</u>.

    (A) you leaving the party

    (B) you leaving from the party

    (C) your leaving the party

    (D) your leaving from the party

    (E) the party being left by you

68. With promptness, you might have arrived in time for the first act.

    Begin with <u>If you</u>.

    (A) would have been prompt

    (B) were prompt

    (C) had been prompt

    (D) showed promptness

    (E) could have been prompt

69. By the recurrence of identical sounds, the emotions are aided in being awakened.

    Begin with <u>The recurrence</u>.

    (A) has a great deal to do with awakening the emotions.

    (B) gives help in awakening the emotions.

    (C) help to awaken the emotions.

    (D) helps to awaken the emotions.

    (E) is of help in awakening the emotions.

70. Susan was inline skating and she tripped on a crack in the sidewalk.

    Begin with <u>Inline skating</u>.

    (A) Susan tripped on a crack

    (B) a crack tripped Susan

    (C) a crack caused Susan to trip

    (D) a crack made Susan trip

    (E) Susan was tripped on a crack

71. The company manufactured all kinds of tools including cutting tools, grinding tools, and polishing tools.

    Change <u>all kinds of tools</u> to <u>several kinds of tools</u>.

    (A) They were cutting tools

    (B) They are cutting tools

    (C) ; cutting tools

    (D) : cutting tools

    (E) , cutting tools

72. The speed limit was reduced to fifty-five miles per hour on open highways in America primarily because it had been determined that a significant amount of gasoline would be saved.

    Omit <u>primarily because</u>.

    (A) thus saving

    (B) in order to save

    (C) thereby determining that

    (D) and that was how

    (E) and we saved

73. The main reason that interstellar travel is considered improbable in the near future is that the fuel for such a lengthy trip has not yet been compounded.

    Begin with <u>The fuel for such a lengthy trip</u>.

    (A) compounded because

    (B) compounded and

    (C) compounded, and

    (D) compounded, while

    (E) compounded; therefore

74. Hardcover novels have declined so in popularity that it is beginning to make economic sense to publish first in paperback.

    Begin with <u>Publishing first</u>.

    (A) because

    (B) therefore

    (C) in spite of the fact that

    (D) moreover

    (E) although

75. Prior to and during the Depression, high protective tariff barriers were erected throughout the Western world in futile attempts to protect and stimulate domestic industries.

Begin with The attempts by.

(A) led to Depression.

(B) protected and stimulated domestic industries.

(C) constituted an exercise in futility.

(D) proved futile.

(E) erected high protective tariff barriers.

76. I learned the art of spiritual peace during my forty years in China from many friends, who, though illiterate, were wise and sophisticated.

Begin with During my forty years in China.

(A) wisdom among many friends

(B) peace, were wise and sophisticated

(C) peace from many friends

(D) learned the art of the peaceful spirit

(E) the art of peace, though illiterate

77. When man lived in a cave with only stone implements at his disposal, his mind no less than his actions was grooved into simple channels.

Begin with Living in a cave.

(A) mankind was both mind and action

(B) man was actively and simply grooved

(C) man of mind and action was grooved

(D) man, mind, actions, all were grooved

(E) man, in both his mind and his actions

78. Certainty that the students alone were to blame for the discipline problems in the high school caused the school board to retain the principal.

Change the noun certainty to the adjective sure.

(A) was retained

(B) will retain

(C) retained

(D) has been retained

(E) had retained

79. Greece has a claim upon our attention because we are by our spiritual and mental inheritance partly Greek.

Begin with Because our spiritual.

(A) inheritance is partly Greek, Greece

(B) inheritance are partly Grecian, Greece

(C) inheriting for the most part Greece, and the Greek

(D) inheritance for the most part is Greek, Greece

(E) inheritance is partly Greek; Greece

80. The odes of Keats contain lush imagery.

Change the proper name Keats to its possessive form.

(A) Keats'es odes

(B) His odes (Keats')

(C) His (Keats's) odes

(D) Keats' odes

(E) Odes from Keats

81. The film ended and the sobbing crowd arose.

Change The film to As soon as the film.

(A) ended; the sobbing

(B) ended and the sobbing

(C) ended, the sobbing

(D) ended before the sobbing

(E) ended: the sobbing

82. I eat fried potatoes often even though they are not good for me.
Change <u>even though</u> to <u>which</u>.
   (A) consequently
   (B) results that
   (C) however
   (D) I consider
   (E) I doubt if

83. The results of the poll had little or no effect on the actions of the legislature.
Begin with <u>The actions of the legislature</u>.
   (A) was barely effected
   (B) was barely affected
   (C) was hardly under effect
   (D) were hardly affected
   (E) were hardly effected

84. We could find no precedent for the judge's outrageous ruling in this case.
Begin with <u>No precedent</u>.
   (A) can be found
   (B) could be found
   (C) is being found
   (D) cannot be found
   (E) can find

85. Such fallacious reasoning can quickly and easily be detected by an experienced debater.
Begin with <u>An experienced debater</u>.
   (A) easily detect such
   (B) easy detection but
   (C) easily but fallaciously
   (D) easy and quick detecting
   (E) easily detected such

86. I'm trying to concentrate, so please be quiet.
Eliminate <u>so</u>.
   (A) concentrate; please
   (B) concentrate, please
   (C) concentrate and please
   (D) concentrate: please
   (E) concentrating; pleasing

87. Just why some individuals choose one way of adjusting to their difficulties and others choose another way is not known.
Begin with <u>It is</u>.
   (A) completely unknown why some people
   (B) not knowable why some individuals
   (C) not known why some individuals
   (D) complete and unknown why some people
   (E) not known why just some people

88. Control of the Mississippi had always been the goal of nations having ambitions in the New World.
Begin with <u>Nations having ambitions</u>.
   (A) had forever maintained the right to control the Mississippi
   (B) had always had the goal of controlling the Mississippi
   (C) had forever had the goal to control of the Mississippi
   (D) had always had the goal of Mississippi control
   (E) had always maintained control of the Mississippi

89. There is a very simple way in which technical terminology can lose contact with reality.
Begin with <u>Technical terminology can</u>.
   (A) in reality with
   (B) with reality in
   (C) really in contact with
   (D) in contact with
   (E) with contact in

90. Today Venice seems to provide artists with such obvious subjects to paint that we are apt to forget that it was not always so.
Delete the conjunction <u>that</u>.
   (A) painting; we are
   (B) to paint, however being
   (C) to paint, we are
   (D) to paint—we are
   (E) to paint; we are

Directions: In each of the following questions you are given four sentences and a question that asks for the best sequence to make a clear, sensible paragraph. Choose the option that reflects the best ordering of the sentences for a clear, sensible paragraph.

91. I.   The laws of war are those portions of international law that deal with the inception of war, the conduct of war, and the cessation of war.

    II. They regulate the relations between states at war and the relationships of those states which claim to be neutral powers.

    III. The popular view of war is that war is uncontrolled violence and barbarism, near the bottom in the annals of man's inhumanity to man.

    IV. Actually, war is a political act, usually undertaken only when it appears that all other alternatives have failed.

    Which of the following presents the BEST sequence of the sentences above to make a clear, sensible paragraph?

    (A) I, IV, II, III
    (B) III, I, II, IV
    (C) III, IV, I, II
    (D) IV, III, I, II
    (E) IV, I, II, III

92. I.   Inertial guidance systems are used today in airplanes, submarines, and spacecraft.

    II. Inertial systems serve a need on fast-moving vehicles moving in a three-dimensional plane, where position information is required by the pilot almost constantly.

    III. These are very important items to have readily available, whether one is in a high-speed vehicle with very low visibility due to poor weather or in a spacecraft traveling in lunar orbit.

    IV. They display for the pilot his pitch, roll and yaw angles, heading, speed, and latitude and longitude.

    Which of the following presents the BEST sequence of the sentences above to make a clear, sensible paragraph?

    (A) I, IV, III, II
    (B) II, IV, I, III
    (C) III, II, I, IV
    (D) III, I, II, IV
    (E) IV, I, II, III

93. I.   The intensified agricultural produc-
          tion required in these countries has
          potential adverse side effects on other
          resources.

     II. Some other problems include water-
          logging, soil erosion, increased popu-
          lation of pests, and agricultural
          pollution.

     III. The disruptive effects of absent reser-
          voirs are self-evident.

     IV. In most Asian countries, where rice is
          the principal food crop, increased cul-
          tivation has barely met the demands
          of the growing populations.

Which of the following presents the BEST
sequence of the sentences above to make
a clear, sensible paragraph?

(A) I, II, III, IV
(B) I, III, II, IV
(C) IV, II, III, I
(D) IV, I, III, II
(E) IV, I, II, III

94. I.   The business of the private security
          sector is not only to sell safety and
          security but to educate people in the
          many ways they can protect themselves.

     II. This important service makes private
          security a natural ally of the police
          and a formidable foe of the criminal.

     III. Together they can fashion a program
          that will foster public understanding
          and enlist public assistance in com-
          bating crime.

     IV. Both police and private security stand
          to gain, but more importantly, the
          public stands to gain the most.

Which of the following presents the BEST
sequence of the sentences above to make
a clear, sensible paragraph?

(A) I, II, III, IV
(B) I, III, IV, II
(C) II, III, IV, I
(D) IV, I, II, III
(E) IV, III, II, I

95. I.   Thus, even Third World nations must
          get most of their news from the big
          four Western news agencies, and they
          are thereby susceptible to cultural
          imperialism.

     II. These stories are written and filed
          the day before they are transmitted,
          and the stories are not updated dur-
          ing the day.

     III. The news agencies of Third World
          countries can afford to keep few, if
          any, foreign correspondents.

     IV. Even attempts to pool Third World
          resources have had limited success;
          Interlink, the wire service of Inter
          Press Service (IPS), the Third World's
          largest news agency and the world's
          sixth largest (after the big four and
          TASS, the news agency of the former
          Soviet Union), carries only about ten
          stories a day.

Which of the following presents the BEST
sequence of the sentences above to make
a clear, sensible paragraph?

(A) II, I, III, IV
(B) II, III, IV, I
(C) III, I, II, IV
(D) IV, III, II, I
(E) III, IV, II, I

96. I. When television is good, nothing—not the theater, not magazines, nor newspapers—is better.

II. I invite you to sit down in front of your television set when your station goes on the air and stay there without a book, correspondence, handicrafts project, or anything else to distract you and keep your eyes glued to that set until the station signs off.

III. I can assure you that you will observe a vast wasteland.

IV. But when television is bad, nothing is worse.

Which of the following presents the BEST sequence of the sentences above to make a clear, sensible paragraph?

(A) I, II, III, IV
(B) I, IV, II, III
(C) II, I, III, IV
(D) II, III, IV, I
(E) III, IV, I, II

97. I. The larger arsenals for chemical-biological warfare may be restricted to the major powers, but there is little doubt that an increasing capability is proliferating in some of the smaller and developing countries.

II. The reasons are that the nations, including some of the smaller ones, are already downstream too far.

III. And it is most difficult to dispense with this first reaction.

IV. The first reaction one has to the question of viable approaches to the control of chemical and biological weapons is that there are no such approaches.

Which of the following presents the BEST sequence of the sentences above to make a clear, sensible paragraph?

(A) I, II, IV, III
(B) I, II, III, IV
(C) IV, III, II, I
(D) IV, I, II, III
(E) IV, II, I, III

98. I. No one person decides anything; each decision of any importance is the product of an intricate process of brokerage involving individuals inside and outside the organization who feel some reason to be affected by the decision or who have special knowledge to contribute to it.

II. The increase in the extent to which each individual is personally responsible to others is most noticeable in a large bureaucracy.

III. The more varied the organization's constituency, the more outside "veto groups" will need to be taken into account.

IV. But even if no outside consultations were involved, sheer size would produce a complex process of decision.

Which of the following presents the BEST sequence of the sentences above to make a clear, sensible paragraph?

(A) I, II, III, IV

(B) II, I, IV, III

(C) II, I, III, IV

(D) III, II, I, IV

(E) IV, III, II, I

99. I. In its beginning, the conflict between Christianity and Islam was violent.

II. But throughout this long period there were sometimes peaceful and more rational dialogues and debates.

III. The dialogue with Islam has a long history.

IV. One could cite here the Muslim conquests in the seventh and eighth centuries, the Crusades, the Inquisition in Spain, religious persecution, and the missionary movements.

Which of the following presents the BEST sequence of the sentences above to make a clear, sensible paragraph?

(A) I, II, III, IV

(B) I, III, IV, II

(C) III, II, IV, I

(D) III, I, II, IV

(E) III, I, IV, II

100. I. Courts have ruled that sexual harassment in the workplace can be considered illegal sexual discrimination because it results in an untenable environment for the victim.

II. It is illegal for employers to discriminate against employees on the basis of race, gender, religion, or national origin.

III. However, the line between harassment and discrimination is not precise, and courts often differ when deciding if an employer's conduct rises to the level of illegal discrimination.

IV. But mere offensive utterances or casual comments will not violate the law, even if the employee might find them annoying and distasteful.

Which of the following presents the BEST sequence of the sentences above to make a clear, sensible paragraph?

(A) I, II, III, IV

(B) II, I, III, IV

(C) III, IV, I, II

(D) IV, I, III, II

(E) I, III, IV, II

101. I. If we make a long, dedicated search that fails, we will not have wasted our time.

II. We will have developed important technology, with applications to many other aspects of our own civilization.

III. We will surely have added greatly to our knowledge of the physical universe.

IV. Whether the search for extraterrestrial intelligence succeeds or fails, its consequences will be extraordinary.

Which of the following presents the BEST sequence of the sentences above to make a clear, sensible paragraph?

(A) IV, I, II, III

(B) II, IV, I, III

(C) III, II, I, IV

(D) II, III, IV, I

(E) III, I, II, IV

102. I. Professionals in the business and the conscientious test publishers know the limitations as well as the values.

II. But they have no jurisdiction over users; a test can be administered by almost anyone, whether he knows how to interpret it or not.

III. They write these things into test manuals and in critiques of available tests.

IV. Nor can the difficulty be controlled by limiting sales to qualified users; some attempts to do so have been countered by restraint-of-trade suits.

Which of the following presents the BEST sequence of the sentences above to make a clear, sensible paragraph?

(A) I, II, III, IV

(B) I, III, IV, II

(C) I, IV, II, III

(D) I, III, II, IV

(E) III, I, II, IV

103.
I. When reading "Oedipus Rex," one may think that the play reflects man's subjection to an inevitable fate or the will of the gods.

II. Such a reading removes all dignity and courage, which are necessary qualities in the hero of a tragedy, if he is to move us to pity and fear.

III. It is in Oedipus' search for the truth in spite of the prophecies, in his freedom to determine their meaning and their relation to his own life, that his heroism is demonstrated.

IV. While the gods in the play know what will happen, but they do not cause it to happen.

Which of the following presents the BEST sequence of the sentences above to make a clear, sensible paragraph?

(A) I, II, III, IV

(B) I, II, IV, III

(C) III, I, II, IV

(D) III, IV, I, II

(E) IV, I, II, III

104.
I. Yet, the land cannot be moved.

II. Land, property, real estate, or territory, by whatever name one chooses to call it, is a powerful force for both contentment and strife.

III. Because of this last reality, wars have been fought.

IV. The location of the land determines the quality and quantity of the sustenance it provides, the nature of the shelter and the ease with which it may be obtained, and indeed, the very quality of life.

Which of the following presents the BEST sequence of the sentences above to make a clear, sensible paragraph?

(A) I, II, III, IV

(B) II, III, IV, I

(C) II, IV, I, III

(D) II, I, III, IV

(E) IV, III, II, I

105. I. Was not the American policy of Manifest Destiny a foreshadowing of Hitler's justification of his action by Germany's alleged need for living space?

    II. Thus, some would argue that the American government's policy toward Native Americans amounted to genocide.

    III. The indigenous population of the continental United States declined from an estimated 12.5 million in the year 1500 to fewer than 250,000 by the beginning of the twentieth century.

    IV. Native groups were removed from their homelands and relocated or kept under military guard for years—situations that decimated their populations.

Which of the following presents the BEST sequence of the sentences above to make a clear, sensible paragraph?

(A) II, I, III, IV

(B) III, IV, I, II

(C) III, II, IV, I

(D) IV, III, I, II

(E) IV, I, III, II

106. I. The technique begins with the assembling of a list of all the activities needed to accomplish an overall task.

    II. The time required for each activity is estimated by simple statistical techniques by the persons who will be responsible for the work, and the time required to complete the entire string of activities along each sequential path through the network is then calculated.

    III. One of the specific administrative techniques for program management is Program Evaluation Review Technique (PERT).

    IV. The next step consists of arranging these activities in a sequential network showing both how much time each activity will take and which activities must be completed before others can begin.

Which of the following presents the BEST sequence of the sentences above to make a clear, sensible paragraph?

(A) I, II, IV, III

(B) II, I, IV, III

(C) I, IV, III, II

(D) III, I, II, IV

(E) III, I, IV, II

107. I. Along with the useful potential of genetic engineering comes the frightening prospect of its misuse.

II. Unscrupulous researchers might experiment with humans and create "Frankenstein's monsters."

III. If we choose to predetermine the heredity of humans and to "breed to order," who has the right to choose which shall be super-intelligent and which only marginally functional?

IV. And unanswered questions arise: When the ability to do so arrives, should we breed genetic "supermen" along with a lower species of human being to do distasteful work?

Which of the following presents the BEST sequence of the sentences above to make a clear, sensible paragraph?

(A) I, II, III, IV

(B) I, III, IV, II

(C) I, II, IV, III

(D) I, IV, II, III

(E) I, III, II, IV

108. I. Contradictory as it may sound, the more slowly a person reads, the less he absorbs.

II. This is probably because heavier concentration is required for rapid reading, and concentration enables a reader to grasp important ideas contained in the reading material.

III. The more rapidly he reads, the more he understands and retains.

IV. The two basic elements in reading interpretation are speed and comprehension.

Which of the following presents the BEST sequences of the sentences above to make a clear, sensible paragraph?

(A) I, II, III, IV

(B) I, III, II, IV

(C) IV, III, II, I

(D) IV, I, III, II

(E) IV, I, II, III

109. I. Demonstrating citizens have greatest access to public streets and to public property that is regularly open to the public.

II. Obviously, the purpose of assembly and demonstration is to be seen and heard; therefore, locations with high visibility are most often targeted.

III. Subject to safety considerations, the more public the area, the greater the citizens' right to assemble and/or demonstrate.

IV. This latter category includes areas such as public parks and transportation facilities.

Which of the following presents the BEST sequence of the sentences above to make a clear, sensible paragraph?

(A) I, II, IV, III

(B) II, I, IV, III

(C) II, III, I, IV

(D) III, IV, I, II

(E) III, IV, II, I

110. I. The manager should be particularly sensitive when personal issues are reached in the course of an interview.

II. They may ask for advice, but actually they want only a chance to express themselves.

III. Even when advice-giving is successful, there is the danger that the subordinate may become overly dependent on the superior officer and run to her whenever he has a minor problem.

IV. In situations like this, what most people want is a sympathetic, understanding listener rather than an advisor.

Which of the following presents the BEST sequence of the sentences above to make a clear, sensible paragraph?

(A) I, IV, II, III

(B) IV, I, II, III

(C) III, IV, II, I

(D) II, IV, III, I

(E) IV, II, III, I

ANSWER KEY AND EXPLANATIONS

Knowledge Questions

1.	B	15.	A	29.	C	43.	B	57.	A
2.	B	16.	C	30.	B	44.	D	58.	B
3.	D	17.	B	31.	B	45.	C	59.	B
4.	B	18.	C	32.	A	46.	A	60.	C
5.	C	19.	D	33.	B	47.	B	61.	C
6.	A	20.	A	34.	A	48.	D	62.	B
7.	A	21.	B	35.	C	49.	C	63.	D
8.	C	22.	D	36.	B	50.	D	64.	B
9.	D	23.	D	37.	A	51.	C	65.	D
10.	D	24.	C	38.	B	52.	D	66.	A
11.	B	25.	C	39.	D	53.	C	67.	D
12.	D	26.	D	40.	A	54.	D	68.	D
13.	D	27.	C	41.	A	55.	A	69.	C
14.	A	28.	A	42.	B	56.	D	70.	D

Maps: Europe—Questions 36 to 39

1. Portugal
2. Spain
3. France
4. Switzerland
5. Italy
6. Yugoslavia (now Serbia and Montenegro)
7. Albania
8. Greece
9. Turkey
10. Bulgaria
11. Romania
12. U.S.S.R. (now the Commonwealth of Independent States)
13. Mallorca (Spain)
14. Sardinia (Italy)
15. Corsica (France)
16. Sicily (Italy)
17. Malta
18. Crete (Greece)
19. Cyprus (Turkey/Greece)
20. Iceland
21. Ireland
22. England/Scotland/Wales
23. Northern Ireland
24. Norway
25. Sweden
26. Finland
27. Denmark
28. German Democratic Republic (East Germany) (now part of Germany)
29. Czechoslovakia (now the Czech Republic and Slovakia)
30. Hungary

Maps: Middle East and the Indian Subcontinent—Questions 58 to 60

1. Turkey
2. Syria
3. Jordan
4. Israel
5. Lebanon
6. Iraq Emirates
7. Saudi Arabia
8. Iran
9. Afghanistan
10. Pakistan
11. Yemen
12. People's Democratic Republic of Yemen (now part of Yemen)
13. Oman
14. Kuwait
15. United Arab Emirates
16. India
17. Sri Lanka
18. Bangladesh
19. Nepal
20. Bhutan

1. **The correct answer is (B).** In *Schenck v. United States* (1919), Oliver Wendell Holmes, speaking for a unanimous Supreme Court, held that "free speech would not protect a man falsely shouting fire in a theater and causing a panic." He went on to say that Schenck's writings in wartime created a "clear and present danger" to the American people and government.

2. **The correct answer is (B).** A nation would not unilaterally disarm if it wished to maintain a balance of power. By unilaterally disarming, the nation would in effect make itself powerless, which would drastically upset the balance of power.

3. **The correct answer is (D).** This has to do with relative costs and comparative advantages. By specializing and trading, total production will go up in both countries and consumers can have more of both goods. This would be beneficial for both countries.

4. **The correct answer is (B).** Aaron Copland explored American folk traditions when he composed two ballets based on themes from cowboy songs and a third ballet based on traditional Shaker music. Carl Sandburg was a poet and historian. Much of his poetry centered around the evils of industrialization at the turn of the twentieth century. His biography of Abraham Lincoln earned him the Pulitzer Prize for history. Agnes De Mille was a dancer–choreographer whose use of traditional folk themes in ballets and musical comedy formed the basis for a distinctly American dance style.

5. **The correct answer is (C).** A consular official sending diamonds to his home country in a diplomatic pouch is in violation of international law. According to the Vienna Convention on Diplomatic Relations (1961), "The packages constituting the diplomatic bag must bear visible external marks of their character and may contain only diplomatic documents or articles intended for official use."

6. **The correct answer is (A).** A division chief who wishes to restrict promotions to supervisory positions in his division exclusively to employees in his division is limiting himself to the possible benefits of external employees who may be better suited for the job. This is the same concept as the isolationist country not availing itself of imports that may be produced better and cheaper.

7. **The correct answer is (A).** The equilibrium level of national income is OK. At point C, the line $C + I + G$ intersects the 45° line. The level of national income is equal to the level of national expenditures, i.e., $C + I + G = Y$. There is no reason to change the level of output, for unintended inventories are equal to zero.

8. **The correct answer is (C).** At equilibrium level of national income OK, consumption spending is KG. In equilibrium, $C + I + G = C + S + T$, so CG would be equal to $S + T$ which is equal to $I + G$. Alternatively, consumption spending, investment spending, and government spending equal consumption, saving, and taxes, if there are no exports or imports.

9. **The correct answer is (D).** Hegemonic stability theory argues that overwhelming dominance by one country is necessary for the existence of an open and stable world economy. As the dominant maritime power in the world in the nineteenth century as well as the first nation to industrialize, Great Britain assumed that position for much of the nineteenth century.

10. **The correct answer is (D).** According to the 2000 census, Hispanics are the fastest growing minority in the United States. The following statistics show the rate of increase from 1990 to 2000: Hispanic—57.9%, Asian-American—48.3%, Native American—26.4%, African-American—15.6%.

11. **The correct answer is (B).** The United States officially declared war against England (1776 and 1812), Spain (1898), and Italy (1944). The United States has never officially declared war against Russia.

12. **The correct answer is (D).** In 1994, civil war between the Hutu and the Tutsi broke out in Rwanda after the country's President Juvenal Habyarimana, a Hutu, was killed. During the massacres of April 1994, it is estimated that as many as 500,000 people died, most of them Tutsi.

13. **The correct answer is (D).** The Tiananmen Square massacre would have been the earliest event to have occurred from the list provided. The dates are as follows: Tiananmen Square—1989; Earth Summit—1992; United Nation's fiftieth anniversary—1995; Wye River Accord—1998.

14. **The correct answer is (A).** *Amicus curiae* is a legal term meaning "friend of the court." The term is used to refer to someone who is not a party to a trial, but is brought in to advise the court on a matter of law relating to the case.

15. **The correct answer is (A).** Costa Gavras is a famed director of politically themed films. He directed *Z* in 1969 and *State of Siege* in 1973.

16. **The correct answer is (C).** Of the choices given, local control over the curriculum has generated the least amount of controversy. The majority of controversy surrounding the other three focuses on the extent to which the federal government has become involved with them.

17. **The correct answer is (B).** The Congress of Vienna was able to bring a lasting peace to Europe for nearly a century (1815–1914). It was one of the most significant meetings of political leaders in the history of Europe. It set the precedent for later meetings that would create the League of Nations and the United Nations.

18. **The correct answer is (C).** A paucity, or scarcity, of political information is not a reason for the decline in voter turnout. With the use of television, radio, newspapers, magazines, and the Internet, voters are actually given more information now than in any other period in history.

19. **The correct answer is (D).** Reagan's Strategic Defense Initiative (SDI), later dubbed "Star Wars," was designed to protect the people of the United States against potential nuclear attacks by the Soviet Union. This was to be accomplished by using combined space- and Earth-based sensors, lasers, and missiles to intercept ICBMs in flight.

20. **The correct answer is (A).** The purpose of a grand jury is to inquire as to whether or not a crime has been committed. The purpose of a petit jury is to determine the guilt or innocence of the

answers

accused. The only federal court in the United States that uses both forms of juries is the District Court.

21. **The correct answer is (B).** Both schedules indicate constant costs. As the production of clothing increases, the production of food decreases at a steady proportional rate for both countries.

22. **The correct answer is (D).** If Nation A places a protective tariff against the textile exports of Nation B, they are doing so in order to protect the textile industries of their own country. By establishing the tariff, they can insure that their textiles will be economically competitive within their own country.

23. **The correct answer is (D).** Russia had a history of political absolutism under the reign of the Romanovs; sought a warm-water port in both World War I and World War II; experienced a communist revolution in 1917 and a second revolution in 1991 that led to the dissolution of the Soviet Union; and, along with the United States formed a bipolar global system during most of the last half of the twentieth century.

24. **The correct answer is (C).** The assassination of Archduke Francis Ferdinand and his wife Sophie in Bosnia led Austria to declare war on Serbia. That declaration of war set off a series of actions that would eventually escalate into World War I.

25. **The correct answer is (C).** If the output–capital ratio is 1:3 and a net saving of 5 percent of national income is needed to maintain per capita incomes at their present level, then the population rate must increase by $\frac{1}{3}$ of 5 percent, or $1\frac{2}{3}$ percent.

26. **The correct answer is (D).** One of the three stated purposes of the International Monetary Fund was to stabilize currency exchange rates. This was to be accomplished by having each nation agree to set a par value for its currency.

27. **The correct answer is (C).** An export effects the U.S. balance of payments by bringing revenue into the country. The only example provided that would also bring revenue into the country would be an American receiving a birthday check from relatives in the Netherlands.

28. **The correct answer is (A).** Ruth Benedict's *Chrysanthemum and the Sword* (1946) was an anthropological study of Japan.

29. **The correct answer is (C).** Colombia-based drug trafficking organizations continue to direct the cocaine trade under the Cali and Medellin cartels. In 2001, approximately 80 to 90 percent of all cocaine smuggled into the United States came from Colombia.

30. **The correct answer is (B).** Increases in productivity create a steady demand for labor. As long as the demand for labor increases so will real wages.

31. **The correct answer is (B).** During World War II, there were two Theatres of Operation, the European Theatre and the Pacific Theatre. Within the European Theatre, there were two fronts: the eastern front along the German/Russian border and the western front on the French border. In order to maintain control of areas acquired in Eastern Europe, Stalin was insistent that England and the United States attack Germany from the west.

32. **The correct answer is (A).** This excerpt is from Woodrow Wilson's War Message to Congress delivered on April 2, 1917.

33. **The correct answer is (B).** Although liberals have historically opposed any governmental regulations pertaining to abortions as a violation of a woman's right to make her own decision, political realities are such that some sort of concession is warranted for political survival. Most contemporary liberals would be willing to support restricting a

woman's choice on abortion to the first trimester.

34. The correct answer is (A). Point II covered freedom of the seas. Point IV covered reduction of armaments. Point XIV covered the establishment of a general federation of nations. None of the fourteen points dealt with freedom of the press.

35. The correct answer is (C). When President Reagan spoke of the excesses of government being pushed onto our children, he was referring specifically to future costs of interest payments on national debt. Governmental excesses reduce the possibility of lowering the national debt. More often than not they lead to increases in the national debt, which would naturally lead to increased interest payments in the future.

36. The correct answer is (B). On this map, country number 9 is Turkey and country number 12 is the Commonwealth of Independent States. The only thing these two areas would have in common is that they are both on the same continent.

37. The correct answer is (A). During World War II, a pro-German government was set up in Norway with Vidkun Quisling, a Norwegian Nazi sympathizer, placed in charge.

38. The correct answer is (B). Quisling became a term applied to anyone who helps an enemy power conquer his or her country. It is derived from the name of Vidkun Quisling, who proclaimed himself premier of a Nazi-controlled government set up in Norway during World War II.

39. The correct answer is (D). Northern Ireland has a history of conflict between Protestants and Catholics. The real issue centers around whether Northern Ireland should be part of the United Kingdom or the Republic of Ireland.

40. The correct answer is (A). A balance-of-payments deficit occurs when a country imports more than it exports. To eliminate the deficit using exchange controls, a country would limit its imports to the amount of its exports.

41. The correct answer is (A). This quote deals with cause and effect with the effect being a positive outcome or benefit. A fixed tax surcharge affecting everyone equally has no positive benefit. The benefit would be neutral.

42. The correct answer is (B). Dr. Daniel Hale Williams was an African-American surgeon who performed the first successful open-heart surgery as well as founding the National Medical Association for black doctors. Garrett A. Morgan was an African-American inventor who patented the safety hood and invented electric traffic signals. Benjamin Banneker was an African-American astronomer, mathematician, and inventor. Eli Whitney is the only individual listed who was not black. He was a white inventor best known for inventing the cotton gin.

43. The correct answer is (B). In *Texas v. Johnson* (1989), Justice Brennan wrote that, "Government may not prohibit the expression of an idea because society finds the idea itself offensive or disagreeable." This ruling overturned Johnson's conviction for burning a flag in front of a Dallas building in 1984.

44. The correct answer is (D). The most important reason would be that once the plane landed in Israel the occupants of the plane would be subject to Israeli law. Israel has extremely strict drug laws, and the teenagers would be subject to those laws.

45. The correct answer is (C). The Berlin Wall was a 12-foot-high, 103-mile-long barrier surrounding West Berlin. It served only one purpose: to keep East Germans from being able to defect to the West.

46. **The correct answer is (A).** If a foreign-born immigrant is over the age of 18, they may make a declaration of intent to become a citizen before the clerk of a naturalization court. After residing in the country for five consecutive years, applicants file a petition for citizenship in a state where they have been residing for the last six months.

47. **The correct answer is (B).** *The Christian Science Monitor* was first published in 1908 as a reaction to the rampant sensationalism of the popular press. It has been noted for its insightful and in-depth analysis of the news. Its lack of bias has been one of its strongest selling points.

48. **The correct answer is (D).** A reduction in imports would lessen the amount and variety of goods available to the countries' consumers. The reason for increasing exports would be to have a more favorable balance of trade. Logically, the best alternative would therefore be to increase imports, but not as much as exports have been increased.

49. **The correct answer is (C).** The fact that the technical change is export-biased will change the terms of trade against the nation. If the production of the goods for export that are the result of the technical change increase significantly causing a reduction of their price, then the terms of trade will be a move against the nation.

50. **The correct answer is (D).** Under the guidelines of the Immigration and Nationality Act of 1952, accused Nazi war criminals can be deported even if they have gained U.S. citizenship. The basis for their deportation would be the falsification of their applications where they would have had to of lied about their criminal past.

51. **The correct answer is (C).** In Alternative I, there is a segregation of staff based on personnel subject matter. The only coordination of efforts is via the agency personnel officer. As a result, it is improbable that any personnel advice provided will be based on an integrated basis.

52. **The correct answer is (D).** The U.S. Constitution does not place more emphasis on either national security or freedom of speech over the other. Instead each instance in question is subject to interpretation via self-policing and a set of informal checks and balances.

53. **The correct answer is (C).** The organization or individual putting forth the document would be responsible for classifying its degree of sensitivity. This is not a role reserved solely to the legislative branch.

54. **The correct answer is (D).** Foreign governments tend to begin treaty negotiations with the United States as soon as possible after inauguration day. The logic would be that any treaty then ratified would remain intact for the longest possible period of time.

55. **The correct answer is (A).** The UN Convention on the Law of the Sea was strongly advocated by President Reagan. President Bush however had reservations about whether or not the United States should approve ratification of the treaty.

56. **The correct answer is (D).** Every nation has the primary responsibility for enforcing international law within its borders. Outside forces are only brought in when a nation fails in that responsibility.

57. **The correct answer is (A).** William Henry Hastie was the first black man appointed governor of the Virgin Islands (1946). In 1949, he became the first black judge of the U.S. Circuit Court of Appeals. He was never known for producing spoofs of any type.

answers

58. The correct answer is (B). Bangladesh (formerly East Pakistan) and Pakistan (formerly West Pakistan) were united until East Pakistan was liberated from West Pakistan on December 16, 1971.

59. The correct answer is (B). Syria's strategic location and considerable military power have given it a great deal of political influence on much of the Middle East. Syria has been deeply involved with many of the political problems in the region since World War II.

60. The correct answer is (C). The "top of the world" would be a way of describing the highest elevated point on the planet. Mount Everest, the world's highest peak, is on Nepal's northern border.

61. The correct answer is (C). The quote cited is from Article IV, Section 2.2 of the U.S. Constitution.

62. The correct answer is (B). Of the choices provided, the manner of avoiding deficit trading that would best serve the interests of the United States would be making investments abroad instead of loans. While the other three options could allow the United States to avoid deficit trading, they would not be in the best interests of the country.

63. The correct answer is (D). Either nation could commit war crimes; who was the aggressor has nothing to do with the treatment of prisoners of war. Determining who was the aggressor and who was defending themselves becomes important after the war, in determining the status and distribution of captured territory.

64. The correct answer is (B). Nonviolent activism was the cornerstones of the movements founded by both Mohandas Gandhi and Martin Luther King Jr. As the leader of the CIO, John Lewis would have been more in tune with Booker T. Washington's philosophy of advancement through hard work and money. It is doubtful that Allen W. Dulles, with his involvement with the CIA, was influenced by the concept of nonviolent activism.

65. The correct answer is (D). While all of these items are genuine concerns, the most important concern would be that unhappy employees tend to be riper targets for breaches of security through carelessness or for their personal gain. Productivity may slow a business down, but a security breach can cause infinitely more damage.

66. The correct answer is (A). Prior to the adoption of the Constitution, many cities and states had an established church. The wording of this passage is designed to serve as a non-establishment clause in order to insure both freedom of religion and the separation of church and state.

67. The correct answer is (D). A declining death rate, inflation, population cycles resulting in a smaller work force, and an increase in number of early retirements have all led to a severe drain on the Social Security Trust Fund.

68. The correct answer is (D). The main reason why many of the Third World Asian and African countries chose not to support Argentina in its dispute with Great Britain over the Falkland Islands was that they had fragile boundaries of their own and could potentially be risking their own security if they were to endorse setting a precedent of settling territorial disputes by military means.

69. The correct answer is (C). *Of Human Bondage* deals with a coming to maturity in turn-of-the-century Europe.

70. The correct answer is (D). The Spanish Civil War was primarily a battle between the Nationalists and the Republicans. A Loyalist was defined as a supporter of the Republic during the Spanish Civil War. The Republicans gained much of their support from the Socialists and Anarchists.

English Expression

1.	B	23.	D	45.	C	67.	C	89.	B
2.	E	24.	D	46.	C	68.	C	90.	E
3.	B	25.	E	47.	D	69.	D	91.	C
4.	A	26.	A	48.	A	70.	A	92.	A
5.	B	27.	A	49.	C	71.	D	93.	D
6.	C	28.	E	50.	D	72.	B	94.	A
7.	D	29.	C	51.	E	73.	E	95.	E
8.	E	30.	C	52.	C	74.	A	96.	B
9.	C	31.	D	53.	A	75.	D	97.	C
10.	E	32.	C	54.	C	76.	C	98.	C
11.	C	33.	D	55.	B	77.	E	99.	E
12.	A	34.	C	56.	B	78.	C	100.	B
13.	A	35.	A	57.	E	79.	A	101.	A
14.	C	36.	A	58.	D	80.	D	102.	D
15.	B	37.	D	59.	A	81.	C	103.	B
16.	B	38.	C	60.	B	82.	C	104.	C
17.	B	39.	B	61.	E	83.	D	105.	B
18.	D	40.	C	62.	C	84.	B	106.	E
19.	E	41.	C	63.	A	85.	A	107.	C
20.	C	42.	E	64.	B	86.	A	108.	D
21.	D	43.	D	65.	A	87.	C	109.	B
22.	D	44.	B	66.	D	88.	B	110.	A

1. **The correct answer is (B).** There are *fewer* calories in a bagel than in a doughnut.

2. **The correct answer is (E).** This sentence is correct.

3. **The correct answer is (B).** He had a large *number* of friends until he lost all his money.

4. **The correct answer is (A).** *Because* she was a newcomer to our organization, Rose was shy.

5. **The correct answer is (B).** The florist asked three of us, Dan, Edward, and *me*, to carry the plants down to the loading dock.

6. **The correct answer is (C).** My father, along with hundreds of other workers, *has* been on strike since New Year's Day.

7. **The correct answer is (D).** The child dislikes green vegetables: broccoli, spinach, kale, *etc.*

8. **The correct answer is (E).** This sentence is correct.

9. **The correct answer is (C).** Neither John nor his children *are* likely to attend the ceremonies.

10. **The correct answer is (E).** This sentence is correct.

11. **The correct answer is (C).** The constant rise of prices and wages *brings* about inflation.

12. **The correct answer is (A).** He saw the *same* plaid jacket on sale for ten dollars less two weeks after he bought it.

13. **The correct answer is (A).** If I *weren't* hungry, I wouldn't even consider eating that peanut butter and jelly sandwich.

14. **The correct answer is (C).** It was not quite clear whether it was his friend or *he* who had requested the favor.

15. **The correct answer is (B).** After he had paid the fee and *had seen* the pictures, he was quite satisfied.

16. **The correct answer is (B).** Further acquaintance with the memoirs of Elizabeth Barrett Browning and Robert Browning *enables* us to appreciate the depth of influence that two people of talent can have on one another.

17. **The correct answer is (B).** Because she has always been active *and has good eating habits*, she enjoys good health and physical fitness at the age of 70.

18. **The correct answer is (D).** Having studied your report carefully, I am convinced that neither of your solutions *is* correct.

19. **The correct answer is (E).** This sentence is correct.

20. **The correct answer is (C).** In spite of his youth, no faster runner than *he* will be found on our Olympic team.

21. **The correct answer is (D).** Because of the poor lighting, they mistakenly supposed the intruder to be *me*.

22. **The correct answer is (D).** None of the diplomats at the conference was able either to comprehend or *to* solve the problem.

23. **The correct answer is (D).** It was agreed by a majority of the signers of the compact that truth as well as justice was to be *their* rule of life.

24. **The correct answer is (D).** Everybody was up early on Monday because our local store was having *its* annual sale.

25. **The correct answer is (E).** This sentence is correct.

26. **The correct answer is (A).** What *effect* the law will have on our drivers and how it will affect our lives remain to be seen.

27. **The correct answer is (A).** If I *were* you, I should be careful of who my friends are.

28. **The correct answer is (E).** This sentence is correct.

29. **The correct answer is (C).** Although his story had aspects of truth about it, I *could hardly* believe what he said. Or, Although his story had aspects of truth about it, I *couldn't* believe what he said.

30. **The correct answer is (C).** I would have invited you to join me at the performance if you *had told* me that you enjoy chamber music.

31. **The correct answer is (D).** You decide whether to buy the red shirt or the blue one; I like *both* of them.

32. **The correct answer is (C).** A torrential downpour, in addition to long stretches of road construction that made it necessary to slow down to fifteen miles an hour, *has* so delayed us that we shall not be able to be on hand for the ceremony.

33. **The correct answer is (D).** The soprano alleged that the dampness in the concert hall caused her to sing *terribly*.

34. **The correct answer is (C).** It was he, not I, who became *nauseated* because of the boat's motion.

35. **The correct answer is (A).** Although Richard graduated *from* high school with honors, he failed three subjects as a college freshman.

36. **The correct answer is (A).** At first, Shakespeare's plays were performed more for the roles they provided the actors than for the truth of their characterizations or the beauty of their verse.

37. **The correct answer is (D).** Desiring to insure the continuity of their knowledge,

the chiefs transmit magical lore to their descendants.

38. **The correct answer is (C).** Both diplomats have this point in common: their forte lies not so much in administrative routine or social activities *as in* securing the greatest advantage to their country at the conference table.

39. **The correct answer is (B).** If the parent *had shown* more interest, her daughter would be in college today.

40. **The correct answer is (C).** The judge instructed the jury *to deliberate carefully before announcing its* verdict.

41. **The correct answer is (C).** Crossing the bridge, *we caught a glimpse of the islands.*

42. **The correct answer is (E).** This book has been *lying* here for weeks.

43. **The correct answer is (D).** When the officer *returns*, I'll tell him you called.

44. **The correct answer is (B).** After he graduated *from* school, he entered the army.

45. **The correct answer is (C).** A secure person is one who can make a joke even if it's embarrassing to *him.*

46. **The correct answer is (C).** Sitting around the fire, *each of us told* mystery stories.

47. **The correct answer is (D).** The loud noise of the subway trains and the trolley cars *frightens* country people.

48. **The correct answer is (A).** Inspecting the final report, the director could find no fault with the committee's recommendations.

49. **The correct answer is (C).** *Because he overslept,* he arrived at work late.

50. **The correct answer is (D).** *I could not help feel* that her reasons for coming here were not honest.

51. **The correct answer is (E).** *She never has done* and she *never will do any work.*

52. **The correct answer is (C).** The customized vehicle resembles a production sports car, but its design is *unique.*

53. **The correct answer is (A).** Did you read Yeats's poem "Byzantium?"

54. **The correct answer is (C).** Security Officers perform investigative and protective services in the United States and overseas; are responsible for the security of U.S. facilities, operations, and personnel abroad; and combat *worldwide* criminal, intelligence, and terrorist activities that might threaten American lives and property.

55. **The correct answer is (B).** The budget figures *implied our company faced financial difficulties; from this I inferred* it was not a good time to ask for a salary raise.

56. **The correct answer is (B).** Each day during the two weeks *that have passed* since her vacation, Kelly has remembered it.

57. **The correct answer is (E).** The reason Frank is going to Arizona is that *he needs a dry climate.*

58. **The correct answer is (D).** When noon arrives, *we may have photographed* five rabbits.

59. **The correct answer is (A).** I know a bank *whereon* the wild thyme grows.

60. **The correct answer is (B).** The student *asked a question because* he was not sure he understood the assignment.

61. **The correct answer is (E).** Whomever the gods wish to destroy, *they first make mad.*

62. **The correct answer is (C).** The language of Faulkner's novels *is somewhat like that of Proust's.*

63. **The correct answer is (A).** Try to be patient since *we can assist but one of you* at a time.

64. **The correct answer is (B).** By tomorrow *the book will have lain* on the shelf two weeks.

65. **The correct answer is (A).** Asia *is as valuable as and is more fully developed* than Africa.

66. **The correct answer is (D).** Neither the diplomats *nor our president was to blame* for the fiasco.

67. **The correct answer is (C).** Instead of *your leaving the party*, you should introduce yourself to the other guests.

68. **The correct answer is (C).** If you *had been prompt*, you might have arrived in time for the first act.

69. **The correct answer is (D).** The recurrence of identical sounds *helps to awaken the emotions*.

70. **The correct answer is (A).** Inline skating, *Susan tripped on a crack* in the sidewalk.

71. **The correct answer is (D).** The company manufactured several kinds of tools*: cutting tools*, grinding tools, and polishing tools.

72. **The correct answer is (B).** The speed limit was reduced to fifty-five miles per hour on open highways in America *in order to save* a significant amount of gasoline.

73. **The correct answer is (E).** The fuel for such a lengthy trip has not yet been *compounded; therefore,* interstellar travel is considered improbable in the near future.

74. **The correct answer is (A).** Publishing first in paperback is beginning to make economic sense *because* hardcover novels have declined so in popularity.

75. **The correct answer is (D).** The attempts by the Western world to protect and stimulate domestic industries prior to and during the Depression by erecting high protective tariff barriers *proved futile*.

76. **The correct answer is (C).** During my forty years in China I learned the art of spiritual *peace from many friends*, who, though illiterate, were wise and sophisticated.

77. **The correct answer is (E).** Living in a cave with only stone implements at his disposal, *man, in both his mind and his actions*, was grooved into simple channels.

78. **The correct answer is (C).** Sure that the students alone were to blame for the discipline problems in the high school, the school board *retained* the principal.

79. **The correct answer is (A).** Because our spiritual and mental *inheritance is partly Greek, Greece* has a claim upon our attention.

80. **The correct answer is (D).** *Keats' odes* contain lush imagery.

81. **The correct answer is (C).** As soon as the film *ended, the sobbing* crowd arose.

82. **The correct answer is (C).** I eat fried potatoes often which, *however,* are not good for me.

83. **The correct answer is (D).** The actions of the legislature *were hardly affected* by the results of the poll.

84. **The correct answer is (B).** No precedent *could be found* for the judge's outrageous ruling in this case.

85. **The correct answer is (A).** An experienced debater can quickly and *easily detect such* fallacious reasoning.

86. **The correct answer is (A).** I'm trying to *concentrate; please* be quiet.

87. **The correct answer is (C).** It is *not known why some individuals* choose one way of adjusting to their difficulties and others choose another way.

88. **The correct answer is (B).** Nations having ambitions in the New World *had always had the goal of controlling the Mississippi*.

answers

89. **The correct answer is (B).** Technical terminology can lose contact *with reality in* a very simple way.

90. **The correct answer is (E).** Today Venice seems to provide artists with such obvious subjects to *paint; we are* apt to forget that it was not always so.

91. **The correct answer is (C).**

92. **The correct answer is (A).**

93. **The correct answer is (D).**

94. **The correct answer is (A).**

95. **The correct answer is (E).**

96. **The correct answer is (B).**

97. **The correct answer is (C).**

98. **The correct answer is (C).**

99. **The correct answer is (E).**

100. **The correct answer is (B).**

101. **The correct answer is (A).**

102. **The correct answer is (D).**

103. **The correct answer is (B).**

104. **The correct answer is (C).**

105. **The correct answer is (B).**

106. **The correct answer is (E).**

107. **The correct answer is (C).**

108. **The correct answer is (D).**

109. **The correct answer is (B).**

110. **The correct answer is (A).**

PRACTICE TEST 3 ANSWER SHEET

Knowledge Questions

1. Ⓐ Ⓑ Ⓒ Ⓓ	21. Ⓐ Ⓑ Ⓒ Ⓓ	41. Ⓐ Ⓑ Ⓒ Ⓓ	61. Ⓐ Ⓑ Ⓒ Ⓓ
2. Ⓐ Ⓑ Ⓒ Ⓓ	22. Ⓐ Ⓑ Ⓒ Ⓓ	42. Ⓐ Ⓑ Ⓒ Ⓓ	62. Ⓐ Ⓑ Ⓒ Ⓓ
3. Ⓐ Ⓑ Ⓒ Ⓓ	23. Ⓐ Ⓑ Ⓒ Ⓓ	43. Ⓐ Ⓑ Ⓒ Ⓓ	63. Ⓐ Ⓑ Ⓒ Ⓓ
4. Ⓐ Ⓑ Ⓒ Ⓓ	24. Ⓐ Ⓑ Ⓒ Ⓓ	44. Ⓐ Ⓑ Ⓒ Ⓓ	64. Ⓐ Ⓑ Ⓒ Ⓓ
5. Ⓐ Ⓑ Ⓒ Ⓓ	25. Ⓐ Ⓑ Ⓒ Ⓓ	45. Ⓐ Ⓑ Ⓒ Ⓓ	65. Ⓐ Ⓑ Ⓒ Ⓓ
6. Ⓐ Ⓑ Ⓒ Ⓓ	26. Ⓐ Ⓑ Ⓒ Ⓓ	46. Ⓐ Ⓑ Ⓒ Ⓓ	66. Ⓐ Ⓑ Ⓒ Ⓓ
7. Ⓐ Ⓑ Ⓒ Ⓓ	27. Ⓐ Ⓑ Ⓒ Ⓓ	47. Ⓐ Ⓑ Ⓒ Ⓓ	67. Ⓐ Ⓑ Ⓒ Ⓓ
8. Ⓐ Ⓑ Ⓒ Ⓓ	28. Ⓐ Ⓑ Ⓒ Ⓓ	48. Ⓐ Ⓑ Ⓒ Ⓓ	68. Ⓐ Ⓑ Ⓒ Ⓓ
9. Ⓐ Ⓑ Ⓒ Ⓓ	29. Ⓐ Ⓑ Ⓒ Ⓓ	49. Ⓐ Ⓑ Ⓒ Ⓓ	69. Ⓐ Ⓑ Ⓒ Ⓓ
10. Ⓐ Ⓑ Ⓒ Ⓓ	30. Ⓐ Ⓑ Ⓒ Ⓓ	50. Ⓐ Ⓑ Ⓒ Ⓓ	70. Ⓐ Ⓑ Ⓒ Ⓓ
11. Ⓐ Ⓑ Ⓒ Ⓓ	31. Ⓐ Ⓑ Ⓒ Ⓓ	51. Ⓐ Ⓑ Ⓒ Ⓓ	
12. Ⓐ Ⓑ Ⓒ Ⓓ	32. Ⓐ Ⓑ Ⓒ Ⓓ	52. Ⓐ Ⓑ Ⓒ Ⓓ	
13. Ⓐ Ⓑ Ⓒ Ⓓ	33. Ⓐ Ⓑ Ⓒ Ⓓ	53. Ⓐ Ⓑ Ⓒ Ⓓ	
14. Ⓐ Ⓑ Ⓒ Ⓓ	34. Ⓐ Ⓑ Ⓒ Ⓓ	54. Ⓐ Ⓑ Ⓒ Ⓓ	
15. Ⓐ Ⓑ Ⓒ Ⓓ	35. Ⓐ Ⓑ Ⓒ Ⓓ	55. Ⓐ Ⓑ Ⓒ Ⓓ	
16. Ⓐ Ⓑ Ⓒ Ⓓ	36. Ⓐ Ⓑ Ⓒ Ⓓ	56. Ⓐ Ⓑ Ⓒ Ⓓ	
17. Ⓐ Ⓑ Ⓒ Ⓓ	37. Ⓐ Ⓑ Ⓒ Ⓓ	57. Ⓐ Ⓑ Ⓒ Ⓓ	
18. Ⓐ Ⓑ Ⓒ Ⓓ	38. Ⓐ Ⓑ Ⓒ Ⓓ	58. Ⓐ Ⓑ Ⓒ Ⓓ	
19. Ⓐ Ⓑ Ⓒ Ⓓ	39. Ⓐ Ⓑ Ⓒ Ⓓ	59. Ⓐ Ⓑ Ⓒ Ⓓ	
20. Ⓐ Ⓑ Ⓒ Ⓓ	40. Ⓐ Ⓑ Ⓒ Ⓓ	60. Ⓐ Ⓑ Ⓒ Ⓓ	

English Expression

1. Ⓐ Ⓑ Ⓒ Ⓓ Ⓔ	31. Ⓐ Ⓑ Ⓒ Ⓓ Ⓔ	61. Ⓐ Ⓑ Ⓒ Ⓓ Ⓔ	91. Ⓐ Ⓑ Ⓒ Ⓓ Ⓔ
2. Ⓐ Ⓑ Ⓒ Ⓓ Ⓔ	32. Ⓐ Ⓑ Ⓒ Ⓓ Ⓔ	62. Ⓐ Ⓑ Ⓒ Ⓓ Ⓔ	92. Ⓐ Ⓑ Ⓒ Ⓓ Ⓔ
3. Ⓐ Ⓑ Ⓒ Ⓓ Ⓔ	33. Ⓐ Ⓑ Ⓒ Ⓓ Ⓔ	63. Ⓐ Ⓑ Ⓒ Ⓓ Ⓔ	93. Ⓐ Ⓑ Ⓒ Ⓓ Ⓔ
4. Ⓐ Ⓑ Ⓒ Ⓓ Ⓔ	34. Ⓐ Ⓑ Ⓒ Ⓓ Ⓔ	64. Ⓐ Ⓑ Ⓒ Ⓓ Ⓔ	94. Ⓐ Ⓑ Ⓒ Ⓓ Ⓔ
5. Ⓐ Ⓑ Ⓒ Ⓓ Ⓔ	35. Ⓐ Ⓑ Ⓒ Ⓓ Ⓔ	65. Ⓐ Ⓑ Ⓒ Ⓓ Ⓔ	95. Ⓐ Ⓑ Ⓒ Ⓓ Ⓔ
6. Ⓐ Ⓑ Ⓒ Ⓓ Ⓔ	36. Ⓐ Ⓑ Ⓒ Ⓓ Ⓔ	66. Ⓐ Ⓑ Ⓒ Ⓓ Ⓔ	96. Ⓐ Ⓑ Ⓒ Ⓓ Ⓔ
7. Ⓐ Ⓑ Ⓒ Ⓓ Ⓔ	37. Ⓐ Ⓑ Ⓒ Ⓓ Ⓔ	67. Ⓐ Ⓑ Ⓒ Ⓓ Ⓔ	97. Ⓐ Ⓑ Ⓒ Ⓓ Ⓔ
8. Ⓐ Ⓑ Ⓒ Ⓓ Ⓔ	38. Ⓐ Ⓑ Ⓒ Ⓓ Ⓔ	68. Ⓐ Ⓑ Ⓒ Ⓓ Ⓔ	98. Ⓐ Ⓑ Ⓒ Ⓓ Ⓔ
9. Ⓐ Ⓑ Ⓒ Ⓓ Ⓔ	39. Ⓐ Ⓑ Ⓒ Ⓓ Ⓔ	69. Ⓐ Ⓑ Ⓒ Ⓓ Ⓔ	99. Ⓐ Ⓑ Ⓒ Ⓓ Ⓔ
10. Ⓐ Ⓑ Ⓒ Ⓓ Ⓔ	40. Ⓐ Ⓑ Ⓒ Ⓓ Ⓔ	70. Ⓐ Ⓑ Ⓒ Ⓓ Ⓔ	100. Ⓐ Ⓑ Ⓒ Ⓓ Ⓔ
11. Ⓐ Ⓑ Ⓒ Ⓓ Ⓔ	41. Ⓐ Ⓑ Ⓒ Ⓓ Ⓔ	71. Ⓐ Ⓑ Ⓒ Ⓓ Ⓔ	101. Ⓐ Ⓑ Ⓒ Ⓓ Ⓔ
12. Ⓐ Ⓑ Ⓒ Ⓓ Ⓔ	42. Ⓐ Ⓑ Ⓒ Ⓓ Ⓔ	72. Ⓐ Ⓑ Ⓒ Ⓓ Ⓔ	102. Ⓐ Ⓑ Ⓒ Ⓓ Ⓔ
13. Ⓐ Ⓑ Ⓒ Ⓓ Ⓔ	43. Ⓐ Ⓑ Ⓒ Ⓓ Ⓔ	73. Ⓐ Ⓑ Ⓒ Ⓓ Ⓔ	103. Ⓐ Ⓑ Ⓒ Ⓓ Ⓔ
14. Ⓐ Ⓑ Ⓒ Ⓓ Ⓔ	44. Ⓐ Ⓑ Ⓒ Ⓓ Ⓔ	74. Ⓐ Ⓑ Ⓒ Ⓓ Ⓔ	104. Ⓐ Ⓑ Ⓒ Ⓓ Ⓔ
15. Ⓐ Ⓑ Ⓒ Ⓓ Ⓔ	45. Ⓐ Ⓑ Ⓒ Ⓓ Ⓔ	75. Ⓐ Ⓑ Ⓒ Ⓓ Ⓔ	105. Ⓐ Ⓑ Ⓒ Ⓓ Ⓔ
16. Ⓐ Ⓑ Ⓒ Ⓓ Ⓔ	46. Ⓐ Ⓑ Ⓒ Ⓓ Ⓔ	76. Ⓐ Ⓑ Ⓒ Ⓓ Ⓔ	106. Ⓐ Ⓑ Ⓒ Ⓓ Ⓔ
17. Ⓐ Ⓑ Ⓒ Ⓓ Ⓔ	47. Ⓐ Ⓑ Ⓒ Ⓓ Ⓔ	77. Ⓐ Ⓑ Ⓒ Ⓓ Ⓔ	107. Ⓐ Ⓑ Ⓒ Ⓓ Ⓔ
18. Ⓐ Ⓑ Ⓒ Ⓓ Ⓔ	48. Ⓐ Ⓑ Ⓒ Ⓓ Ⓔ	78. Ⓐ Ⓑ Ⓒ Ⓓ Ⓔ	108. Ⓐ Ⓑ Ⓒ Ⓓ Ⓔ
19. Ⓐ Ⓑ Ⓒ Ⓓ Ⓔ	49. Ⓐ Ⓑ Ⓒ Ⓓ Ⓔ	79. Ⓐ Ⓑ Ⓒ Ⓓ Ⓔ	109. Ⓐ Ⓑ Ⓒ Ⓓ Ⓔ
20. Ⓐ Ⓑ Ⓒ Ⓓ Ⓔ	50. Ⓐ Ⓑ Ⓒ Ⓓ Ⓔ	80. Ⓐ Ⓑ Ⓒ Ⓓ Ⓔ	110. Ⓐ Ⓑ Ⓒ Ⓓ Ⓔ
21. Ⓐ Ⓑ Ⓒ Ⓓ Ⓔ	51. Ⓐ Ⓑ Ⓒ Ⓓ Ⓔ	81. Ⓐ Ⓑ Ⓒ Ⓓ Ⓔ	
22. Ⓐ Ⓑ Ⓒ Ⓓ Ⓔ	52. Ⓐ Ⓑ Ⓒ Ⓓ Ⓔ	82. Ⓐ Ⓑ Ⓒ Ⓓ Ⓔ	
23. Ⓐ Ⓑ Ⓒ Ⓓ Ⓔ	53. Ⓐ Ⓑ Ⓒ Ⓓ Ⓔ	83. Ⓐ Ⓑ Ⓒ Ⓓ Ⓔ	
24. Ⓐ Ⓑ Ⓒ Ⓓ Ⓔ	54. Ⓐ Ⓑ Ⓒ Ⓓ Ⓔ	84. Ⓐ Ⓑ Ⓒ Ⓓ Ⓔ	
25. Ⓐ Ⓑ Ⓒ Ⓓ Ⓔ	55. Ⓐ Ⓑ Ⓒ Ⓓ Ⓔ	85. Ⓐ Ⓑ Ⓒ Ⓓ Ⓔ	
26. Ⓐ Ⓑ Ⓒ Ⓓ Ⓔ	56. Ⓐ Ⓑ Ⓒ Ⓓ Ⓔ	86. Ⓐ Ⓑ Ⓒ Ⓓ Ⓔ	
27. Ⓐ Ⓑ Ⓒ Ⓓ Ⓔ	57. Ⓐ Ⓑ Ⓒ Ⓓ Ⓔ	87. Ⓐ Ⓑ Ⓒ Ⓓ Ⓔ	
28. Ⓐ Ⓑ Ⓒ Ⓓ Ⓔ	58. Ⓐ Ⓑ Ⓒ Ⓓ Ⓔ	88. Ⓐ Ⓑ Ⓒ Ⓓ Ⓔ	
29. Ⓐ Ⓑ Ⓒ Ⓓ Ⓔ	59. Ⓐ Ⓑ Ⓒ Ⓓ Ⓔ	89. Ⓐ Ⓑ Ⓒ Ⓓ Ⓔ	
30. Ⓐ Ⓑ Ⓒ Ⓓ Ⓔ	60. Ⓐ Ⓑ Ⓒ Ⓓ Ⓔ	90. Ⓐ Ⓑ Ⓒ Ⓓ Ⓔ	

KNOWLEDGE QUESTIONS

70 Questions • 2 Hours

Directions: Each of the questions or incomplete statements below is followed by four possible answers. Select the best answer for each question and then blacken the corresponding space on the answer sheet. Some sets of questions are presented with material such as reading passages, plans, graphs, tables, etc. Answers to such questions may require interpretation of the material and/or outside knowledge relevant to its content.

1. Congress has approved the opening of a U.S. mission in the country of Bangurm. An administrative officer in the State Department assigned to compare the costs of buying, leasing, or building facilities for this mission should consider which of the following?

   I.   Linear break-even analysis
   II. Present-worth comparison
   III. Depreciation
   IV. Program Evaluation and Review Technique

   (A) I only
   (B) II and III only
   (C) I, II, and IV only
   (D) I, II, III, and IV

2. Franklin D. Roosevelt's famous "Four Freedoms" included all of the following EXCEPT

   (A) freedom of religion.
   (B) freedom from want.
   (C) freedom from fear.
   (D) freedom from discrimination.

3. A latent function of a primitive rain dance is to

   (A) aid the rainfall.
   (B) provide a prelude to puberty rites in the United States.
   (C) solidify the group.
   (D) provide a *rite de passage*.

4. Which one of the following resulted from the Cuban Missile Crisis of October, 1962?

   (A) Cuba was subsequently invaded, unsuccessfully, by 1,000 U.S.-trained anti-Castro troops.
   (B) Castro was temporarily removed from power, but then regained power several years later.
   (C) Soviet missiles were removed from Cuba, and U.S. Jupiter missiles were later removed from Turkey.
   (D) The United States diplomatically recognized Castro's Cuba.

practice test 3

5. During the 1990s, U.S. defense spending
   (A) increased slightly as a percentage of the federal budget.
   (B) decreased as a percentage of the federal budget.
   (C) increased substantially as a percentage of the federal budget.
   (D) increased, then decreased, then increased again as a percentage of the federal budget.

6. From 1866 to 1915, around 25 million immigrants came to America. The main reason behind this massive influx was probably
   (A) the desire for economic betterment.
   (B) industrial expansion and the increased use of farm machinery in Europe.
   (C) political and religious persecution.
   (D) improved transportation technology.

7. If you were to locate the majority of Americans on the "political spectrum"—left, center, and right—that majority would be found at or on the political
   (A) left.
   (B) center.
   (C) right.
   (D) far right.

8. In which was the second event a result of the first?
   (A) Outbreak of the Napoleonic Wars—Enactment of the Embargo Act
   (B) Passage of the Missouri Compromise—*Alabama* claims
   (C) Tariff of 1828—Calling of the Hartford Convention
   (D) Homestead Act—Establishment of "pet banks"

9. For a treaty to be ratified in the American political system, what must happen?
   (A) The House of Representatives and U.S. Senate must approve the treaty by majority vote.
   (B) The Senate must approve by a three-quarters vote.
   (C) The House must approve by a majority and the Senate must approve by a two-thirds vote.
   (D) The Senate must approve by a two-thirds vote.

10. When the German colonies in central Africa were mandated to Great Britain and France following World War I, the mandatories assumed all of the following obligations EXCEPT
   (A) deny themselves special economic advantages.
   (B) prepare the colonies for immediate self-government.
   (C) guarantee freedom of conscience and religion.
   (D) prevent the establishment of military bases.

11. Tariffs are imposed to protect a producer who, perhaps for reasons that are not in any way that producer's own fault, is at a disadvantage in the larger economy. While the tariffs are in existence, the larger economy suffers because all the units of a given good are not being produced in a way that maximizes the quality of the product and minimizes the cost of production. In imposing the tariffs, one hopes, however, to promote the development of the protected constituency. When the protected constituency is a geographic region, that development includes social and political goals as well as economic ones. Ideally, with the assistance of temporary protection, the protected producer will eventually be able to forego the protection, meld with the larger economy as a healthy producer (or, sometimes, also as a healthy social and political actor), and carry the production of the larger economy to new heights. The short-term goals of a tariff include

I. bolstering of the general economy.

II. maximizing the quality of the product.

III. punishment of protected producers.

IV. development of a weak producer.

(A) I and II only

(B) II, III, and IV only

(C) IV only

(D) None of these

12. All modern governments have developed specific procedures to ensure accountability for the receipt and expenditure of public funds. The steps in one such procedure are given below, out of their logical order. Select the option that BEST presents these stages in their logical sequence.

(1) Disbursing officers provide for the payment of cash or check to satisfy the liability.

(2) The central financial authority (treasury) places money at the disposal of disbursing officers.

(3) The heads of agencies extend to designated officials within the agency the authorization to incur obligations. Designated officials award contracts for goods and services and incur obligations for the payment of salaries.

(4) The legislature authorizes the chief executive to make expenditure authority available to administrative agencies. The executive authority responsible for the execution of the budget, in accordance with legislative action, extends to the agencies' authorization to incur obligations.

(5) Fiscal officers within agencies prepare and certify vouchers to show that obligations are due and payable by disbursing officers. Orders for payment are prepared by fiscal officers and submitted to disbursing officers.

(A) 2, 5, 4, 1, 3

(B) 3, 2, 5, 1, 4

(C) 4, 3, 2, 5, 1

(D) 5, 1, 3, 4, 2

13. Which of the following is a political characteristic found in both the United States and Great Britain?

    (A) A vote of "no confidence"

    (B) Popular election

    (C) A unitary system

    (D) The fusion of the executive and legislative branches

14. American dance companies with both classical and contemporary works in their repertoires include all of the following EXCEPT the

    (A) New York City Ballet.

    (B) American Ballet Theater.

    (C) Alwin Nikolais Dance Company.

    (D) City Center Joffrey Ballet.

15. The concept of "collective security" is most CLOSELY associated with the

    (A) North Atlantic Treaty Organization.

    (B) League of Nations.

    (C) United Nations General Assembly.

    (D) European Union.

16. The names of Colin Powell, Henry Kissinger, Cyrus Vance, John Foster Dulles, and Dean Rusk are all associated with the position of

    (A) National Security Adviser.

    (B) Secretary of Defense.

    (C) Secretary of State.

    (D) United Nations Ambassador.

17. Prior to the nineteenth century, state formation in the interior of East Africa was stimulated by all of the following EXCEPT

    (A) the growth of long-distance trade.

    (B) the development of an economy based on fixed cultivation.

    (C) a need to control conquered territory.

    (D) introduction of European forms of political organization.

18. In American public opinion, the "attentive public" refers to

    (A) the small percentage of the public that is politically informed.

    (B) just another name for the "mass public."

    (C) only those individuals who are actually in the government.

    (D) those citizens who are actually interviewed by the national opinion polls.

QUESTION 19 IS BASED ON THE GRAPH BELOW:

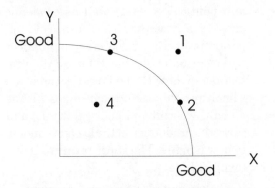

19. Which of the following statements is correct concerning the production–possibilities frontier for the economy shown above?

    (A) Point 1 is the maximum output at full employment.

    (B) The economy is better off at point 3 than at point 2.

    (C) The economy is better off at point 2 than at point 3.

    (D) Production at point 4 involves substantial unemployment.

20. Historically, patterns of population change during the process of industrialization generally have shown that
    (A) the birth rate drops markedly and is followed by decreases in the death rate.
    (B) the birth and death rates show marked and simultaneous reductions.
    (C) the death rate falls initially and is followed by reductions in the birth rate.
    (D) both birth and death rates remain fairly constant until very high levels of material prosperity are achieved.

21. During the last half of the nineteenth century, an important aim of Japan in modernizing itself was to
    (A) improve the living conditions of the peasants.
    (B) remove Western European nations from China.
    (C) resist threats of foreign domination.
    (D) increase the power of the feudal lords.

22. Which of the following is an intangible component of national/international power?
    (A) National will
    (B) Number of troops in the army
    (C) Economic productivity and growth rates
    (D) The trade balance: export vs. import revenue

23. In which of the following paired events did the first event lead directly to the second?
    (A) Bombing of Pearl Harbor—Annexing of Hawaii by the United States of America
    (B) Purchase of Alaska—Cold war with Russia
    (C) Failure of the League of Nations—World War I
    (D) Assassination of President Garfield—Passage of the Pendleton Civil Service Act

QUESTIONS 24 TO 26 ARE BASED ON THE FOLLOWING MAP:

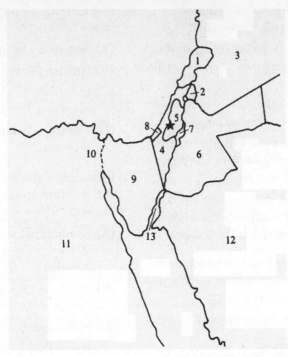

24. The starred city is
    I. holy to Muslims, Jews, and Christians.
    II. administered by an international committee.
    III. a bargaining chip in all manners of Middle East negotiations.
    IV. divided into sectors that are rigidly restricted to members of specific groups.
    (A) I only
    (B) I and II only
    (C) II, III, and IV only
    (D) I, III, and IV only

25. Area number 7 is
    (A) a territory over which 4, 5, and 6 are constantly at war.
    (B) the only neutral country in the Middle East.
    (C) the source of waters that irrigate lands to its south.
    (D) a rich source of salt and minerals.

26. The entire area represented by this map is of importance to U.S. foreign policy because of
    I. its militarily strategic location.
    II. the natural resources it possesses or controls.
    III. the historic/religious significance of the area.
    IV. the possibility of Russian influence.
    (A) I and II only
    (B) I, II, and III only
    (C) II, III, and IV only
    (D) I, II, and IV only

27. An American novel that greatly influenced lifestyles in the United States and much of Europe in the late 1950s was
    (A) Aleister Crowley's *Liber Trigrammaton.*
    (B) Jack Kerouac's *On the Road.*
    (C) Vladimir Nabokov's *Lolita.*
    (D) Aldous Huxley's *Brave New World.*

28. Which of the following is NOT consistent with the writings of Karl Marx?

    (A) The primacy of the class struggle

    (B) The growing poverty of the proletariat

    (C) The withering away of the state

    (D) Accumulation of individual profit

29. The Treaties of Rome in March 1957 produced a number of pacts serving various purposes. Among these were the

    I.   European Maritime Convention.

    II. Inter-European Agreement on Guest Labor.

    III. European Economic Community.

    IV. European Atomic Energy Community.

    (A) I and III only

    (B) II and IV only

    (C) III and IV only

    (D) II, III, and IV only

30. The writings of John Maynard Keynes have been influential in justification of

    (A) lower interest and availability of money.

    (B) German reparation payments to England.

    (C) high interest rates.

    (D) deficit financing.

31. With the general abandonment of some of the basic requirements of the traditional gold standard, the par value for each of the monetary units of the world

    (A) no longer exists.

    (B) is adjusted unilaterally by countries in the light of their balance of payments position.

    (C) is adjusted through the International Monetary Fund.

    (D) is regulated by regional agreements such as the European Payments Union.

32. Which of the following can BEST be classified as nations marked by low birth rates and low death rates?

    (A) Communist China, India, the United Arab Republic

    (B) The United States, Brazil, Indonesia

    (C) Austria, France, Great Britain

    (D) Ghana, Mexico, Spain

33. With respect to which of the following is there the GREATEST similarity between the countries of the Middle East and those of Latin America?

    (A) The traditional lack of a middle class

    (B) The lack of economic viability

    (C) Dependence on agricultural products for export earnings

    (D) Type of government organization

34. "He set out to fulfill the American dream of a public school system that was the chief training ground for democracy. He advocated a curriculum that had meaning for an urban age. He taught, moreover, that curriculum and subject matter should be adapted to the needs and capabilities of children." Who of the following most STRONGLY advocated the principles stated above?

    (A) Horace Mann

    (B) John Dewey

    (C) Henry Thoreau

    (D) Henry James

35. Which of the following is generally characteristic of modern underdeveloped countries?

   (A) Rising nationalism, population problems, middle-class philosophy

   (B) Low savings rate, inequality of wealth, need for land reform

   (C) Poor endowment of natural resources, failure of the wealthy to invest in manufacturing, security of foreign investments

   (D) Desire for Western material goods, large role of government investment, full utilization of manpower

36. The right to use the airways is controlled by the government in which of the following countries?

   I.   The former Soviet Union

   II. The United States

   III. Great Britain

   IV. Lebanon

   (A) I and IV only

   (B) II and III only

   (C) I, II, and III only

   (D) I, II, III, and IV

37. If the president were faced with an international crisis, he would most likely rely LEAST upon which advisory group?

   (A) National Security Council

   (B) Joint Chiefs of Staff

   (C) The Cabinet

   (D) U.S. senators on the Foreign Relations Committee

38. The reply was to the effect that the "Creative Power," when he made the earth, made no marks, no lines of division or separation upon it, and that it should be allowed to remain as then made. The earth was his mother. He was made of earth and grew up on its bosom. The earth, as his mother and nurse, was sacred to his affections, too sacred to be valued by or sold for silver or gold. He could not consent to sever his affections from the land that bore him. He was content to live upon such fruits as the "Creative Power" placed within and upon it, and unwilling to barter these and his free habits away for the new modes of life proposed by us.

This reply was MOST likely made by

   (A) a Massachusetts Puritan to the English Privy Council.

   (B) an American Indian to a U.S. government commission.

   (C) a Mormon leader to the governor of the Utah Territory.

   (D) a Mexican official to American settlers in Texas.

39. In which United Nations body are all member-states represented?

   (A) The Security Council

   (B) The Economic and Social Council

   (C) The General Assembly

   (D) The Trusteeship Council

40. All of the following former or current world leaders are correctly matched with his or her nation EXCEPT

   (A) Vladimir Putin—Russia

   (B) Saddam Hussein—Iraq

   (C) Andres Pastrana—Mexico

   (D) Anwar Sadat—Egypt

41. Worldwide hostage-taking had become a major problem during the twentieth century. The most important reason for NOT negotiating with terrorists is

    (A) to avoid granting legitimacy to their movements.

    (B) that the cost of ransom may become staggering.

    (C) that you can't trust terrorists to negotiate in good faith.

    (D) that negotiation and compromise sets a precedent that encourages future hostage-taking for gain.

42. John K. Galbraith's concept of countervailing power leads to the conclusion that

    (A) more government action and regulation is necessary to restore competition.

    (B) a spontaneous growth of economic forces has, in effect, curbed the power of oligopoly.

    (C) oligopoly will, in due time, replace competition.

    (D) competition is doomed in any highly advanced industrial country.

43. A comparison of the general situation in Europe at the opening of the twentieth century with that at the opening of the eighteenth century would show the greatest difference with respect to the

    (A) character of the social class structure.

    (B) practice of balance-of-power diplomacy.

    (C) interest in imperialism.

    (D) role of technology in the economy.

QUESTIONS 44 AND 45 ARE BASED ON THE FOLLOWING PARAGRAPH:

In-basket tests are often used to assess managerial potential. The exercise consists of a set of papers that would be likely to be found in the in-basket of an administrator or manager at any given time and requires the individuals participating in the examination to indicate how they would dispose of each item found in the in-basket. In order to handle the in-basket effectively, participants must successfully manage their time, refer and assign some work to subordinates, juggle potentially conflicting appointments and meetings, and arrange for follow-up of problems generated by the items in the in-basket. In other words, the in-basket test is attempting to evaluate the participants' abilities to organize their work, set priorities, delegate, control, and make decisions.

44. To succeed in an in-basket test, an administrator must

    (A) be able to read very quickly.

    (B) have a great deal of technical knowledge.

    (C) know when to delegate work.

    (D) arrange a lot of appointments and meetings.

45. All of the following abilities are indications of managerial potential EXCEPT the ability to

    (A) organize and control.

    (B) manage time.

    (C) conform to social norms.

    (D) make appropriate decisions.

46. In this world of high-speed travel, electronic transfer of money, and instant communications, events in one country can have a profound effect on events in many other countries. If, in the Tokyo market, the dollar drops sharply against the Japanese yen,

    (A) the price of gold will rise in London.

    (B) the dollar will strengthen against the German mark.

    (C) trading will cease on the New York stock exchange.

    (D) American tourism in Japan will increase radically.

47. The concept of the economic man in the history of economic thought relates to an individual who

    (A) seeks to further his economic self-interest above anything else.

    (B) seeks to create a balance and equilibrium among the factors of consumption, production, distribution, and exchange.

    (C) seeks to interpret politics mainly in the light of economic factors.

    (D) seeks to make the superiority of capitalism over socialism a reality.

48. The original signatories to the NAFTA agreement were

    (A) Peru, Ecuador, and Brazil.

    (B) Mexico, Honduras, and Argentina.

    (C) Mexico, Canada, and the United States.

    (D) Chile, Brazil, and the United States.

49. The "Camp David" Accords occurred during which administration and involved which two nations?

    (A) President Carter—Israel and Egypt

    (B) President Ford—China and Taiwan

    (C) President Clinton—Haiti and Cuba

    (D) President George W. Bush—Northern Ireland and Great Britain

50. The Maastrict Treaty, signed in December 1991, provided for

    (A) a new arms control treaty between Russia and the United States.

    (B) a new peace agreement between Great Britain and Northern Ireland.

    (C) NATO "enlargement" involving Poland, the Czech Republic, and Hungary.

    (D) new steps in the political-economic integration of Europe.

51. Which of the following descriptions is MOST consistent with "a favorable balance of trade"?

    (A) Goods and services available for domestic use exceed the value of domestic production

    (B) Domestic holdings of gold increase

    (C) Domestic exports of merchandise exceed imports of merchandise

    (D) Net foreign investment is negative

52. In the field of international relations, the effectiveness of nuclear deterrence is most CLOSELY associated with

    (A) diplomatic ingenuity and international treaty-making.

    (B) total disarmament and verification by international inspectors.

    (C) mutual second-strike capability and survivability.

    (D) espionage and counter-intelligence operations.

53. The term "laws of war" on its surface appears to be an oxymoron. One's first impression is that war is lawless. Actually, the laws of war as they apply to non-hostile contacts between the warring parties are generally observed and are quite effective. Non-hostile contacts include such activities as

(A) flags of truce, armistices, and safe passage.

(B) bomb shelters, demilitarized zones, and armistices.

(C) espionage, peace treaties, and first aid stations.

(D) respect for the dead, flags of truce, and mine sweeping.

54. Film is a powerful art form. It may be used to educate, to entertain, to make moral statements, and to make political statements. Under the guarantees of free speech, the statement made by a film might not always be for the common good, as witness the film below, which openly praises the Ku Klux Klan and implicitly condemns miscegenation. This film is

(A) Arthur Penn's *Bonnie and Clyde.*

(B) Jean Renoir's *The Rules of the Game.*

(C) Man Ray's *Return to Reason.*

(D) D. W. Griffith's *The Birth of a Nation.*

55. Which one of the following was NOT provided for in the Treaty of Rome (1957), which established the European Economic Community?

(A) Common action will be taken to improve living and working conditions for employees

(B) Monetary policies of the members are to be coordinated

(C) The colonies and associated territories of the members are to be excluded from the Common Market

(D) Trade barriers are to be gradually eliminated among the six members over a period of years

QUESTIONS 56 TO 58 ARE BASED ON THE MAP BELOW:

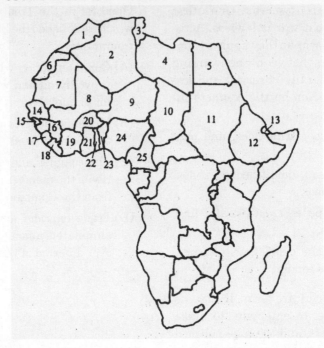

56. While much of Africa is rich in natural resources and a large part of the continent is fertile and productive, the economic situation of the continent, as a whole, is very bleak. Large areas of the continent are arid, and every ten years or so, there is a prolonged drought that creates severe famine and widespread starvation. Corruption, exploitation, and poor transportation and distribution all contribute to economic problems. In an attempt to better the lot of his people by channeling funds from his military defense budget to his economic development budget, the leader of one country made an innovative and courageous peace overture to an enemy of long standing. This ruler came from

  (A) 1.

  (B) 5.

  (C) 12.

  (D) 20.

57. The influence of Italy on the African continent has been minimal, but in a show of his "superior military power," Mussolini invaded and easily conquered a weak, unprepared African country. That country was

  (A) 5.

  (B) 11.

  (C) 12.

  (D) 13.

58. When one thinks of oil one thinks of the Middle East, but some African nations are oil-producing and some belong to OPEC. Among the OPEC nations are

  (A) 2 and 3.

  (B) 4 and 5.

  (C) 5 and 11.

  (D) 4 and 24.

59. The doctrine of purchasing-power-parity indicates that the balance of payments disequilibrium that is due to inflation may be corrected by

(A) depreciation of the foreign exchange rate by a percentage equal to the price rise.

(B) appreciation of the foreign exchange rate by the same percentage as the price rise.

(C) an increase in the money supply by the same amount as prices.

(D) increased taxes so as to reduce purchasing power.

60. In the middle of the night, five people—a mother, father, their adult son, and two young teenage daughters—approach the American embassy in a foreign country and beg for asylum. They claim that they are being harassed because of their religious beliefs, that their home is regularly searched and pillaged, that they are unable to earn a living, and that the daughters have been molested by official police and by soldiers. Under further questioning, they admit that the son is facing a number of criminal charges, but they insist that these are trumped-up charges and that the son has been framed. They fear for his safety and, indeed, for his life. They are quite certain that they were observed as they approached the embassy. If the family is permitted temporary residence in the legation until long-range plans for their safety are completed, they will be following a precedent typified by

(A) Archbishop Stepinac in our legation in Yugoslavia.

(B) Cardinal Mindzenty in our legation in Budapest.

(C) Cardinal Wyszynski in our legation in Warsaw.

(D) Archbishop Iacovos in our legation in Athens.

61. According to Julius Nyerere, former President of Tanzania, a two-party system is justified only when parties differ on a fundamental issue—when one group fights to remove a grievous wrong from society that hurts all of society. In any other situation, a two-party system merely reduces politics to the level of a football match, as both sides agree on the general goals of society but haggle over which group or class will get a greater share of the nation's wealth or power, thereby hindering their effort to increase the prosperity and well-being of the nation.

While Nyerere's assessment might hold true in his country, the two-party system served a real social purpose in the United States right after the turn of the twentieth century. Rivalries between the parties provided for

(A) an arena in which to settle arguments by debate rather than by violence.

(B) extensive social services to new immigrants in hopes of cultivating their support once they became citizens.

(C) clubhouses that kept men off the street at night.

(D) efforts to eliminate sweatshops and to improve working conditions.

62. Which is a TRUE statement about the United States and the Vietnam War?

(A) The United States was successful in preserving the independence of South Vietnam.

(B) The United States relied exclusively on air power to try and defeat the Communist forces.

(C) The War generated only a small degree of protest in the United States.

(D) The United States underestimated the resolve of the North Vietnamese.

63. The common conception—or misconception—of the Native American is that of the painted savage or fierce warrior. Secondarily, Native Americans are thought of as line artisans and artists and as skillful woodsmen. In truth, Native Americans—as typified by Standing Bear, Red Cloud, and John Logan—are especially to be admired for their skill and success as

(A) songwriters.

(B) physicians.

(C) calligraphers.

(D) orators.

64. Under Title VII of the Civil Rights Act and the Equal Employment Opportunity Act, persons of certain race and national origin categories are singled out for special consideration. For Affirmative Action programs giving preference to members of certain minority groups, American Indians and Alaskan natives qualify ONLY if

(A) they have lived at least 70 percent of their lives on reservations.

(B) they have left the reservation.

(C) they maintain cultural identification through tribal affiliation or community recognition.

(D) they have made an honest attempt at assimilation.

65. The rationale for the rule in question 64 is that Affirmative Action is meant to

(A) hasten assimilation of ethnic minorities.

(B) help specific disadvantaged individuals to acquire advanced training that they could not otherwise afford.

(C) atone for past discrimination by promoting minority workers more quickly through the ranks.

(D) assist representative members of a racial group that has deficiencies of background created by prior discrimination, thereby helping to move the group into the economic mainstream.

66. The Constitution of the United States is a very short document and is specific on very few subjects; however, it does state "The Congress shall have Power To Promote the Progress of Science and useful Arts, by securing for limited Times to Authors and Inventors the exclusive Right to their respective Writings and Discoveries." By guaranteeing the protection of patents and copyrights, the Constitution establishes that

(A) there will be free enterprise in the United States.

(B) Congress will closely regulate granting of patents and copyrights.

(C) scientists and authors will have freedom of speech.

(D) authors and inventors are a superior class of citizen.

67. If the end result was arms reduction and reversal of nuclear proliferation along with national security, the impetus that brought the Soviet Union and the United States to the bargaining table and led to the agreement was immaterial. The chief reason that the Soviet Union proposed such talks and agreements was

(A) the pressure of international criticism that the nuclear arms race was irresponsible.

(B) budgetary pressures and economic reality.

(C) fear of "nuclear winter."

(D) fear that the deployment of "Star Wars" would leave the Soviet Union vulnerable.

68. The subject matter and emphases of the musical shows *The Red Mill* and *Stop the World I Want to Get Off* would make them good openers for lively discussion at a convention of

    (A) psychiatrists.

    (B) feminists.

    (C) prohibitionists.

    (D) socialists.

69. An impressive statistic coming from many Communist LDCs is the low infant mortality rate—not just a reduced mortality rate from the pre-communist era but truly a low rate and often a rate considerably lower than that in highly developed, capitalistic nations. The most LIKELY explanation of this phenomenon is which of the following?

    (A) Communist countries have a controlled press and may manipulate figures to impress the world.

    (B) In capitalist countries, there is competition for public health dollars, so the rate of infant mortality is exaggerated in local reporting in order to get greater funding for research and services.

    (C) Health care is visible and is always appreciated, so Communist regimes invest in it disproportionately as a means of satisfying their own citizens and displaying their humanity to the world.

    (D) The LDCs are less industrialized, have less pollution, less stress, and healthier lifestyles.

70. Every major unit of government has interests that may not entirely correspond with those of the State Department. In a large embassy, this state of affairs leads to

    (A) an administrative challenge in coordinating these varying interests in light of space, personnel, and equipment allotments.

    (B) frequent shake-ups of high-ranking personnel in the political, economic, and cultural sections.

    (C) a fragmented portrayal of the American position to the government of the host country.

    (D) a strict hierarchical structure within the embassy.

ENGLISH EXPRESSION

110 Questions • 60 Minutes

> **Directions:** The following sentences contain problems in grammar, usage, diction (choice of words), and idiom. Some sentences are correct. No sentence contains more than one error.
>
> You will find that the error, if there is one, is underlined and lettered. Assume that all other elements of the sentence are correct and cannot be changed. In choosing answers, follow the requirements of standard written English. If there is an error, select the one underlined part that must be changed in order to make the sentence correct, and fill in the corresponding oval on the answer sheet. If there is no error, mark answer choice (E).

1. Before registering, the student <u>had</u> time
   　　　　　　　　　　　　　　　A
   to study the catalogue, <u>choose</u> his classes,
   　　　　　　　　　　　　B
   and <u>deciding</u> which section he
   　　　　C
   <u>would attend</u>. <u>No error</u>
   　　D　　　　　E

2. When one <u>prepares</u> systematically and
   　　　　　　A
   diligently for the examination, <u>you</u> can
   　　　　　　　　　　　　　　　B
   <u>be confident</u> of <u>passing</u> it. <u>No error</u>
   　　C　　　　　D　　　　E

3. Jones seems <u>slow</u> on the track, but you
   　　　　　　A
   will find few men <u>quicker</u> <u>than</u> <u>him</u> on the
   　　　　　　　　　B　　　C　　D
   basketball court. <u>No error</u>
   　　　　　　　　E

4. We had <u>swam</u> <u>across</u> the lake <u>before</u> the
   　　　　A　　　B　　　　　　　C
   sun <u>rose</u>. <u>No error</u>
   　　D　　　E

5. As Martha <u>dived</u> off the springboard, she
   　　　　　　A
   was <u>horrified</u> to see that the water in the
   　　　B
   pool <u>was not cleaned</u> for <u>several weeks</u>.
   　　　　C　　　　　　　　D
   <u>No error</u>
   E

6. <u>Their</u> are <u>still</u> people who say that it has
   　A　　　B
   never <u>really</u> been <u>proved</u> that the Earth is
   　　　C　　　　　D
   round. <u>No error</u>
   　　　　E

7. John Kennedy <u>effected</u> many <u>executive</u>
   　　　　　　　A　　　　　B
   reforms during the <u>tragically</u> few years
   　　　　　　　　　　C
   that he served as <u>president</u>. <u>No error</u>
   　　　　　　　　　D　　　　　E

8. Mary was so <u>disinterested</u> in the <u>baseball</u>
   　　　　　　　A　　　　　　B
   game <u>that</u> she yawned <u>unashamedly</u>.
   　　　C　　　　　　　D
   <u>No error</u>
   E

9. <u>For</u> ten years, the rancher <u>had arose</u> at
   A   B

   <u>dawn</u> in order <u>to feed</u> his cattle. <u>No error</u>
   C   D   E

10. Clearly visible on the desk <u>were</u>
                                A

    <u>those letters</u> he <u>claimed</u> to <u>have mailed</u>
    B   C   D

    yesterday. <u>No error</u>
                 E

11. <u>An inexperienced liar</u>, Mary explained her
         A

    absence from work with an <u>incredulous</u>
                            B

    tale <u>of daring</u> in which she played the
        C

    <u>role</u> of the heroine. <u>No error</u>
    D   E

12. The <u>loud noise</u> of the cars and trucks
         A

    <u>aggravates</u> those <u>who</u> live <u>near the road</u>.
    B   C   D

    <u>No error</u>
    E

13. <u>Irregardless</u> of <u>what people say</u>, I must
    A   B

    repeat that these are the <u>facts concerning</u>
                          C

    the <u>requirements for the position</u>.
                  D

    <u>No error</u>
    E

14. There <u>is</u> no <u>objection to him</u> joining the
        A   B

    party <u>if he is</u> willing to <u>fit in with</u> the
         C   D

    plans of the group. <u>No error</u>
                      E

15. <u>Rather than</u> <u>go with John</u>, he <u>decided</u> to
    A   B   C

    stay <u>at home</u>. <u>No error</u>
         D   E

16. <u>You</u> telling the truth in the face of such
    A

    <u>dire</u> consequences <u>required</u> great <u>moral</u>
    B   C   D

    courage. <u>No error</u>
            E

17. <u>We have</u> no idea <u>what</u> <u>are</u> in <u>those</u>
    A   B   C   D

    abandoned storage tanks. <u>No error</u>
                          E

18. For <u>convenience</u> sake, she <u>chose</u> to take
        A   B

    the job <u>that</u> was located <u>nearer to</u> her
            C   D

    home. <u>No error</u>
          E

19. As we <u>waited</u> for the light to <u>change</u>, we
         A   B

    heard a <u>loud</u> crash that attracted her
          C

    attention and <u>me</u>. <u>No error</u>
             D   E

20. Placing his <u>longbow</u> on the grass
              A

    <u>beside him</u>, Robin Hood, <u>who had had</u> an
    B   C

    exciting day, <u>laid down</u> to rest. <u>No error</u>
             D   E

21. I was <u>not at all</u> surprised <u>to hear</u> of Jim
         A   B

    <u>Dolan winning</u> the election
    C

    <u>for town councilman</u>. <u>No error</u>
    D   E

22. She saw that there was nothing <u>else</u> she
                                      A

    could <u>do</u>; the room was clean <u>like</u> it had
          B   C

    <u>never been</u> before. <u>No error</u>
    D   E

23. The instructor was <u>justly</u> annoyed by <u>him</u>
                        A   B

    walking in <u>late</u> and <u>disturbing</u> the class.
              C   D

    <u>No error</u>
    E

24. Each of the golfers <u>were</u> <u>scrupulously</u>
                         A   B

    careful <u>about</u> proper form of <u>his swing</u>.
            C   D

    <u>No error</u>
    E

25. I <u>enjoy</u> eating in <u>good</u> restaurants and
      A   B

    <u>to go</u> to the theater <u>afterwards</u>. <u>No error</u>
    C   D   E

26. His <u>sworn</u> statement, <u>together with</u> the
        A   B

    testimony and statements <u>from other</u>
                             C

    witnesses, <u>were</u> made a part of the file.
               D

    <u>No error</u>
    E

27. <u>Being able</u> to trust <u>his</u> <u>sources, it</u> is
    A   B   C

    <u>indispensable for</u> the investigative
    D

    reporter. <u>No error</u>
              E

28. <u>No one</u> among the staff <u>was</u> more
    A   B

    <u>disgruntled</u> than <u>she</u> when the assignment
    C   D

    was handed out. <u>No error</u>
                    E

29. The government, announcing a bill of

    rights for <u>its</u> citizens, <u>promising</u> them
               A   B

    equal rights <u>under the law</u> and
                 C

    <u>due process</u> in the courts. <u>No error</u>
    D   E

30. Neither rain <u>or</u> wind <u>stopped</u> her from
                 A   B

    <u>taking</u> her walk <u>around</u> the park. <u>No error</u>
    C   D   E

31. The <u>victim's mother</u>, <u>besides herself</u>
        A   B

    <u>with grief</u>, could give no <u>coherent</u> account
    C   D

    of the accident. <u>No error</u>
                     E

32. If he <u>had had</u> the <u>forethought</u> to arrange
          A   B

    an <u>appointment</u>, his reception
       C

    <u>would have been</u> more friendly. <u>No error</u>
    D   E

33. His education had filled him <u>with anger</u>
                                 A

    against those <u>whom</u> he <u>believed</u> had hurt
                  B   C

    or <u>humiliated</u> him. <u>No error</u>
       D   E

34. I <u>can't</u> decide <u>as to whether</u> <u>I'll</u> go to see a
  A   B   C

film or <u>visit</u> the art museum on Sunday.
        D

<u>No error</u>
  E

35. <u>When you go</u> to the library tomorrow,
         A

please <u>bring</u> this book to the
        B

<u>librarian who sits</u> behind the desk on the
        C

<u>far right of the reference room.</u> <u>No error</u>
              D   E

Directions: In each of the following sentences, some part or all of the sentence is underlined. Below each sentence you will find five ways of rephrasing the underlined part. Select the answer that produces the most effective sentence, one that is clear and exact without awkwardness or ambiguity, and fill in the corresponding oval on your answer sheet. In choosing answers, follow the requirements of standard written English. Choose the answer that best expresses the meaning of the original sentence. Choice (A) is always the same as the underlined part. Choose choice (A) if you think the original sentence needs no revision.

---

36. <u>Marchand is more concerned with demonstrating that racial prejudice exists than preventing it from doing harm, which explains</u> why his work is not always highly regarded.

(A) Marchand is more concerned with demonstrating that racial prejudice exists than preventing it from doing harm, which explains

(B) Marchand is more concerned with demonstrating that racial prejudice exists than with preventing it from doing harm, and this explains

(C) Marchand is more concerned with demonstrating that racial prejudice exists than with preventing it from doing harm, an explanation of

(D) Marchand's greater concern for demonstrating that racial prejudice exists than preventing it from doing harm this explains

(E) Marchand's greater concern for demonstrating that racial prejudice exists than for preventing it from doing harm explains

37. <u>Throughout this history of the American West there runs a steady commentary on the deception and mistreatment of the Indians.</u>

(A) Throughout this history of the American West there runs a steady commentary on the deception and mistreatment of the Indians.

(B) There is steady commentary provided on the deception and mistreatment of the Indians and it runs throughout this history of the American West.

(C) The deception and mistreatment of the Indians provide a steady comment that runs throughout this history of the American West.

(D) Comment on the deception and mistreatment of the Indians is steadily provided and runs throughout this history of the American West.

(E) Running throughout this history of the American West is a steady commentary that is provided on the deception and mistreatment of the Indians.

38. <u>If he would have known</u> of the dangerous working conditions, he would not have taken the job.

    (A) If he would have known

    (B) If he would've known

    (C) If he knew

    (D) If he had known

    (E) If he had knowledge of

39. <u>The findings resulted</u> from extensive international cooperation, it was impossible to select fairly a single recipient for the prize.

    (A) The findings resulted

    (B) Seeing as the findings resulted

    (C) Since the findings resulted

    (D) Although the findings resulted

    (E) The findings being resultant

40. The fans cheered quickly, loudly, <u>and with great enthusiasm</u>.

    (A) and in an enthusiastic manner

    (B) and enthusiastically

    (C) and by acting enthusiastic

    (D) and also used enthusiasm

    (E) and from enthusiasm

41. European film distributors originated the art of "dubbing"—<u>the substitution of lip synchronized translations</u> in foreign languages for the original soundtrack voices.

    (A) —the substitution of lip-synchronized translations

    (B) ; the substitution of lip-synchronized translations

    (C) —the substitutions of translations synchronized by the lips

    (D) , the lip-synchronized substitution of translations

    (D) . The substitution of lip-synchronized translations

42. <u>The crisis we face deals with</u> a growing population and diminishing food supply.

    (A) The crisis we face deals with a

    (B) The crisis we must face up to deals with a

    (C) We face a crisis of

    (D) The crisis we face deal with a

    (E) We face a crisis that concerns a

43. <u>Although it is contrary</u> to popular belief, handling frogs does not cause warts.

    (A) Although it is contrary

    (B) Contrarily

    (C) Contrary

    (D) Although contrary

    (E) Although it is contrary

44. The epidemic worsened because <u>of overcrowded conditions and they were unsanitary</u>.

    (A) of overcrowded conditions and they were unsanitary

    (B) of overcrowded and unsanitary conditions

    (C) of overcrowded conditions and unsanitary ones

    (D) they were overcrowded and unsanitary conditions

    (E) of there being overcrowded and unsanitary conditions

45. To read the difficult and complex material <u>it requires much concentration</u>.

    (A) it requires much concentration.

    (B) it has to be concentrated on a lot

    (C) it requires much concentrating

    (D) much concentration is required

    (E) requires much concentration

46. The parties agreed <u>to abide with</u> the arbitrator's decision.

    (A) to abide with
    (B) to abiding on
    (C) to abide on
    (D) to abide by
    (E) to abiding from

47. <u>Honor as well as profit are to be gained by this work.</u>

    (A) Honor as well as profit are to be gained by this work.
    (B) Honor as well as profit is to be gained by this work.
    (C) Honor in addition to profit are to be gained by this work.
    (D) Honor, as well as profit, are to be gained by this work.
    (E) Honor and profit is to be gained by this work.

48. <u>He was neither in favor of or opposed to the plan.</u>

    (A) He was neither in favor of or opposed to the plan.
    (B) He was not in favor of or opposed to the plan.
    (C) He was neither in favor of the plan or opposed to it.
    (D) He was neither in favor of the plan or opposed to the plan.
    (E) He was neither in favor of nor opposed to the plan.

49. <u>I don't enjoy those kinds of films.</u>

    (A) I don't enjoy those kinds of films.
    (B) I don't enjoy those kind of films.
    (C) I don't enjoy films that are of that kind.
    (D) I don't enjoy films that are of that type.
    (E) I don't enjoy those kinds of film.

50. The doctor was startled to learn of the <u>amount of new cases</u> of the rare disease.

    (A) amount of new cases
    (B) number of new cases
    (C) number of new incidents
    (D) new case figure amounts
    (E) amount of new instances

51. The group called a rally <u>to demonstrate how it was opposed</u> to the proposed construction.

    (A) to demonstrate how it was opposed to
    (B) to demonstrate how it was in opposition to
    (C) to demonstrate its opposition to
    (D) to remonstrate its opposition to
    (E) for a demonstration of its being opposed to

52. By 2 o'clock, the child <u>will have lain</u> in his bed for ten solid hours.

    (A) will have lain
    (B) will have lied
    (C) will have laid
    (D) will have lay
    (E) will be laying

53. Because they were unaware of his interest in the building, they did not understand <u>why he felt so bad about it's</u> being condemned.

    (A) why he felt so bad about it's
    (B) why he felt so badly about it's
    (C) why he felt so badly about its
    (D) why he felt so bad about its
    (E) the reason why he felt so bad about its

54. Support Communications Officers are assigned to overseas posts and to <u>Washington, D.C., and often work</u> on rotating shifts as well as performing call-in/stand-by duties involving a variety of activities.

(A) Washington, D.C., and often work

(B) Washington, D.C. and often work

(C) Washington, D.C., often working

(D) Washington, D.C., and they often work

(E) Washington, D.C., and work often

55. A "cliometrician" is <u>an economist or economic historian who works with mathematical statistics to solve historical problems</u>.

(A) an economist or economic historian who works with mathematical statistics to solve historical problems

(B) an economist or economic historian which works with mathematical statistics to solve historical problems

(C) an economist or economical historian who works with mathematical statistics to solve historical problems

(D) an economist or economic historian who works with mathematics and statistics in the solution of historical problems

(E) an economist or economic historian who works with mathematical statistics to solve historic problems

Directions: In each of the following questions you are given a complete sentence to be rephrased according to the directions that follow it. You should rephrase the sentence mentally to save time, although you may make notes in your test book if you wish.

Below each sentence and its directions are listed words or phrases that may occur in your revised sentence. When you have thought out a good sentence, look in the choices (A) through (E) for the word or entire phrase that is included in your revised sentence, and fill in the corresponding oval on the answer sheet. The word or phrase you choose should be the most accurate and most nearly complete of all the choices given, and should be part of a sentence that meets the requirements of standard written English.

Of course, a number of different sentences can be obtained if the sentence is revised according to the directions, and not all of these possibilities can be included in only five choices. If you should find that you have thought of a sentence that contains none of the words or phrases listed in the choices, you should attempt to rephrase the sentence again so that it includes a word or phrase that is listed.

Although the directions may at times require you to change the relationship between parts of the sentence or to make slight changes in meaning in other ways, make only those changes that the directions require. Keep the meaning the same or as nearly the same as the directions permit. If you think that more than one good sentence can be made according to the directions, select the sentence that is most exact, effective, and natural in phrasing and construction.

56. Owing to her conservative fiscal policy, the governor attracted many voters.

    Begin with <u>Many people voted for the governor</u>

    (A) so

    (B) while

    (C) although

    (D) because

    (E) and

57. It displeases the director when Richard and I arrive late for work.

    Begin with <u>The director does not approve</u>.

    (A) of me and Richard arriving

    (B) of Richard and me arriving

    (C) of Richard's and my arriving

    (D) when Richard and me arrive

    (E) about Richard and me arriving

58. She shows laziness which annoys me.

    Change <u>shows laziness</u> to <u>is lazy</u>.

    (A) which annoys me.

    (B) and this annoys me.

    (C) and this habit annoys me.

    (D) which is something that annoys me.

    (E) which is annoying.

59. There is a stain on my tie so can you remove it?

    Eliminate <u>so</u>.

    (A) , can you remove the stain?

    (B) , can you remove it?

    (C) ; can you remove it?

    (D) . Can you remove it?

    (E) . Can you remove the stain?

60. The storm, as it seems, will soon be upon us.

Begin with It looks.

(A) like the storm

(B) like as if the storm

(C) as if the storm

(D) as though the storm

(E) like that the storm

61. Miss Talbot resisted the temptation to expand too quickly beyond the company's financial means, so BonTon grew slowly and steadily.

Begin with BonTon grew slowly and steadily.

(A) in spite of

(B) in light of

(C) although

(D) whenever

(E) because of

62. She is one of those people of the type who complain all the time.

Change of the type who to who.

(A) are always complaining

(B) complain and complain and complain.

(C) complain.

(D) complain quite a bit.

(E) complain unceasingly.

63. We buy only cherry plums since those are the kind we like best of all.

Instead of since those, use since we.

(A) are very fond of cherry plums.

(B) like cherry plums most of all.

(C) eat cherry plums frequently.

(D) like that kind best.

(E) just adore cherry plums.

64. That he felt defeated was clearly indicated by his slumping posture.

Begin with His slumping posture.

(A) clearly implied

(B) clearly inferred

(C) clearly marked

(D) implied a clear inference

(E) clearly inferred and implied

65. At this time kick your feet in the water in the way that Gregory just did.

Begin with Now.

(A) like Gregory just done.

(B) just like Gregory did.

(C) like Gregory just did.

(D) just as Gregory did.

(E) as Gregory just did.

66. Carson's sells merchandise of equal quality while having a lower price.

Change while to and.

(A) prices its merchandise lower.

(B) sells at a lower price.

(C) is having a lower price.

(D) has a lower price.

(E) its prices are lower.

67. The virtuoso is playing in Saturday's concert, so I don't want to miss his performance.

Change so to and.

(A) I don't want to miss the concert.

(B) I don't want to miss it.

(C) I don't want to miss Saturday.

(D) I don't want to take a chance to miss it.

(E) I don't want to miss his concerted performance.

68. It is more rewarding to make friends than it is being antisocial.

Begin with <u>Making friends</u>.

(A) than to be antisocial

(B) than being antisocial

(C) than to be like an antisocial person

(D) than it is to be antisocial

(E) than antisocial

69. I called you last night and I called several times.

Begin with <u>Last night</u>.

(A) I have called you several times.

(B) I kept calling you several times.

(C) I called you several times.

(D) I had called you several times

(E) several times did I call you.

70. Help was asked of Tom and me by the distraught traveler.

Begin with <u>The distraught traveler</u>.

(A) of Tom and me to help.

(B) me and Tom to help.

(C) Tom and I to help.

(D) I and Tom to help.

(E) help from Tom and me.

71. Was she really the one whom you saw last night?

Begin with <u>Was it really</u>.

(A) she which

(B) she who

(C) her who

(D) her whom

(E) she whom

72. Saying only that she was a friend of Mary's, she left without giving her name.

Change <u>Saying only</u> to <u>She said</u>.

(A) and didn't give her name.

(B) , and left without giving her name.

(C) , she left without giving her name.

(D) and left without giving her name.

(E) ; and left without giving her name.

73. Fugitive slaves in the North were counted as slaves rather than as free blacks, hence increasing the percentage of slaves in the total black population.

Begin with <u>The percentage of slaves</u>.

(A) and counted as

(B) by the counting of

(C) the count was made

(D) because the way they counted

(E) the count of

74. Jules Verne has been called the father of modern science fiction. In his tales of adventure and romance, he predicted many scientific achievements of the twentieth century.

Rewrite as one sentence beginning with <u>In his tales</u>.

(A) ; he was called

(B) which made him

(C) leading to his being called

(D) because he was called

(E) calling him

75. A federal employee must restrict the expression of his political sympathies to the voting booth.

Begin with <u>As a federal employee</u>.

(A) restrictions on

(B) and restricting

(C) restrict and

(D) have to restrict

(E) have to restricted

76. The psychologist could find no reason for the man's outrageous conduct.

Begin with <u>No reason</u>.

(A) can be found

(B) could be found

(C) is being found

(D) cannot be found

(E) can find

77. The tenant thought that the rent was too high, but he did not want to leave the apartment.

Omit <u>but he</u>.

(A) Since the
(B) Although the
(C) When thinking
(D) After concluding
(E) Having though

78. Unless we have both wage and price controls, inflation cannot be stopped.

Begin with <u>To stop inflation</u>.

(A) is a necessity
(B) there are needed
(C) there has to be
(D) must be had
(E) must have

79. Extremely low wages are paid to migrant workers, and they must live and work under substandard conditions. Cesar Chavez saw the development of strong unions as the way to improve their lot.

Write as one sentence, beginning with <u>Cesar Chavez had developed</u>.

(A) to improve the conditions
(B) along with the conditions
(C) thereby improving the conditions
(D) with improved conditions
(E) wages; in addition, the conditions

80. The often expressed wish of the negotiators was that, if the cultural exchange program were initiated, that event would begin an era of increasingly cordial relations between the two countries.

Delete <u>if</u>.

(A) program's initiation
(B) program being initiated
(C) the initiation of
(D) to be initiated
(E) by the initiation of

81. There are times when the medical profession appears to be a mystical cabal and not a scientific field.

Substitute <u>appears more</u> for <u>appears to be</u>.

(A) than a scientific field
(B) being a scientific field
(C) rather than a mystical cabal
(D) and less than scientific
(E) and being mystical as well as

82. When we lived with our parents and depended on them for all our needs, life was much simpler and our daily routine more circumscribed.

Begin with <u>Living with our parents</u>.

(A) when we depended on them
(B) and having depended on them
(C) depending on them
(D) since we depended on them
(E) having to depend on them

83. It delights my students when the principal of the school and I disagree on an issue.

Begin with <u>My students approve</u>.

(A) of the principal of the school and me disagreeing
(B) of the school principal's and my disagreeing
(C) of the school principal and I disagreeing
(D) when the principal of the school and me disagree
(E) of I and the principal of the school disagreeing

84. It was very kind of you to arrange for the meeting to be postponed, but now it will be impossible to reschedule his appearance.

Begin with <u>Although</u>.

(A) postponed. But

(B) postponed, but

(C) impossible for rescheduling

(D) postponed, now

(E) impossible to postpone

85. The agent recommended planting a stand of alfalfa to restore nitrogen to the farmer's acreage.

Begin with <u>Following the agent's recommendation</u>.

(A) planting a stand

(B) alfalfa restored

(C) acreage is planted

(D) nitrogen restored

(E) planted a stand

86. Every normal human being learns at least one language in childhood, which he continues to use throughout life.

Begin with <u>At least one language</u>.

(A) throughout life by learning

(B) throughout living and learning by

(C) throughout life had been learned of

(D) throughout life is learned

(E) throughout life is learned about

87. It was abundantly clear to Sir Winston Churchill that the long-term aims of the three principal allies were very different.

Begin with <u>The long-term aims</u>.

(A) different, it was

(B) differently so it was a fact

(C) different (a fact that was

(D) different; a fact that

(E) different and so it was

88. A pilot leaving London will arrive in New York at the hour, by the clock, at which he departed.

Start with <u>Flying from London</u>.

(A) at the hour of departure

(B) to New York, a plane landed

(C) a plane shall be arriving

(D) a pilot is arriving in New York

(E) to New York, a pilot will arrive

89. The enemy's air bombardment began and continued for five successive days.

Begin with <u>For five successive days</u>.

(A) enemy's bombarded us

(B) had been bombarded by us

(C) we were bombarded from

(D) we bombarded the enemy

(E) we had bombarded from

90. Willie Mays was a successful hitter and an extraordinary outfielder.

Begin with <u>Willie Mays was not only</u>.

(A) hitter, but fielded

(B) hitter as well as

(C) hitter, an extraordinary

(D) hitter and also

(E) hitter but also

Directions: In each of the following questions you are given four sentences and a question that asks for the best sequence to make a clear, sensible paragraph. Choose the option that reflects the best ordering of the sentences for a clear, sensible paragraph.

91. I. The state that best epitomizes this ideal and hopefully foreshadows the United States of the future is Hawaii.

II. Such a person should be told that there are many successful multi-ethnic communities in which people of diverse backgrounds and cultures live and work together in harmony.

III. Just as events in Third World nations may be distorted in the American press, so also events in the United States may be selectively reported and sensationalized in the foreign press.

IV. Hence, a foreigner with any hostility towards the United States is apt to seize upon the status of American race relations.

Which of the following presents the BEST sequence of the sentences above to make a clear, sensible paragraph?

(A) III, IV, II, I
(B) IV, II, I, III
(C) III, II, I, IV
(D) I, III, IV, II
(E) I, IV, III, II

92. I. Most of the migrants came with the intention of working for a few years and then going back to their home countries.

II. Whether called "guest worker," "migrant," "temporary labor," or "immigrant," the foreign laborer consistently appeared on the scene in the industrialized nations of Northern and Western Europe, shocking nations that had been culturally and racially homogeneous for centuries.

III. One of the greatest changes in Western Europe after World War II was the arrival of the immigrant worker.

IV. However, many of these "migrants" have ended up staying in the West, and there is not a country in Europe where they do not suffer from some degree of prejudice and discrimination.

Which of the following presents the BEST sequence of the sentences above to make a clear, sensible paragraph?

(A) III, I, II, IV
(B) III, II, I, IV
(C) II, I, IV, III
(D) II, III, I, IV
(E) I, II, IV, III

93. I. This implies a duty to accept the verdict of the courts if we challenge the law and our challenge is not vindicated.

II. To be amorally justified in such a stance, one must be prepared to submit to legal prosecution for violation of the law and accept the punishment if his attack is unsuccessful.

III. He should even demand that the law be enforced and then be willing to acquiesce in the ultimate judgment of the courts.

IV. The assumption that a law is a valid target of civil disobedience is filled with moral and legal responsibility that cannot be taken lightly.

Which of the following presents the BEST sequence of the sentences above to make a clear, sensible paragraph?

(A) II, I, III, IV
(B) III, II, I, IV
(C) III, I, IV, II
(D) IV, II, III, I
(E) IV, III, II, I

94. I. Life and its perpetuation was what the animal world seemed to be about—indeed, the only thing it seemed to be about—and until Darwin, there was no one, large, encompassing idea under which the great variety of animal life could be gathered and related.

II. Zoology then set upon a sometimes fantastic journey from the mythical, moralizing bestiaries of medieval times through the rigid classifying methods of the eighteenth century and the charm and naïveté of its popular natural history phase to the broader, sounder science of more modern times.

III. Despite these scientific ups and downs and the vagaries and trends of scientific fashion, the core phenomenon of zoology has remained constant throughout the phenomenon of life.

IV. As they did with nearly all the sciences, the Greeks set zoology off on the right road, but with their decline, the scientific pathways became overgrown and were finally lost.

Which of the following presents the BEST sequence of the sentences above to make a clear, sensible paragraph?

(A) I, II, III, IV
(B) I, II, IV, III
(C) III, I, II, IV
(D) IV, III, I, II
(E) IV, II, III, I

95.
I. The first is that, in any enforcement action, the great powers must necessarily bear the predominant burden.

II. The second is that the organization must depend for its strength upon the essential solidarity of the great powers.

III. Open as it is, on theoretical democratic grounds, to serious objection, the system of economic sanctions provided for the Covenant of the League of Nations rests on two basic assumptions.

IV. If this solidarity fails, then the security of enforcement arrangements will surely fail as well.

Which of the following presents the BEST sequence of the sentences above to make a clear, sensible paragraph?

(A) I, II, III, IV
(B) I, II, IV, III
(C) III, I, II, IV
(D) III, IV, I, II
(E) IV, I, II, III

96.
I. The former arrangement was called the contract system, while the latter came to be known as the piece–price system.

II. Prisoners were typically either leased to private companies who set up shop in the prison or used by prison officials to produce finished goods for a manufacturer who supplied the raw materials to the prison.

III. When the United States replaced corporal punishment with confinement as the primary punishment for criminals in the early nineteenth century, the private sector was the most frequent employer of convict labor.

IV. Private enterprise is no stranger to the American prison.

Which of the following presents the BEST sequence of the sentences above to make a clear, sensible paragraph?

(A) I, II, III, IV
(B) III, II, I, IV
(C) II, I, III, IV
(D) IV, II, I, III
(E) IV, III, II, I

97.
I. The Communists' preoccupation with economic growth and their whole attitude toward economic progress have been shaped by Marx's theory of long-run development of human society.

II. This theory places economic development at the center of the entire social philosophy, and it is impossible to study the Marxists' political, social, and economic views without referring to it.

III. Without the knowledge of this theory, it is difficult to understand the Communists' dogmatic belief in the superiority of their system, whatever the observable facts are, and their faith in the final victory over capitalism.

IV. Economic development has to lead, sooner or later, to socialism and communism, and it is necessary to build socialism and, later, communism to make future economic growth possible.

Which of the following presents the BEST sequence of the sentences above to make a clear, sensible paragraph?

(A) I, II, III, IV
(B) II, III, I, IV
(C) III, IV, I, II
(D) IV, III, I, II
(E) IV, III, II, I

98.
I. They had a press.

II. The founding fathers knew precisely what they were dealing with.

III. Indeed, the founding fathers were themselves often at the point end of the press sword.

IV. And the press of their time was not only guilty of bad taste and inaccuracy; it was partisan, reckless, and sometimes vicious.

Which of the following presents the BEST sequence of the sentences above to make a clear, sensible paragraph?

(A) III, IV, I, II
(B) I, III, II, IV
(C) II, I, III, IV
(D) I, II, III, IV
(E) III, I, II, IV

99.
I. Such parents may not teach their children the necessary limits to self-expression.

II. The role of a parent is not only to feed and shelter a child, but also to inculcate social and moral values, including self-discipline.

III. Some parents, whom educators refer to as parent advocates, develop a relationship with their children that resembles friendship rather than leadership.

IV. They may complain that a school dress code violates the child's rights, and if informed a child has misbehaved in school, insist that the child was merely expressing important parts of his or her personality.

Which of the following presents the BEST sequence of the sentences above to make a clear, sensible paragraph?

(A) I, II, III, IV
(B) I, IV, III, II
(C) II, I, III, IV
(D) II, III, I, IV
(E) III, I, IV, II

100.
I. Thus form and content cannot be meaningfully separated, and to paraphrase a text's meaning is to destroy the aesthetic experience.

II. Yet these elements must also be considered as parts of a whole in order to understand their relationship and the structure of the work.

III. For a formalist critic, a literary text can only be understood by considering intrinsic literary features.

IV. The first task of such a critic is to explicate elements such as the text's genre, diction, imagery, and tone.

Which of the following presents the BEST sequence of the sentences above to make a clear, sensible paragraph?

(A) IV, III, II, I
(B) I, II, III, IV
(C) III, IV, II, I
(D) III, I, IV, II
(E) IV, II, I, III

101.

I. Women were trained in "women's work"—housework or fieldwork according to the nature of the society.

II. Along with their training in defense of the community and support for their families, men were instructed in the structure of that community and were trained to sit on its councils.

III. Men were taught the history and folklore of their nations, the religious beliefs and practices, and the healing arts.

IV. From the very earliest times, boys and young men have been educated in the ways of their people.

Which of the following presents the BEST sequence of the sentences above to make a clear, sensible paragraph?

(A) I, II, III, IV

(B) II, III, IV, I

(C) III, II, IV, I

(D) IV, II, III, I

(E) IV, III, II, I

102.

I. It seems that in instances in which the predictions may have life-and-death consequences, the meteorologists serve us well; but we had best not count on the weather for our picnic tomorrow.

II. Countless lives have been saved by the weather service's timely warning of the approach of severe weather.

III. To the meteorologists' credit, scientific weather forecasting can claim many successes.

IV. If we will allow for a margin of error either in days or in miles, the range of accuracy rises dramatically.

Which of the following presents the BEST sequence of the sentences above to make a clear, sensible paragraph?

(A) II, III, I, IV

(B) I, III, II, IV

(C) III, II, IV, I

(D) IV, II, III, I

(E) IV, III, II, I

103.

I. No one questions it in calm days, because it is not needed.

II. And the reverse is true also; only when free utterance is suppressed is it needed, and when it is needed, it is most vital to justice.

III. I reply with the sad truth that only in time of stress is freedom of utterance in danger.

IV. You say that freedom of utterance is not for time of stress.

Which of the following presents the BEST sequence of the sentences above to make a clear, sensible paragraph?

(A) I, II, IV, III

(B) III, I, II, IV

(C) IV, I, II, III

(D) IV, III, I, II

(E) IV, I, III, II

104. I. The American university is a direct descendant of the ancient universities in Europe.

II. These are the oldest institutions, aside from the church itself, in Western civilization.

III. But the tradition of learning and of scholarly inquiry has lived on.

IV. They have survived many periods of trouble, of revolution, and of persecution.

Which of the following presents the BEST sequence of the sentences above to make a clear, sensible paragraph?

(A) I, II, IV, III

(B) I, IV, III, II

(C) II, I, IV, III

(D) II, IV, III, I

(E) III, II, I, IV

105. I. In most regions of the world, recorded history is short relative to the time between the largest earthquakes.

II. Historical records as such rarely constitute an adequate or, more important, reliable basis for estimating earthquake potential.

III. It may alternatively be due to the short length of available records relative to the long repeat time for large earthquakes.

IV. Thus, the fact that there have been no historic earthquakes larger than a given size does not make us confident that they will also be absent in the future.

Which of the following presents the BEST sequence of the sentences above to make a clear, sensible paragraph?

(A) I, IV, III, II

(B) II, I, III, IV

(C) II, I, IV, III

(D) I, II, III, IV

(E) I, III, IV, II

106. I. Third World development plans have been largely based on energy-intensive industries (such as steel, metals, and paper), energy-intensive agriculture (using petroleum-based fertilizers as well as harvesting combines), and increased transportation.

II. High energy prices have created many problems for the Non-Oil-Producing Less Developed Countries (NOLDCs) and, in turn, for the rest of the world.

III. As these programs are cut back, the NOLDCs have even less money from foreign exchange to pay for imported food and oil.

IV. High oil prices have caused cutbacks in these programs.

Which of the following presents the BEST sequence of the sentences above to make a clear, sensible paragraph?

(A) I, II, IV, III

(B) I, II, III, IV

(C) II, III, I, IV

(D) II, I, IV, III

(E) IV, II, I, III

107.
I. In all cases, supervisors on all levels must be alert to discover the needs of their employees for training.

II. Such conditions can be observed without any formal analysis in most cases.

III. Many conditions can signal training needs: poor work performance, poor service, low employee morale, etc.

IV. The need for training can be brought more sharply into focus, however, if time is spent on a survey of the problems.

Which of the following presents the BEST sequence of the sentences above to make a clear, sensible paragraph?

(A) I, IV, II, III

(B) II, III, IV, I

(C) III, II, IV, I

(D) IV, I, III, II

(E) III, IV, I, II

108.
I. But to reach this conclusion would change the subject from what happened during a particular era to the question of how knowledge is arrived at.

II. Both primary and secondary source accounts of the encounters between settlers and natives in seventeenth-century New England contain conflicting and sometimes even irreconcilable descriptions of events.

III. This could cause one to adopt a perspectivist point of view—all facts are only facts within the perspective from which they are discussed.

IV. The result would be to empty statements of their content, which would eliminate the possibility of writing history of the relations between settlers and natives.

Which of the following presents the BEST sequence of the sentences above to make a clear, sensible paragraph?

(A) II, III, IV, I

(B) II, I, III, IV

(C) II, IV, III, I

(D) III, IV, I, II

(E) IV, III, II, I

109. I.   As a unit, these ten amendments are referred to as the Bill of Rights.

II. Although it spelled out the law of the land, it truly did not provide sufficient protection for individuals against the power and might of the newly formed federal republic.

III. This lack of protection for individuals led to the first ten amendments to the Constitution.

IV. When the U.S. Constitution was originally written, the framers realized that the Constitution by itself left something to be desired.

Which of the following presents the BEST sequence of the sentences above to make a clear, sensible paragraph?

(A) I, III, II, IV

(B) II, IV, III, I

(C) IV, III, II, I

(D) IV, II, I, III

(E) IV, II, III, I

110. I.   It would be unthinkable today for the public to be unaware of the extent of a president's physical disability, as was the case when Franklin D. Roosevelt was president.

II. The media have also caused loss of trust by increasing coverage of corruption and scandal and by focusing on information about the personal lives of public figures.

III. In America, the increasing distrust of the government and its institutions began in the 1960s, and it has been fueled by the media's presentation of news.

IV. Vietnam was the first televised war, and the immediacy of imagery of both the war and demonstrations against it made people feel that they, rather than the government, understood the situation.

Which of the following presents the BEST sequence of the sentences above to make a clear, sensible paragraph?

(A) I, II, III, IV

(B) I, II, IV, III

(C) II, I, III, IV

(D) III, IV, II, I

(E) IV, III, II, I

ANSWER KEY AND EXPLANATIONS

Knowledge Questions

1.	B	15.	A	29.	C	43.	D	57.	C
2.	D	16.	C	30.	D	44.	C	58.	D
3.	C	17.	D	31.	A	45.	C	59.	B
4.	C	18.	A	32.	C	46.	A	60.	B
5.	B	19.	D	33.	A	47.	A	61.	B
6.	A	20.	C	34.	B	48.	C	62.	D
7.	B	21.	C	35.	B	49.	A	63.	D
8.	A	22.	A	36.	D	50.	D	64.	C
9.	D	23.	D	37.	C	51.	C	65.	D
10.	D	24.	A	38.	B	52.	C	66.	A
11.	C	25.	D	39.	C	53.	A	67.	B
12.	C	26.	D	40.	C	54.	D	68.	B
13.	B	27.	B	41.	D	55.	C	69.	C
14.	C	28.	B	42.	B	56.	B	70.	A

Maps: Israel and Its Neighbors—Questions 24 to 26

1. Lebanon
2. Golan Heights/Syria
3. Syria
4. Israel
5. West Bank/Judea and Samaria
6. Jordan
7. Dead Sea
8. Gaza Strip
9. Sinai Peninsula/Egypt
10. Suez Canal
11. Egypt
12. Saudi Arabia
13. Gulf of Aqaba

Maps: Northern Africa—Questions 56 to 58

1. Morocco
2. Algeria
3. Tunisia
4. Libya
5. Egypt
6. Western Sahara
7. Mauritania
8. Mali
9. Niger
10. Chad
11. Sudan
12. Ethiopia
13. Djibouti
14. Senegal
15. Guinea-Bissau
16. Guinea
17. Sierra Leone
18. Liberia

19. Ivory Coast

20. Birkana Faso

21. Ghana

22. Togo

23. Benin

24. Nigeria

25. Cameroon

1. **The correct answer is (B).** If property is to be acquired, it would be important to look at both the present-worth and depreciation.

2. **The correct answer is (D).** Roosevelt's "Four Freedoms" included freedom of speech, freedom of religion, freedom from want, and freedom from fear.

3. **The correct answer is (C).** A latent function is one that is present but not overtly revealed. In this instance, it would refer to how rain dances serve to solidify the group by their taking part in the religious or social ceremony.

4. **The correct answer is (C).** The Bay of Pigs invasion occurred in 1961, prior to the Cuban Missile Crisis. Castro was never removed from power, and the United States has never diplomatically recognized Castro's Cuba. The Soviet missiles were removed from Cuba, and later, the United States removed its Jupiter missiles from Turkey.

5. **The correct answer is (B).** During the Clinton Administration, defense spending decreased as a percentage of the federal budget.

6. **The correct answer is (A).** The main reason for the post–Civil War influx of immigrants was the attraction of economic opportunities in the United States. Labor-recruiting agents, steamship companies, and land-grant railroads all advertised the abundant opportunities available in the United States.

7. **The correct answer is (B).** The majority of Americans today would be at the political center. When there are only one or two relevant issues, it is easier to polarize a group. Given the large number of issues involved in American politics today, political divisions become less rigidly defined.

8. **The correct answer is (A).** In an attempt to keep America out of the Napoleonic Wars in Europe, Thomas Jefferson secured passage of the Embargo Act in 1807. He hoped that depriving England and France of American supplies would compel them to respect American shipping.

9. **The correct answer is (D).** According to Article II, Section 2.2 of the U.S. Constitution, a two-thirds vote by the Senate is required for the ratification of a treaty.

10. **The correct answer is (D).** When the League of Nations mandated the German colonies in central Africa to Great Britain and France after World War I, they were obligated to follow certain guidelines and procedures. They were not prevented from establishing military bases. Those bases would be necessary in order to insure political stability as well as to carry out their other obligations in the region.

11. **The correct answer is (C).** The short-term goal of a tariff is to assist with the development of a weak producer. It gives them the time they need to ideally develop their business well enough to be able to compete in the larger economy as a healthy producer.

12. **The correct answer is (C).** Permission is given to spend money, services are contracted for, money is set aside to make payments, payments for services rendered are submitted, and payments are made.

13. **The correct answer is (B).** Of the choices provided, the only characteristic shared by both nations is the use of the popular election for the selection of political representatives.

14. The correct answer is (C). The Alwin Nikolais Dance Company is noted for its use of abstract dances free of conventional patterns.

15. The correct answer is (A). NATO was formed out of a desire by western nations to form a measure of "collective security" against the spread of communism following the conclusion of World War II.

16. The correct answer is (C). Colin Powell was Secretary of State from 2001–2005. Henry Kissinger was Secretary of State from 1973–1977. Cyrus Vance was Secretary of State from 1977–1980. John Foster Dulles was Secretary of State from 1953–1959. Dean Rusk was Secretary of State from 1961–1969.

17. The correct answer is (D). Prior to the nineteenth century, Europeans were busy colonizing the interior of East Africa. It would not be until after the nineteenth century that they would begin to introduce European forms of political organization to the region.

18. The correct answer is (A). The "attentive public" is the part of the public that is paying attention and keeps informed as to what is going on around them. Equating this to public opinion, it would be the small percentage of Americans that is politically informed.

19. The correct answer is (D). Point 1 is NOT the maximum output at full employment. Points 2 and 3 are both at equilibrium. Production at point 4 is far below equilibrium, so substantial unemployment can be expected.

20. The correct answer is (C). While there are many theories to explain the reason for it, patterns of population change during the process of industrialization have shown that the death rate falls initially and is then followed by reductions in the birth rate.

21. The correct answer is (C). Having witnessed what happened in China as a result of imperialism, one of Japan's primary aims following the Meiji Restoration was to retain their sovereignty by resisting foreign dominance.

22. The correct answer is (A). National will is an intangible component of national/international power. Number of troops, economic productivity, growth rates, and the trade balance are all tangible factors that can be quantifiably measured.

23. The correct answer is (D). President Garfield was opposed to the idea of the spoils system. He believed appointments should be based on merit alone. Charles J. Guiteau asked Garfield for an appointment that he did not merit, so Garfield refused. Guiteau then resolved to kill him. As a result of this incident, two years later the Pendleton Civil Service Act was passed.

24. The correct answer is (A). Jerusalem is considered a holy city by Muslims, Jews, and Christians.

25. The correct answer is (D). The Dead Sea has an abundance of salt and minerals.

26. The correct answer is (D). The entire area is important to foreign policy because of its location, its natural resources, and the possibility of Russian influence. While the historical/religious significance of the area is of importance, it would not be a factor considered in determining U.S. foreign policy in the region.

27. The correct answer is (B). Jack Kerouac's *On the Road* became the bible of the Beat Movement which gained prominence in the late 1950s in the United States and Europe.

28. The correct answer is (B). Karl Marx, author of the *Communist Manifesto*, believed that all history could be defined as a class struggle over the control of the means of production. As the proletariat was further exploited by the bourgeois, they would eventually rise up and destroy the exploiters of their labor, replacing the state with a classless society. At that point, everyone would share equally in the accumulation of profit. Contrary to his teachings would be the further impoverishment of the proletariat.

29. **The correct answer is (C).** The Treaties of Rome (1957) founded the European Economic Community (EEC) and established the European Atomic Energy Community (Euratom). The six founding nations were Belgium, West Germany, France, Netherlands, Luxembourg, and Italy.

30. **The correct answer is (D).** Keynes argued that the government was responsible for maintaining high levels of employment. Consumers were not the cause of business cycle shifts; business investors and government were. This theory has been influential in justifying deficit financing.

31. **The correct answer is (A).** When the United States removed the dollar from the gold standard in 1971, the requirement of the Bretton Woods Conference that each nation must establish a par value for its currency was abandoned.

32. **The correct answer is (C).** Year 2000 estimates show that Austria has a birth rate of 9.9 and a death rate of 9.91, France has a birth rate of 12.27 and a death rate of 9.14, Great Britain has a birth rate of 11.76 and a death rate of 10.38.

33. **The correct answer is (A).** Of the choices provided, the item that represents the greatest similarity between the countries of the Middle East and those of Latin America would be the traditional lack of a middle class.

34. **The correct answer is (B).** John Dewey was a pioneer in the field of education. His theories formed the basis for the progressive education movement of the first half of the twentieth century in the United States.

35. **The correct answer is (B).** Most modern underdeveloped countries have a low savings rate due to an overall low standard of living, inequality of wealth along with a minimal or non-existent middle-class, and a need for land reform to better utilize what land is available.

36. **The correct answer is (D).** The Paris Convention of 1919 granted sovereignty to each nation for the air space above it. Given that fact, the only logical choice would be all of the countries listed.

37. **The correct answer is (C).** If the president were faced with an international crisis, he would be least likely to approach the Cabinet. The Cabinet is designed to advise the president primarily on domestic issues.

38. **The correct answer is (B).** Native Americans were unable to understand the concept of land ownership. To them, owning the land was as unthinkable as owning the wind, the rain, or the moon.

39. **The correct answer is (C).** Only in the General Assembly are all member-states represented.

40. **The correct answer is (C).** Andres Pastrana became the President of Colombia in a runoff election on June 21, 1998.

41. **The correct answer is (D).** To negotiate with a terrorist is to appease the terrorist. In doing so, you are only encouraging other terrorists to attempt the same things in the future.

42. **The correct answer is (B).** Galbraith's concept of countervailing power leads to the conclusion that competition is "doomed" in advanced industrial countries because large firms and unions will exist to offset the economic power of each. Economies of scale declining average costs with size will lead to most industries consisting of only a few firms that will be

held in check (to some degree) by strong labor unions and government policies, e.g., antitrust.

43. **The correct answer is (D).** The greatest difference would be with respect to the role of technology in the economy. This would not only include production (spinning jenny, power loom, steam engine, etc.) but also transportation (trains, steam-powered ships, etc.).

44. **The correct answer is (C).** To succeed in an in-basket test, an administrator must know when to delegate work. If they attempt to do it all themselves, they will not be able to succeed.

45. **The correct answer is (C).** Based on the in-basket test, the abilities to organize and control, manage time, and make appropriate decisions are all indications of managerial potential. There is no indication that the ability to conform to social norms is relative to managerial potential.

46. **The correct answer is (A).** With a decline in the value of the dollar against the yen, many participants in the foreign exchange market will look for a stable money or commodity. Traditionally, gold has been considered a safe asset to hold in times of uncertainty. Plus, one of the fundamental reasons why the dollar may be declining is due to higher inflation in the United States versus Japan. If the U.S. inflation is higher than the inflation rate in Japan, gold has been an asset that maintains its value during periods of inflation.

47. **The correct answer is (A).** The economic man is one who is fueled by the desire for economic advancement. He would seek to further his economic self-interest above anything else.

48. **The correct answer is (C).** The original signatories of the North American Free Trade Agreement were Mexico, Canada, and the United States.

49. **The correct answer is (A).** The Camp David Accords (1979) occurred during the Carter administration. They resulted in an agreement for mutual recognition and peace between Egypt and Israel.

50. **The correct answer is (D).** The Maastricht Treaty (1991), or Treaty of European Union, was an agreement made by a 12-member European Community to establish a political union and single market in Europe.

51. **The correct answer is (C).** In a favorable balance of trade, a nation brings in more revenue than it expends. This is accomplished by making sure that the domestic exports of merchandise exceed imports of merchandise.

52. **The correct answer is (C).** The effectiveness of nuclear deterrence is that both sides know that regardless of who initiates a first-strike, the other nation will still be able to launch a counter-strike.

53. **The correct answer is (A).** Non-hostile contacts can be defined as activities that are exempt from continued hostilities. Examples of these types of contacts would include flags of truce, armistices, and safe passage.

54. **The correct answer is (D).** Arthur Penn's *Bonnie and Clyde* deals with the actions of criminals. Jean Renoir's *The Rules of the Game* deals with relationships within French society. Man Ray's *Return to Reason* is an avant-garde film. D. W. Griffith's *The Birth of a Nation* focuses on the rise of the Ku Klux Klan and openly supports their activities.

55. **The correct answer is (C).** Nowhere in the Treaty of Rome (1957) is there any mention that colonies and associated territories of the members are to be excluded from the Common Market.

56. **The correct answer is (B).** In 1977, Anwar el-Sadat, President of Egypt, became the first Arab head of state to visit Israel. Two years later, Egypt and Israel signed a peace treaty at the Camp David Accords.

57. **The correct answer is (C).** In 1935, Italy invaded Ethiopia and occupied the country until 1941.

58. **The correct answer is (D).** Libya and Nigeria are both members of the Organization of Petroleum Exporting Countries (OPEC).

59. **The correct answer is (B).** The doctrine of purchasing-power-parity indicates that to counter inflation and achieve equilibrium of the balance of payments, you would need appreciation of the foreign exchange rate by the same percentage as the price rise.

60. **The correct answer is (B).** At dawn on November 4, 1955, Cardinal Mindszenty fled to the U.S. Embassy in Budapest, where he received asylum. He later left the embassy and Hungary under a prior agreement between the Hungarian state, the U.S. administration, and the Vatican.

61. **The correct answer is (B).** During the first decade of the twentieth century, approximately 9 million immigrants entered the United States. Politicians, hoping to cultivate the political support of these new immigrants once they became citizens, generally supported the passage of legislation that provided for extensive social services for the new immigrants. Had it not been for political rivalries, these social services might not have come about.

62. **The correct answer is (D).** It took the United States eleven years, 140 billion dollars and 346,000 American casualties before it finally realized that it had underestimated the resolve of the North Vietnamese.

63. **The correct answer is (D).** Standing Bear was the leader of the Ponca, who later went on to be a lecturer in several American cities. Red Cloud was the chief of the Ogala Sioux during the 1860s. He later became an advocate for peace and gave a number of speeches in Washington. John Logan had close relations with the white man until his family was massacred in 1774. He later wrote *Logan's Lament,* which was widely circulated among the colonies.

64. **The correct answer is (C).** In order for American Indians and Alaskan natives to qualify for Affirmative Action programs, they must maintain cultural identification through tribal affiliation or community recognition.

65. **The correct answer is (D).** The rationale is to benefit the group as well as the individual. It would not be feasible to assist every single individual. However, by assisting representative members that will remain part of the group, the group itself will benefit.

66. **The correct answer is (A).** In a free enterprise or capitalist economy, the economic decisions are made in the marketplace. By guaranteeing the protection of patents and copyrights, the Constitution insures the viability of the market economy.

67. **The correct answer is (B).** In the mid-twentieth century, the Soviet Union began to suffer economic stagnation. As a result of the budgetary pressures and economic reality, the Soviet Union proposed the idea of arms reduction to the United States in the 1980s.

68. **The correct answer is (B).** Victor Herbert's *The Red Mill* tells the story of a young girl imprisoned in a mill by her father for refusing to marry the man he has selected for her. *Stop the World I Want to Get Off* tells the story of how Littlechap achieves success in the world of business and politics after marrying the daughter of his boss.

69. **The correct answer is (C).** Given the oppressive nature of many Communist LDCs, the most likely explanation for the low infant mortality rate is that the government spends a disproportionate amount of money on health care. This not only satisfies the citizenry to a degree, but it also allows them to counter claims of denying basic human rights.

70. **The correct answer is (A).** A major challenge for administrators in large embassies is to coordinate all of the interests of the various units of government with a limited amount of resources.

answers

English Expression

1.	C	23.	B	45.	E	67.	B	89.	C
2.	B	24.	A	46.	D	68.	B	90.	E
3.	D	25.	C	47.	B	69.	C	91.	A
4.	A	26.	D	48.	E	70.	E	92.	B
5.	C	27.	C	49.	A	71.	E	93.	D
6.	A	28.	E	50.	B	72.	D	94.	E
7.	E	29.	B	51.	C	73.	B	95.	C
8.	A	30.	A	52.	A	74.	C	96.	E
9.	C	31.	B	53.	D	75.	D	97.	A
10.	E	32.	E	54.	C	76.	B	98.	C
11.	B	33.	B	55.	A	77.	B	99.	D
12.	B	34.	B	56.	D	78.	E	100.	C
13.	A	35.	B	57.	C	79.	A	101.	E
14.	B	36.	E	58.	B	80.	C	102.	C
15.	E	37.	A	59.	E	81.	A	103.	D
16.	A	38.	D	60.	C	82.	C	104.	A
17.	C	39.	D	61.	E	83.	B	105.	C
18.	E	40.	B	62.	A	84.	D	106.	D
19.	D	41.	A	63.	D	85.	E	107.	C
20.	D	42.	C	64.	A	86.	D	108.	A
21.	C	43.	C	65.	E	87.	C	109.	E
22.	C	44.	B	66.	D	88.	E	110.	D

1. **The correct answer is (C).** Before registering, the student had time to study the catalogue, choose his classes, and *decide* which section he would attend.

2. **The correct answer is (B).** When one prepares systematically and diligently for the examination, *one* can be confident of passing it.

3. **The correct answer is (D).** Jones seems slow on the track, but you will find few men quicker than *he* on the basketball court.

4. **The correct answer is (A).** We had *swum* across the lake before the sun rose.

5. **The correct answer is (C).** As Martha dived off the springboard, she was horrified to see that the water in the pool *had not been cleaned* for several weeks.

6. **The correct answer is (A).** *There* are still people who say that it has never really been proved that the Earth is round.

7. **The correct answer is (E).** This sentence is correct.

8. **The correct answer is (A).** Mary was so *uninterested* in the baseball game that she yawned unashamedly.

9. **The correct answer is (C).** For ten years, the rancher *had risen* at dawn in order to feed his cattle.

10. **The correct answer is (E).** This sentence is correct.

11. **The correct answer is (B)**. An inexperienced liar, Mary explained her absence from work with an *incredible* tale of daring in which she played the role of the heroine.

answers

12. **The correct answer is (B).** The loud noise of the cars and trucks *annoys* those who live near the road.

13. **The correct answer is (A).** *Regardless* of what people say, I must repeat that these are the facts concerning the requirements for the position.

14. **The correct answer is (B).** There is no *objection to his* joining the party if he is willing to fit in with the plans of the group.

15. **The correct answer is (E).** This sentence is correct.

16. **The correct answer is (A).** *Your* telling the truth in the face of such dire consequences required great moral courage.

17. **The correct answer is (C).** We have no idea what *is* in those abandoned storage tanks.

18. **The correct answer is (E).** This sentence is correct.

19. **The correct answer is (D).** As we waited for the light to change, we heard a loud crash that attracted her attention and *mine*.

20. **The correct answer is (D).** Placing his longbow on the grass beside him, Robin Hood, who had had an exciting day, *lay* down to rest.

21. **The correct answer is (C).** I was not at all surprised to hear of Jim *Dolan's* winning the election for town councilman.

22. **The correct answer is (C).** She saw that there was nothing else she could do; the room was clean *as* it had never been before.

23. **The correct answer is (B).** The instructor was justly annoyed by *his* walking in late and disturbing the class.

24. **The correct answer is (A).** Each of the golfers *was* scrupulously careful about proper form of his swing.

25. **The correct answer is (C).** I enjoy eating in good restaurants and *going* to the theater afterwards.

26. **The correct answer is (D).** His sworn statement, together with the testimony and statements from other witnesses, *was* made a part of the file.

27. **The correct answer is (C).** Being able to trust his sources *is* indispensable for the investigative reporter.

28. **The correct answer is (E).** This sentence is correct.

29. **The correct answer is (B).** The government, announcing a bill of rights for its citizens, *promised* them equal rights under the law and due process in the courts.

30. **The correct answer is (A).** Neither rain *nor* wind stopped her from taking her walk around the park.

31. **The correct answer is (B).** The victim's mother, *beside* herself with grief, could give no coherent account of the accident.

32. **The correct answer is (E).** This sentence is correct.

33. **The correct answer is (B).** His education had filled him with anger against those *who* he believed had hurt or humiliated him.

34. **The correct answer is (B).** I can't decide *whether* I'll go to see a film or visit the art museum on Sunday.

35. **The correct answer is (B).** When you go to the library tomorrow, please *take* this book to the librarian who sits behind the desk on the far right of the reference room.

36. **The correct answer is (E).** *Marchand's greater concern for demonstrating that racial prejudice exists than for preventing it from doing harm explains* why his work is not always highly regarded.

37. **The correct answer is (A).** Throughout this history of the American West there runs a steady commentary on the deception and mistreatment of the Indians.

38. **The correct answer is (D).** *If he had known* of the dangerous work conditions, he would not have taken the job.

39. **The correct answer is (D).** *Although the findings resulted* from extensive international cooperation, it was impossible to select fairly a single recipient for the prize.

40. **The correct answer is (B).** The fans cheered quickly, loudly, *and enthusiastically*.

41. **The correct answer is (A).** European film distributors originated the art of "dubbing"—the substitution of lip-synchronized translations in foreign languages for the original soundtrack voices.

42. **The correct answer is (C).** *We face a crisis of* growing population and diminishing food supply.

43. **The correct answer is (C).** *Contrary* to popular belief, handling frogs does not cause warts.

44. **The correct answer is (B).** The epidemic worsened because *of overcrowded and unsanitary conditions*.

45. **The correct answer is (E).** To learn the difficult and complex material *requires much concentration*.

46. **The correct answer is (D).** The parties agreed *to abide by* the arbitrator's decision.

47. **The correct answer is (B).** Honor as well as profit *is* to be gained by this work.

48. **The correct answer is (E).** He was *neither* in favor of *nor* opposed to the plan.

49. **The correct answer is (A).** I don't enjoy those kinds of films.

50. **The correct answer is (B).** The doctor was startled to learn of the *number of new cases* of the rare disease.

51. **The correct answer is (C).** The group called a rally *to demonstrate its opposition to* the proposed construction.

52. **The correct answer is (A).** By 2 o'clock, the child will have lain in his bed for ten solid hours.

53. **The correct answer is (D).** Because they were unaware of his interest in the building, they did not understand *why he felt so bad about its* being condemned.

54. **The correct answer is (C).** Support Communications Officers are assigned to overseas posts and to *Washington, D.C., often working* on rotating shifts as well as performing call-in/stand-by duties involving a variety of activities.

55. **The correct answer is (A).** A "cliometrician" is an economist or economic historian who works with mathematical statistics to solve historical problems.

56. **The correct answer is (D).** Many people voted for the governor *because* of his conservative fiscal policy.

57. **The correct answer is (C).** The director does not approve of *Richard's and my arriving* late for work.

58. **The correct answer is (B).** She is lazy *and this annoys me*.

59. **The correct answer is (E).** There is a stain on my *tie. Can you remove the stain?*

60. **The correct answer is (C).** It looks *as if the storm* will soon be upon us.

61. **The correct answer is (E).** BonTon grew slowly and steadily *because of* Miss Talbot's resistance of the temptation to expand too quickly beyond the company's financial means.

62. **The correct answer is (A).** She is one of those people *who are always complaining*.

63. **The correct answer is (D).** We buy only cherry plums since we *like that kind best*.

64. **The correct answer is (A).** His slumping posture *clearly implied* that he felt his defeat.

65. The correct answer is (E). Now kick your feet in the water *as Gregory just did.*

66. The correct answer is (D). Carson's sells merchandise of equal quality and *has a lower price.*

67. The correct answer is (B). The virtuoso is playing in Saturday's concert, *and I don't want to miss it.*

68. The correct answer is (B). Making friends is more rewarding *than being antisocial.*

69. The correct answer is (C). Last night *I called you several times.*

70. The correct answer is (E). The distraught traveler asked for *help from Tom and me.*

71. The correct answer is (E). Was it really *she whom* you saw last night?

72. The correct answer is (D). She said only that she was a friend of Mary's *and left without giving her name.*

73. The correct answer is (B). The percentage of slaves in the total black population was increased *by the counting of* fugitive slaves in the North as slaves rather than as free blacks.

74. The correct answer is (C). In his tales of adventure and romance, Jules Verne predicted many scientific achievements of the twentieth century *leading to his being called* the father of modern science fiction.

75. The correct answer is (D). As a federal employee you will *have to restrict* the expression of your political sympathies to the voting booth.

76. The correct answer is (B). No reason *could be found* by the psychologist for the man's outrageous conduct.

77. The correct answer is (B). *Although the* tenant though that the rent was too high, he did not want to leave the apartment.

78. The correct answer is (E). To stop inflation we *must have* both wage and price controls.

79. The correct answer is (A). Cesar Chavez had developed strong unions *to improve the conditions* under which migrant workers, who are currently paid extremely low wages, must live and work.

80. The correct answer is (C). The often expressed wish of the negotiators was that *the initiation of* a cultural exchange program would begin an era of increasingly cordial relations between the two countries.

81. The correct answer is (A). There are times when the medical profession appears more a mystical cabal *than a scientific field.*

82. The correct answer is (C). Living with our parents and *depending on them* for all our needs, we found life much simpler and our daily routine more circumscribed.

83. The correct answer is (B). My students approve *of the school principal's and my disagreeing* on an issue.

84. The correct answer is (D). Although it was very kind of you to arrange for the meeting to be *postponed, now* it will be impossible to reschedule his appearance.

85. The correct answer is (E). Following the agent's recommendation, the farmer *planted a stand* of alfalfa to restore nitrogen to his acreage.

86. The correct answer is (D). At least one language which is used *throughout life is learned* in childhood by every normal human being.

87. The correct answer is (C). The long-term aims of the three principal allies were very *different (a fact that was* abundantly clear to Sir Winston Churchill).

88. The correct answer is (E). Flying from London *to New York, a pilot will arrive* at the hour, by the clock, at which he departed.

89. **The correct answer is (C).** For five successive days *we were bombarded from* the air by the enemy.

90. **The correct answer is (E).** Willie Mays was not only a successful *hitter but also* an extraordinary outfielder.

91. **The correct answer is (A).**

92. **The correct answer is (B).**

93. **The correct answer is (D).**

94. **The correct answer is (E).**

95. **The correct answer is (C).**

96. **The correct answer is (E).**

97. **The correct answer is (A).**

98. **The correct answer is (C).**

99. **The correct answer is (D).**

100. **The correct answer is (C).**

101. **The correct answer is (E).**

102. **The correct answer is (C).**

103. **The correct answer is (D)**

104. **The correct answer is (A).**

105. **The correct answer is (C).**

106. **The correct answer is (D)**

107. **The correct answer is (C).**

108. **The correct answer is (A).**

109. **The correct answer is (E).**

110. **The correct answer is (D).**

PART III

APPENDICES

The Essentials of English Grammar

Success in the Foreign Service requires a strong command of the English language. One must be able to speak intelligently and write clearly and concisely. Since a large part of one's success in this area hinges on these skills, this section will give you an overview of some of the more important aspects of English grammar.

PARTS OF SPEECH

Nouns

A noun is the name of a person, a place, a thing, or an idea.

Examples: teacher, city, desk, democracy

There are different kinds of nouns:

- *Common nouns* are general: house, girl, street, city
- *Proper nouns* are specific: White House, Jane, Main Street, New York
- *Collective nouns* name groups: team, crowd, organization, Congress

Nouns have cases:

- *Nominative:* the subject, noun of address, or predicate noun
- *Objective:* the direct object, indirect object, or object of the preposition
- *Possessive:* the form that shows possession

Pronouns

Pronouns can substitute for nouns.

Examples: he, they, ours, those

The noun or noun phrase to which a pronoun refers is the **antecedent**. Every pronoun must have a clear antecedent to give it meaning. A pronoun must agree with its antecedent in gender, person, and number.

Example: *Each* of the boys has *his* lunch.

Each is singular and therefore requires a singular pronoun.

There are several kinds of pronouns.

- *Personal pronoun:*

	Nominative Case	Objective Case	Possessive Case
Singular			
First person	I	me	mine
Second person	you	you	yours
Third person	he, she, it	him, her, it	his, hers
Plural			
First person	we	us	ours
Second person	you	you	your
Third person	they	them	theirs

- *Demonstrative pronoun:* this, that, these, those
- *Indefinite pronoun:* all, any, anybody
- *Interrogative pronoun:* who, which, what

Adjectives

An adjective describes or modifies a noun.

Examples: warm, quick, tall, blue

Adjectives answer the following questions about nouns:

- Which one? I'll take the *red* scarf.
- What kind? A *wool* scarf keeps me warm.
- How many? There are *two* keys on the counter.
- Whose? The *students'* lounge is on the second floor.

Adverbs

An adverb modifies a verb, an adjective, or another adverb.

Examples: fast, slowly, friendly, well

An adverb will answer the following questions about verbs, adjectives, or other adverbs:

- Where? The dog ran *away*.
- When? I woke *early* this morning.
- How? I slept *soundly* last night.
- To what extent? She was *absolutely* certain about the answer.

Verbs

Verbs show action or state of being.

> *Examples:* hit, run, study (action verbs)
>
> be, seem, become (state of being verbs)

A verb changes time by the addition of certain endings and helping verbs.

> *Examples:* I *walk* to school. (present tense)
>
> I *walked* to school yesterday. (past tense)
>
> I *will walk* to school tomorrow. (future tense)
>
> I *have walked* to school every morning this week. (present perfect tense)
>
> I *had walked* halfway to school when the bus arrived. (past perfect tense)
>
> I *will have walked* six blocks before I pass your house. (future perfect tense)

SELECTED RULES OF GRAMMAR

1. The subject of a verb is in the nominative case even if the verb is understood and not expressed.

   Example: They are as old as we. (As we are)

2. The word *who* is in the nominative case.

   Example: The trapeze artist who ran away with the clown broke the lion tamer's heart. (*Who* is the subject of the verb *ran*.)

   Whom is in the objective case.

   Example: The trapeze artist whom he loved ran away with the circus clown. (*Whom* is the object of the verb *loved*.)

3. The word *whoever* is in the nominative case.

   Examples: Whoever comes to the door is welcome to join in the party. (*Whoever* is the subject of the verb *comes*.)

   The process server may leave the summons with whoever answers the doorbell. (*Whoever* is the subject of the verb *answers*. The entire clause is the object of the preposition *with*.)

   Whomever is in the objective case.

   Examples: Invite whomever you wish to accompany you. (*Whomever* is the object of the verb *invite*.)

   Whomever the citizens wish to have govern them, they must first elect. (The order of the sentence is inverted, but *whomever* is the object of the verb *wish*.)

4. Nouns or pronouns connected by a form of the verb *to be* should always be in the nominative case.

    Examples: It is I. (Not me)

    The old man's sight had failed so badly that he thought his son to be *me*. (The infinitive *to be* is serving a linking function. Since *his son* is the object of *thought*, the pronoun linked by the infinitive *to be* must be in the objective case. You may test this type of sentence by reversing the order of noun and pronoun. Thus: The old man's sight had failed so badly that he thought me to be his son.)

5. The object of a preposition or of a transitive verb should use a pronoun in the objective case.

    Examples: It would be impossible for me to do that job alone. (*Me* is the object of the preposition *for*.)

    The attendant gave *me* the keys to the locker. (*Me* is the indirect object of the verb *gave*.)

    NOTE: When the first person pronoun is used in conjunction with one or more proper names, you may confirm the choice of I or me by eliminating the proper names and reading the sentence with the pronoun alone.

    Examples: John, George, Marylou, and (me or I) went to the movies last night. (By eliminating the names you can readily choose that *I went to the movies* is correct.)

    It would be very difficult for Mae and (I or me) to attend the wedding. (Without *Mae* it is clear that it is *difficult for me* to attend.)

6. *Each, either, neither, anyone, anybody, somebody, someone, every, everyone, one, no one,* and *nobody* are singular pronouns. Each of these words takes a singular verb and a singular pronoun.

    Examples: *Neither likes* the pets of the other.

    Everyone must wait *his* turn.

    Each of the patients *carries* insurance.

    Neither of the women *has* completed *her* assignment.

7. When the correlative conjunctions *either/or* and *neither/nor* are used, the number of the verb agrees with the number of the last subject.

    Examples: Neither John nor *Greg eats* meat.

    Either the cat or the *mice take* charge in the barn.

8. A subject consisting of two or more nouns joined by a coordinating conjunction takes a plural verb.

    Example: Paul *and* Sue *were* the last to arrive.

9. The number of the verb is not affected by the addition to the subject of words introduced by *with, together with, no less than, as well as*, etc.

   Example: The *captain*, together with the rest of the team, *was delighted* by the victory celebration.

10. A verb agrees in number with its subject. A verb should not be made to agree with a noun that is part of a phrase following the subject.

    Examples: *Mount Snow*, one of my favorite ski areas, *is* in Vermont.

    The *mountains* of Colorado, like those of Switzerland, *offer* excellent skiing.

11. A verb should agree in number with the subject, not with the predicate noun or pronoun.

    Examples: Poor study *habits are* the leading cause of unsatisfactory achievement in school.

    The leading *cause* of unsatisfactory achievement in school *is* poor study habits.

12. A pronoun agrees with its antecedent in person, number, and gender.

    Example: Since you were absent on Tuesday, you will have to ask Mary or Beth for her notes on the lecture. (Use *her*, not their, because two singular antecedents joined by *or* take a singular pronoun.)

13. *Hardly, scarcely, barely, only,* and *but* (when it means *only*) are negative words. Do NOT use another negative in conjunction with any of these words.

    Examples: **Wrong:**   He *didn't have but* one hat.
    Correct: He had *but* one hat. OR He had *only* one hat.

    Wrong: I *can't hardly* read the small print.
    Correct: I *can hardly* read the small print. OR I *can't* read the small print.

14. *As* is a conjunction introducing a subordinate clause, while *like* is a preposition. The object of a preposition is a noun or phrase.

    Examples: The day was crisp and clear *as* October days often are. (*Days* is the subject of the clause; *are* is its verb.)

    He behaves *like* a fool.

    The gambler accepts only hard currency *like* gold coins.

15. When modifying the words *kind* and *sort*, the words *this* and *that* always remain in the singular.

    Examples: *This kind* of apple makes the best pie.

    That sort of behavior will result in severe punishment.

16. In sentences beginning with *there is* and *there are*, the verb should agree in number with the noun that follows it.

    Examples: There isn't an unbroken bone in her body. (The singular subject *bone* takes the singular verb *is*.)

    There are many choices to be made. (The plural subject *choices* takes the plural verb *are*.)

17. A noun or pronoun modifying a gerund should be in the possessive case.

    Example: Is there any criticism of Arthur's going? (*Going* is a gerund. It must be modified by Arthur's, not Arthur.)

18. Do NOT use the possessive case when referring to an inanimate object.

    Example: **Wrong:** He had difficulty with the *store's* management.

    Correct: He had difficulty with the management of the store.

19. When expressing a condition contrary to fact or a wish, use the subjunctive form *were*.

    Example: I wish I *were* a movie star.

20. Statements equally true in the past and in the present are usually expressed in the present tense. The contents of a book are also expressed in the present tense.

    Examples: He said that Venus is a planet. (Even though he made the statement in the past, the fact remains that Venus *is* a planet.)

    In the book *Peter Pan*, Wendy says, "I can fly." (Every time one reads the book, Wendy *says* it again.)

ANTECEDENTS AND MODIFIERS

1. *It*, when used as a relative pronoun, refers to the nearest noun. In your writing, you must be certain that the grammatical antecedent is indeed the intended antecedent.

    Example: Since the mouth of the cave was masked by underbrush, *it* provided an excellent hiding place. (Do you really mean that the underbrush is an excellent hiding place, or do you mean the cave?)

2. *Which* is another pronoun that is subject to errors of reference. In fact, whenever using pronouns, you must ask yourself whether or not the reference of the pronoun is clear.

    Examples: The first chapter awakens your interest in cloning, which continues to the end of the book. (What continues, cloning or your interest?)

    Jim told Bill that he was about to be fired. (Who is about to be fired? This sentence can be interpreted to mean that Jim was informing Bill about Bill's impending termination or about Jim's own troubles.)

In your writing, you may find that the most effective way to clear up an ambiguity is to recast the sentence.

Examples: The first chapter awakens your interest in cloning. The following chapters build upon this interest and maintain it throughout the book.

Jim told Bill, "I am about to be fired." OR Jim told Bill, "You are about to be fired."

3. Adjectives modify only nouns and pronouns. Adverbs modify verbs, adjectives, and other adverbs.

Examples: **Wrong:** One can swim in a lake as *easy* as in a pool.

Correct: One can swim in a lake as *easily* as in a pool. (The adverb *easily* must modify the verb *can swim.*)

Wrong: I was *real* happy.

Correct: I was *really* happy. (The adverb *really* must be used to modify the adjective *happy.*)

Sometimes context determines the use of adjective or adverb.

Example: The old man looked angry. (*Angry* is an adjective describing the old man [angry old man].)

The old man looked *angrily* out the window. (*Angrily* is an adverb describing the man's manner of looking out the window.)

4. Phrases should be placed near the words they modify.

Example: **Wrong:** The author says that he intends to influence your life *in the first chapter*.

Correct: The author *in the first chapter* says . . . OR *In the first chapter*, the author says . . .

5. Adverbs should be placed near the words they modify.

Example: **Wrong:** The man was *only* willing to sell one horse.

Correct: The man was willing to sell *only* one horse.

6. Clauses should be placed near the words they modify.

Example: **Wrong:** He will reap a good harvest *who sows early*.

Correct: *He who sows early* will reap a good harvest.

7. A modifier must modify something.

Example: **Wrong:** Having forgotten to wind it, the clock stopped at midnight.

Correct: Having forgotten to wind the clock, I found that it had stopped at midnight. (*Having forgotten to wind the clock* modifies *I.*)

Examples: **Wrong:**   While on vacation, the pipes burst. (The pipes were not away on vacation.)

   Correct: While we were away on vacation, the pipes burst.

   Wrong: To run efficiently, the serviceman should oil the lawnmower.

   Correct: The serviceman should oil the lawnmower to make it run efficiently.

NOTE: The best test for the placement of modifiers is to read the sentence literally. If you read a sentence literally and it is literally ridiculous, it is wrong. The meaning of a sentence must be clear to any reader. The words of the sentence must make sense.

CHOOSING THE RIGHT WORD

The term *diction* includes the use of the correct word and the avoidance of excess wordiness. The list that follows presents many of the most commonly misused or confused words in the English language. Read through the list now and put a check next to those words that have given you trouble in the past. You may even recognize some words you have been misusing for years without knowing they were troublesome. Skim lightly over the words you have under control; memorize uses of the others. If you have time, try using each word in a sentence of your own.

accede means *to agree with.*
concede means *to yield,* but not necessarily in agreement.
exceed means *to be more than.*

   We shall *accede* to your request for more evidence.
   To avoid delay, we shall *concede* that more evidence is necessary.
   Federal expenditures now *exceed* federal income.

access means *availability.*
excess means *too much.*

   The lawyer was given *access* to the grand jury records.
   The expenditures this month are far in *excess* of income.

accept means *to take when offered.*
except means *excluding.* (preposition)
except means *to leave out.* (verb)

   The draft board will *accept* all seniors as volunteers before graduation.
   All eighteen-year-olds *except* seniors will be called.
   The draft board will *except* all seniors until after graduation.

adapt means *to adjust to change*.
adopt means *to take as one's own*.
adept means *skillful*.

> Children can *adapt* to changing conditions very easily.
> The war orphan was *adopted* by the general and his wife.
> Proper instruction makes children *adept* in various games.

NOTE: adapt *to*, adopt *by*, adept *in* or *at*.

adapted to implies *original or natural suitability*.
adapted for implies *created suitability*.
adapted from implies *changes to be made suitable*.

> The gills of fish are *adapted to* underwater breathing.
> Atomic energy is constantly being *adapted for* new uses.
> Many of Richard Wagner's opera librettos were *adapted from* old Norse sagas.

addition means *the act or process of adding*.
edition means *a printing of a publication*.

> In *addition* to a dictionary, he always used a thesaurus.
> The first *edition* of Shakespeare's plays appeared in 1623.

advantage means *a superior position*.
benefit means *a favor conferred or earned (as a profit)*.

> He had an *advantage* in experience over his opponent.
> The rules were changed for his *benefit*.

NOTE: to *take* advantage *of*, to *have* an advantage *over*.

adverse (pronounced AD-verse) means *unfavorable*.
averse (pronounced a-VERSE) means *disliking*.

> He took the *adverse* decision in poor taste.
> Many students were *averse* to criticism by their classmates.

advise means *to give advice. Advise* is losing favor as a synonym for *notify*.

> *Acceptable*: The teacher will *advise* the student in habits of study.
> *Unacceptable*: We are *advising* you of a delivery under separate cover. (Use *notifying*)

affect means *to influence*. (verb)
effect means *an influence*. (noun)
effect means *to bring about*. (verb)

> Your education will *affect* your future.
> The *effect* of the last war is still being felt.
> A diploma *effected* a tremendous change in his attitude.

NOTE: *Affect* also has the meaning of *pretend*. She had an *affected* manner.

after is unnecessary with the past participle.

> **Wrong:** *After having checked* (omit *after*) the timetable, I left for the station.
> **Correct:** *After* checking the timetable, I left for the station.

Ain't is an unacceptable contraction for *am not, are not,* or *is not.*

aisle is *a passageway between seats.*
isle is *a small island.*

all ready means *completely ready* or *everyone ready.*
already means *prior to some specific time.*

> By the time I was *all ready* to go to the play, the tickets were *already* all sold.
> They were *all ready* to begin when the teacher arrived.

alright is unacceptable. It should always be written as two words: *all right.*

all together means *in sum, collectively,* or *everybody together.*
altogether means *completely.*

> There are *altogether* too many people to seat in this room when we are *all together.*

all ways means *in every possible way.*
always means *at all times.*

> He was in *all ways* acceptable to the voters.
> His reputation has *always* been spotless.

allude means *to make a reference to.*
elude means *to escape from.*

> Only incidentally does Coleridge *allude* to Shakespeare's puns.
> It is almost impossible for one to *elude* tax collectors.

allusion means *a reference.*
illusion means *a deception of the eye or mind.*

> The student made *allusions* to his teacher's habits.
> *Illusions* of the mind, unlike those of the eye, cannot be corrected with glasses.

alongside of means *side by side with.*
alongside means *parallel to the side.*

> Bill stood *alongside of* Henry.
> Park the car *alongside* the curb.

alot is unacceptable. It should always be written as two words: *a lot.*

among always implies that there are *more than two people or things*.
between is used when there are *only two people or things*.

> The knowledge is secure *among* the members of our club.
> Let us keep this secret *between* you and me.

NOTE: *Between* may be used with more than two objects to show the relationship of each object to the others.

> The teacher explained the difference *between* adjective, adverb, and noun clauses.

amount, **much, less** apply to quantities of objects that *cannot be counted one by one*.
number, **many, fewer** apply to quantities that *can be counted one by one*.

> *Many* raindrops make *much* water.
> If you have *fewer* dollars, you have *less* money.
> The *amount* of property you own depends on the *number* of acres in your lot.

annual means *yearly*.
biannual means *twice a year*. (*Semiannual* means the same thing.)
biennial means *once in two years or every two years*.

anywheres is unacceptable.
anywhere is acceptable.

> We can't find it *anywhere*.

NOTE: *nowhere* (NOT nowheres), *somewhere* (NOT somewheres)

Aren't I is colloquial. Its use is discouraged.

> *Am I not* entitled to an explanation?

as (used as a conjunction) is followed by a verb.
like (used as a preposition) is NOT followed by a verb.

> Do *as* I do, not *as* I say.
> Try not to behave *like* a child.
> **Wrong:** He acts *like* I do.

as far as expresses *distance*.
so far as indicates *a limitation*.

> We hiked *as far as* the next guest house.
> *So far as* we know, the barn was adequate for a night's stay.

as good as should be used *for comparisons only*.

> This motel is *as good as* the next one.

NOTE: *As good as* does NOT mean *practically*.

> **Wrong:** They *as good as* promised us a place in the hall.
> **Correct:** They *practically* promised us a place in the hall.

as if is correctly used in:

> **Correct:** He talked *as if* his jaw hurt him.
> **Wrong:** He talked *like* his jaw hurt him.

ascared does not exist

> The child was *scared* of ghosts.

ascent is *the act of rising*.
assent means *approval*.

> The *ascent* to the top of the mountain was perilous.
> Congress gave its *assent* to the president's emergency directive.

assay means *to try or experiment*. (verb)
essay means an *intellectual effort*. (noun)

> We shall *assay* the ascent of the mountain tomorrow.
> The candidate's views were expressed in a well-written *essay*.

attend to means *to take care of*.
tend to means *to be inclined to*.

> One of the clerks will *attend to* the mail in my absence.
> Lazy people *tend to* gain weight.

back should NOT be used with such words as *refer* and *return* since the prefix *re-* means *back*.

> **Wrong:** Refer *back* to the text, if you have difficulty recalling the facts.

backward, backwards are acceptable and may be used interchangeably as an adverb.

> We tried to run *backward*. (or *backwards*)

berth is a *resting place*.
birth means *the beginning of life*.

> The new liner was given a wide *berth* in the harbor.
> He was a fortunate man from *birth*.

beside is a preposition meaning *by the side of*.
besides is an adverb meaning *in addition to*.

> He sat *beside* his sick father.
> *Besides* his father, his mother also was not well.

better means *recovering*.
well means *completely recovered*.

> He is *better* now than he was a week ago.
> In a few more weeks, he will be *well*.

both means *two considered together*.
each means *one or two or more*.

> *Both* of the applicants qualified for the position.
> *Each* applicant was given a generous reference.

NOTE: Avoid using such expressions as the following:

> *Both* girls had a new typewriter. (Use *each girl* instead.)
> *Both* girls tried to outdo the other. (Use *each girl* instead.)
> They are *both* alike (Omit *both*.)

breath means *an intake of air*.
breathe means *to draw air in and give it out*.
breadth means *width* or *scope*.

> Before you dive in, take a very deep *breath*.
> It is difficult to *breathe* under water.
> We are impressed by the *breadth* of his knowledge

bring means *to carry toward the person who is speaking*.
take means *to carry away from the speaker*.

> *Bring* the books here.
> *Take* your raincoat with you when you go out.

broke is the past tense of *break*.
broke is unacceptable for *without money*.

> He *broke* his arm.

bunch refers to *things*.
group refers to *persons or things*.

> This looks like a delicious *bunch* of bananas.
> What a well-behaved *group* of children!

NOTE: The colloquial use of bunch applied to *persons* is discouraged.

> A *bunch* of the boys were whooping it up. (*Number* is preferable.)

certainly (and *surely*) is an *adverb*.
sure is an *adjective*.

> **Wrong:** He *sure* was learning fast.
> **Correct:** He was *certainly* learning fast.

cite means *to quote*.
sight means *seeing*.
site means *a place for a building*.

> He often *cited* from the Scriptures.
> The *sight* of the wreck was appalling.
> The Board of Education was seeking a *site* for the new school.

coarse means *vulgar* or *harsh*.
course means a *path* or a *study*.

> He was shunned because of his *coarse* behavior.
> The ship took its usual *course*.
> Which English *course* are you taking?

come to be should NOT be replaced with the expression *become to be*, since *become* means *come to be*.

> True freedom will *come to be* when all tyrants have been overthrown.

comic means *intentionally funny*.
comical means *unintentionally funny*.

> A clown is a *comic* figure.
> The peculiar hat she wore gave her a *comical* appearance.

conscience means *sense of right*.
conscientious means *faithful*.
conscious means *aware of oneself*.

> A person's *conscience* prevents her from becoming completely selfish.
> We all depend on him because he is *conscientious*.
> The injured man was completely *conscious*.

considerable is properly used only as an adjective, NOT as a noun.

cease means *to end*.
seize means *to take hold of*.

> Will you please *cease* making those sounds?
> *Seize* him by the collar as he comes around the corner.

cent means *a coin*.
scent means *an odor*.
sent is the past tense of *send*.

> The one-*cent* postal card is a thing of the past.
> The *scent* of roses is pleasing.
> We were *sent* to the rear of the balcony.

calendar is *a system of time*.
colander is *a kind of sieve*.

> In this part of the world, most people prefer the twelve-month *calendar*.
> Fresh vegetables should be washed in a *colander* before cooking.

can means *physically able*.
may implies *permission*.

> I *can* lift this chair over my head.
> You *may* leave after you finish your work.

cannot help must be followed by a gerund.

> We cannot help *feeling* (NOT feel) distressed about this.

capital is *the city*.
capitol is *the building*.

> Paris is the *capital* of France.
> The *Capitol* in Washington is occupied by the Congress. (The Washington *Capitol* is always capitalized.)

NOTE: *Capital* also means wealth.

compare to means *to liken to something that has a different form*.
compare with means *to compare persons or things with each other when they are of the same kind*.
contrast with means *to show the difference between two things*.

> A minister is sometimes *compared to* a shepherd.
> Shakespeare's plays are often *compared with* those of Marlowe.
> The writer *contrasted* the sensitivity of the dancer *with* the grossness of the pugilist.

complement means *a completing part*.
compliment is *an expression of admiration*.

> His wit was a *complement* to her beauty.
> He *complimented* her attractive hairstyle.

consul means *a government representative*.
council means *an assembly that meets for deliberation*.
counsel means *advice*.

> Americans abroad should keep in touch with their *consuls*.
> The City *Council* enacts local laws and regulations.
> The defendant heeded the *counsel* of his friends.

convenient to should be followed by a *person*.
convenient for should be followed by a *purpose*.

> Will these plans be *convenient to* you?
> You must agree that they are *convenient for* the occasion.

copy is *an imitation of an original work*. (not necessarily an exact imitation)
facsimile is *an exact imitation of an original work*.

> The counterfeiters made a crude *copy* of the hundred-dollar bill.
> The official government engraver, however, prepared a *facsimile* of the bill.

could of is unacceptable. (*Should of* is also unacceptable.)
could have is *acceptable*. (*Should have* is also acceptable.)

> **Wrong:** You *could of* won the race.
> **Correct:** You *could have* done better with more care.

NOTE: Also avoid *must of, would of*.

decent means *suitable.*
descent means *going down.*
dissent means *disagreement.*

> The *decent* thing to do is to admit your fault.
> The *descent* into the cave was treacherous.
> Two of the nine justices filed a *dissenting* opinion.

deduction means *reasoning from the general (laws or principles) to the particular (facts).*
induction means *reasoning from the particular (facts) to the general (laws or principles).*

> All men are mortal. Since John is a man, he is mortal. (*deduction*)
> There are 10,000 oranges in this truckload. I have examined 100 from various parts of the load and find that they are all of the same quality. I conclude that the 10,000 oranges are of this quality. (*induction*)

delusion means *a wrong idea that will probably influence action.*
illusion means *a wrong idea that will probably not influence action.*

> People were under the *delusion* that the earth was flat.
> It is just an *illusion* that the earth is flat.

desert (pronounced DEZZ-ert) means *an arid area.*
desert (pronounced di-ZERT) means *to abandon*; also *a reward or punishment.*
dessert (pronounced di-ZERT) means the *final course of a meal.*

> The Sahara is the world's most famous *desert.*
> A parent must not *desert* a child.
> Execution was a just *desert* for his crime.
> We had plum pudding for *dessert.*

different from is acceptable.
different than is unacceptable.

> Florida's climate is *different from* New York's climate.

doubt that is acceptable.
doubt whether is unacceptable.

> **Wrong:** We *doubt whether* you will succeed.
> **Correct:** I *doubt that* you will pass this term.

dual means *relating to two.*
duel means *a contest between two persons.*

> Dr. Jekyl had a *dual* personality.
> Alexander Hamilton was fatally injured in a *duel* with Aaron Burr.

due to is unacceptable at the beginning of a sentence. Use *because of*, *on account of*, or some similar expression.

> **Wrong:** *Due to* rain, the game was postponed.
> **Correct:** *Because of* the rain, the game was postponed.
> **Correct:** The postponement was *due to* the rain.

each other refers to *two persons*.
one another refers to *more than two persons*.

> The two girls have known *each other* for many years.
> Several of the girls have known *one another* for many years.

either . . . or is used when referring to choices.
neither . . . nor is the *negative form*.

> *Either* you *or* I will win the election.
> *Neither* Bill *nor* Henry is expected to have a chance.

eliminate means *to get rid of*.
illuminate means *to supply with light*.

> Let us try to *eliminate* the unnecessary steps.
> Several lamps were needed to *illuminate* the corridor.

emerge means *to rise out of*.
immerge means *to sink onto* (also **immerse**).

> The swimmer *emerged* from the pool.
> The painter *immerged* his brushes in a jar of turpentine.

emigrate means *to leave one's country for another*.
immigrate means *to enter another country*.

> Many Norwegians *emigrated* from their homeland to America in the mid-1860s.
> Government restrictions make it more difficult for foreigners to *immigrate* to this country.

everyone is written as one word when it is a *pronoun*.
every one (two words) is used when each individual is stressed.

> *Everyone* present voted for the proposal.
> *Every one* of the voters accepted the proposal.

NOTE: *Everybody* is always written as one word.

everywheres is unacceptable.
everywhere is acceptable.

> We searched *everywhere* for the missing book.

NOTE: *Everyplace* (one word) is unacceptable.

feel bad means *to feel ill.*
feel badly means *to have a poor sense of touch.*

> I *feel bad* about the accident I saw.
> The numbness in his limbs caused him to *feel badly.*

feel good means *to be happy.*
feel well means *to be in good health.*

> I *feel* very *good* about my recent promotion.
> Spring weather always made him *feel well.*

flout means *to insult.*
flaunt means *to make a display of.*

> He *flouted* the authority of the principal.
> Hester Prynne *flaunted* her scarlet "A."

formally means *in a formal way.*
formerly means *at an earlier time.*

> The letter of reference was *formally* written.
> He was *formerly* a delegate to the convention.

former means *the first of two.*
latter means *the second of two.*

> The *former* half of the book was in prose.
> The *latter* half of the book was in poetry.

forth means *forward.*
fourth comes *after third.*

> They went *forth* like warriors of old.
> The *Fourth* of July is our Independence Day.

get is a verb that strictly means *to obtain.*

> Please *get* my bag.

NOTE: There are many slang forms of *get* that should be avoided.

> **Wrong:** Do you *get* me?
> **Correct:** Do you *understand* me?
> **Wrong:** You can't *get* away with it.
> **Correct:** You won't *avoid* punishment if you do it.
> **Wrong:** *Get* wise to yourself.
> **Correct:** *Use* common sense.
> **Wrong:** We didn't *get* to go.
> **Correct:** We didn't *manage* to go.

got means *obtained*.

> **Correct:** He *got* the tickets yesterday.
> **Wrong:** You've *got* to do it.
> **Correct:** You *have* to do it.
> **Wrong:** We *have got* no sympathy for them.
> **Correct:** We *have* no sympathy for them.
> **Wrong:** They have *got* a great deal of property.
> **Correct:** They *have* a great deal of property.

hanged is used in reference to a *person*.
hung is used in reference to a *thing*.

> The prisoner was *hanged* at dawn.
> The picture was *hung* above the fireplace.

however means *nevertheless*.
how ever means *in what possible way*.

> We are certain, *however*, that you will like this class.
> We are certain, *how ever* you decide to study, you will succeed.

if introduces a *condition*.
whether introduces a *choice*.

> I shall go to Europe *if* I win the prize.
> He asked me *whether* I intended to go to Europe. (not *if*)

if it was implies that *something might have been true in the past*.
if it were implies *doubt*, or indicates *something that is contrary to fact*.

> *If your book was* there last night, it is there now.
> *If it were* summer now, we would all go swimming.

in usually refers to *a state of being*. (no motion)
into is used for *motion from one place to another*.

> The records are *in* that drawer.
> I put the records *into* that drawer.

NOTE: "We were walking in the room" is correct even though there is motion because the motion is *not* from one place to another.

irregardless is unacceptable.
regardless is acceptable.

> **Wrong:** *Irregardless* of the weather, I am going to the game.
> **Correct:** *Regardless* of his ability, he is not likely to win.

its is the possessive of *it*.
it's is the contraction for *it is*.

> *It's* I who put *its* stamp on the letter.
> The house lost *its* roof; *it's* an exposed house now.

kind of, sort of are unacceptable alternatives for *rather*.

> We are *rather* disappointed in you.

last refers to *the final member in a series*.
latest refers to *the most recent in time*.
latter refers to the *second of two*.

> This is the *last* bulletin. There won't be any other bulletins.
> This is the *latest* bulletin. There will be other bulletins.
> Of the two most recent bulletins, the *latter* is more encouraging.

lay means *to place*.
lie means *to recline*.

> You may *lay* the books upon the table.
> Let sleeping dogs *lie*.

NOTE: The verb *to lay*, except when referring to hens, may be used ONLY if you could replace it with the verb *to put*. At all other times use a form of the verb *to lie*.

Note the forms of each verb:

Tense	Lie (Recline)
Present	I *lie* on the grass.
Past	I *lay* on the grass.
Pres. Perf.	I *have lain* on the grass.

Tense	Lay (Place)
Present	I *lay* the book on the desk.
Past	I *laid* the book on the desk.
Pres. Perf.	I *have laid* the book on the desk.

learn means *to acquire knowledge*.
teach means *to impart knowledge*.

> My mother *taught me* all that I know.

lightening is the present participle of *to lighten*.
lightning means *the flashes of light accompanied by thunder*.

> Leaving the extra food behind resulted in *lightening* the pack.
> Summer thunderstorms produce startling *lightning* strikes.

may is used in the *present tense*.
might is used in the *past tense*.

> We are hoping that he *may* come today.
> He *might* have done it if you had encouraged him.

it's I is always acceptable.
it's me is acceptable only in colloquial speech or writing.
it's him is always unacceptable.
it's he is always acceptable.

Noplace is unacceptable for *no place* or *nowhere*.

> You now have *nowhere* to go.

number is singular *when the total is intended*.

> The *number* (of pages in the book) is 500.

number is plural *when the individual units are referred to*.

> A *number of pages* (in the book) were printed in italic type.

of any (and *of anyone*) is unacceptable for *of all*.

> His was the highest mark *of all*.

off of is unacceptable.

> He took the book *off* the table.

out loud is unacceptable for *aloud*.

> He read *aloud* to his family every evening.

outdoor (and *out-of-door*) is an adjective.
outdoors (and *out-of-doors*) is an adverb.

> We spent most of the summer at an *outdoor* music camp.
> Most of the time we played string quartets *outdoors*.

people comprise *a united or collective group of individuals*.
persons are *individuals that are separated and unrelated*.

> The *people* of New York City have enthusiastically accepted "Shakespeare-in-the-Park" productions.
> Only five *persons* remained in the theater after the first act.

persecute means *to make life miserable for someone*. (Persecution is illegal.)
prosecute means *to conduct a criminal investigation*. (Prosecution is legal.)

> Some racial groups insist upon *persecuting* other groups.
> The District Attorney is *prosecuting* the racketeers.

precede means *to come before*.
proceed means *to go ahead*. (*Procedure* is the noun.)
supersede means *to replace*.

> What were the circumstances that *preceded* the attack?
> We can then *proceed* with our plan for resisting a second attack.
> It is then possible that Plan B will *supersede* Plan A.

principal means *chief* or *main* (as an adjective); *a leader* (as a noun).
principle means *a fundamental truth or belief*.

> His *principal* supporters came from among the peasants.
> The *principal* of the school asked for cooperation from the staff.
> Humility was the guiding *principle* of Buddha's life.

NOTE: *Principal* may also mean *a sum placed at interest*.

> Part of his monthly payment was applied as interest on the *principal*.

sit means *to take a seat*. (intransitive verb)
set means *to place*. (transitive verb)
Note the forms of each verb:

Tense	Sit
Present	He sits on a chair.
Past	He sat on the chair.
Pres. Perf.	He has sat on the chair.

Tense	Set
Present	He sets the lamp on the table.
Past	He set the lamp on the table.
Pres. Perf.	He has set the lamp on the table.

some time means *a portion of time*.
sometime means *at an indefinite time in the future*.
sometimes means *occasionally*.

> I'll need *some time* to make a decision.
> Let us meet *sometime* after twelve noon.
> *Sometimes* it is better to hesitate before signing a contract.

somewheres is unacceptable.
somewhere is acceptable.

stationary means *standing still*.
stationery means *writing materials*.

> In ancient times people thought the earth was *stationary*.
> We bought writing paper at the *stationery* store.

stayed means *remained*.
stood means *remained upright or erect*.

> The army *stayed* in the trenches for five days.
> The soldiers *stood* at attention for one hour.

sure for *surely* is unacceptable.

> You *surely* (NOT *sure*) are not going to write that!

take in is unacceptable in the same sense of *deceive* or *attend*.

> We were *deceived* (NOT *taken in*) by his manner.
> We should like to *attend* (NOT *take in*) a few plays during our vacation.

their means *belonging to them*.
there means *in that place*.
they're means *they are*.

> We took *their* books home with us.
> You will find your books over *there* on the desk.
> *They're* going to the ballpark with us.

theirselves is unacceptable for *themselves*.

> Most children of school age are able to care for *themselves* in many ways.

these kind is unacceptable.
this kind is acceptable.

> I am fond of *this kind* of apples.

NOTE: *These kinds* would also be acceptable.

through meaning *finished* or *completed* is unacceptable.

> We'll *finish* (NOT *be through with*) the work by five o'clock.

try to is acceptable.
try and is unacceptable.

> *Try to* come (NOT *Try and* come).

NOTE: *Plan on going* is unacceptable; *plan to go* is acceptable.

two is the *numeral 2*.
to means *in the direction of*.
too means *more than* or *also*.

> There are *two* sides to every story.
> Three *two's* (or 2's) equal six.
> We shall go *to* school.
> We shall go, *too*.
> The weather is *too* hot for school.

unique means *unequaled*. Since only one object can be unique, the word does not allow for comparative or superlative forms. *Uniquer* and *uniquest*, or *more unique* and *most unique*, are logical impossibilities. Some other words that fall into this same category are: *round*, *square*, *perfect*, *equal*, and *entirely*.

were is used when something is *contrary to fact* (not a fact).

> I wish I *were* in Bermuda.

ways is unacceptable for *way*.

> We climbed a little way (NOT *ways*) up the hill.

went and took (*went and stole*, etc.) is unacceptable.

> They *stole* (NOT *went and stole*) our tools.

when (and *where*) should NOT be used to introduce a definition of a noun.

> A tornado *is a* twisting, high wind on land (NOT *is when a* twisting, high wind is on land).
> A pool *is a place for swimming* (NOT *is where people swim*).

whereabouts is unacceptable for *where*.

> *Where* (NOT *whereabouts*) do you live?

NOTE: *Whereabouts* as a noun meaning a place is *acceptable*.

> Do you know his *whereabouts*?

whether should NOT be preceded by *of* or *as to*.

> The president will consider the question *whether* (NOT *of whether*) it is better to ask for or demand higher taxes now.
> He inquired *whether* (NOT *as to whether*) we were going or not.

which as a relative pronoun refers only to *objects*.
who, **whom** refer only to *people*.
that as a relative pronoun may refer to *either objects* or *people*.

> This is the vase *which* the cat knocked over.
> This is the vase *that* the cat knocked over.
> The boy *who* won the prize is over there.
> The boy *that* won the prize is over there.

while is unacceptable for *and* or *though*.

> The library is situated on the south side; (OMIT *while*) the laboratory is on the north side.
> *Though* (NOT *while*) I am in your office every day, do not attempt to see me.

whose is the possessive of *who*.
who's is the contraction for *who is*.

> *Whose* car is in the street?
> Do you know *who's* ringing the doorbell?

your is the possessive of *you*.
you're is the contraction for *you are*.

> I hope *you're* planning to leave *your* muddy boots outside.

SENTENCE STRUCTURE

1. Every sentence must contain a verb. A group of words without a verb is a sentence fragment, not a sentence. A verb may consist of one, two, three, or four words.

    Examples: The boy *studies* hard.

    > The boy *will study* hard.

    > The boy *has been studying* hard.

    > The boy *should have been studying* hard.

    The words that make up a single verb may be separated.

    Examples: It *is* not *snowing*.

    > It *will* almost certainly *snow* tomorrow.

2. Every sentence must have a subject. The subject may be a noun, a pronoun, or a word or group of words functioning as a noun.

Examples: *Fish* swim. (noun)

She is young. (pronoun)

Running is good exercise. (gerund)

To argue is pointless. (infinitive)

That he was tired was evident. (noun clause)

In commands, the subject is usually not expressed but is understood to be you.

Example: Mind your own business.

3. A phrase cannot stand by itself as a sentence. A phrase is any group of related words that has no subject or predicate and which is used as a single part of speech. Phrases may be built around prepositions, participles, gerunds, or infinitives.

Examples: The boy *with curly hair* is my brother. (Prepositional phrase used as an adjective modifying *boy*)

My favorite cousin lives *on a farm*. (Prepositional phrase used as an adverb modifying *lives*)

Beyond the double white line is out of bounds. (Prepositional phrase used as a noun, the subject of the sentence)

A thunderstorm *preceding a cold front* is often welcome. (Participial phrase used as an adjective modifying *thunderstorm*)

We eagerly awaited the pay envelopes *brought by the messenger*. (Participial phrase used as an adjective modifying *envelopes*)

Running a day camp is an exhausting job. (Gerund phrase used as a noun, subject of the sentence)

The director is paid well for *running the day camp*. (Gerund phrase used as a noun, the object of the preposition *for*)

To breathe unpolluted air should be every person's birthright. (Infinitive phrase used as a noun, the subject of the sentence)

The child began *to unwrap his gift*. (Infinitive phrase used as a noun, the object of the verb *began*)

The boy ran away from home *to become a marine*. (Infinitive phrase used as an adverb modifying *ran away*)

4. A *main, independent*, or *principal* clause can stand alone as a complete sentence. A main clause has a subject and a verb. It may stand by itself or be introduced by a coordinating conjunction.

Example: The sky darkened ominously and rain began to fall. (Two independent clauses joined by a coordinating conjunction)

A subordinate or dependent clause must never stand alone. It is not a complete sentence, only a sentence fragment, despite the fact that it has a subject and a verb. A subordinate clause usually is introduced by a subordinating conjunction. Subordinate clauses may act as adverbs, adjectives, or nouns. Subordinate adverbial clauses are generally introduced by the subordinating conjunctions when, while, because, as soon as, if, after, although, as before, since, than, though, until, and unless.

Examples: *While we were waiting for the local*, the express roared past.

           The woman applied for a new job *because she wanted to earn more money*.

Although a *subordinate clause* contains both subject and verb, *it cannot stand alone* because it is introduced by a *subordinating word*.

Subordinating adjective clauses may be introduced by the pronouns *who, which,* and *that*.

Examples: The play *which he liked best* was a mystery.

           I have a neighbor *who served in the Peace Corps*.

Subordinate noun clauses may be introduced by *who, what,* or *that*.

Examples: The stationmaster says *that the train will be late*.

           I asked the waiter *what the stew contained*.

           I wish I knew *who backed into my car*.

5. Two independent clauses cannot share one sentence without some form of connective. If they do, they form a run-on sentence. Two principle clauses may be joined by a coordinating conjunction, by a comma followed by a coordinating conjunction, or by a semicolon. They may also form two distinct sentences. Two main clauses may NEVER be joined by a comma without a coordinating conjunction. This error is called a comma splice.

Examples: **Wrong:**   A college education has never been more important than it is today it has never cost more.

           Wrong: A college education has never been more important than it is today, it has never cost more.

           Wrong: A college education has never been more important than it is today and it has never cost more.

           Wrong: A college education has never been more important than it is today; and it has never cost more.

Correct: A college education has never been more important than it is today, and it has never cost more.

Correct: A college education has never been more important than it is today; it has never cost more.

Correct: A college education has never been more important than it is today. It has never cost more.

Correct: A college education has never been more important than it is today. And it has never cost more.

Correct: While a college education has never been more important than it is today, it has never cost more.

6. Direct quotations follow all the rules of sentence formation. Beware of comma splices in divided quotations.

Examples: **Wrong:**   "Your total is wrong," he said, "add the column again."

         Correct: "Your total is wrong," he said. "Add the column again." (The two independent clauses form two separate sentences.)

         Wrong: "Are you lost?" she asked, "may I help you?"

         Correct: "Are you lost?" she asked. "May I help you?" (Two main clauses; two separate sentences.)

7. Comparisons must be logical and complete.

Examples: **Wrong:**   Wilmington is larger than any city in Delaware.

         Correct: Wilmington is larger than any *other* city in Delaware.

         Wrong: He is fat, if not fatter, than his uncle.

         Correct: He is as fat *as*, if not fatter than, his uncle.

         Wrong: I hope to find a summer job other than a lifeguard.

         Correct: I hope to find a summer job other than that of lifeguard.

         Wrong: Law is a better profession than an accountant.

         Correct: Law is a better profession than accounting.

8. Avoid the "is when" and "is where" construction.

Examples: **Wrong:**   A limerick is when a short poem has a catchy rhyme.

         Correct: A limerick is a short poem with a catchy rhyme.

         Wrong: To exile is where a person must live in another place.

         Correct: To exile a person is to force him to live in another place.

9. Errors in parallelism are often quite subtle, but you should learn to recognize and avoid them. The Foreign Service Officer Exam relies upon difficult questions to differentiate highly qualified candidates from adequate candidates.

Examples: **Wrong:**   Skiing and to skate are both winter sports.

            Correct: *Skiing* and *skating* are both winter sports.

            Wrong: She spends all her time eating, asleep, and on her studies.

            Correct: She spends all her time *eating*, *sleeping*, and *studying*.

            Wrong: The work is neither difficult nor do I find it interesting.

            Correct: The work is neither *difficult* nor *interesting*.

            Wrong: His heavy drinking and the fact that he gambles makes him a poor role model.

            Correct: His heavy *drinking* and *gambling make* him a poor role model.

10. Avoid needless shifts in point of view. A shift in point of view is a change within the sentence from one tense or mood to another, from one subject or voice to another, or from one person or number to another. Shifts in point of view destroy parallelism within the sentence.

Examples: After he *rescued* the kitten, he *rushes* down the ladder to find its owner. (Shift from past tense to present tense)

         Change to: After he rescued the kitten, he rushed down the ladder to find its owner.

         First *stand* at attention and then you *should salute* the flag. (Shift from imperative to indicative mood)

         Change to: First *stand* at attention and then *salute* the flag.

         Mary especially likes math, but history is also enjoyed by her. (The subject shifts from *Mary* to *history*; the mood shifts from active to passive.)

         Change to: Mary especially likes math, but she also enjoys history.

         George rowed around the island and soon the mainland came in sight. (The subject changes from *George* to *the mainland*.)

         Change to: George rowed around the island and soon came in sight of the mainland.

         The captain welcomed *us* aboard, and the crew enjoyed showing *one* around the boat. (The object shifts from first to third person.)

         Change to: The captain welcomed us aboard, and the crew enjoyed showing us around the boat.

         One should listen to the weather forecast so that *they* may anticipate a hurricane. (The subject shifts from singular to plural.)

         Change to: *One* should listen to the weather forecast so that *he* may anticipate a hurricane.

Other Careers with the Department of State

U.S. FOREIGN COMMERCIAL SERVICE

Founded in 1980, the U.S. Commercial Service is a Commerce Department agency that helps U.S. companies, particularly small and medium-sized businesses, make sales in international markets. The agency's network includes 107 U.S. Export Assistance Centers throughout the country, and more than 150 offices overseas. Last year, the U.S. Commercial Service facilitated more than $23 billion in U.S. exports and conducted nearly 150,000 counseling sessions with American companies.

Foreign Service Officer

Foreign Service Officers in the Commercial Service work out of both foreign and domestic field offices and the headquarters located in Washington, D.C. Their job is to promote the export of U.S. goods and services and defend U.S. commercial interests abroad.

Application Process

The Commercial Service Assessment is a competitive oral and written examination, used to recruit new, tenure-track Foreign Service Officers into the Commercial Service. Successful candidates are placed on a Rank Order Register. Candidates whose scores on the Commercial Service Assessment merit placement on the Registry may be tendered conditional offers of employment, pending successful completion of a security clearance, a medical clearance, and drug testing. Offers of employment are made off the Rank Order Register, as vacancies become available, according to the needs of the Service. The Commercial Service Assessment is offered every two years. The next test will be offered in 2005. In the interim, please review the 2003 Assessment Information Package found at www.export.gov/comm_svc/pdf/03CSAssessment.pdf for information on the Commercial Service and the traits that the agency seeks in applicants.

appendix b

Internships and Co-Ops

Domestic Opportunities

If you are interested in internship opportunities at one of the domestic Export Assistance Centers, log on to www.jobs.doc.gov. If you are interested in learning more about Internship and Co-Op opportunities at the International Trade Administration headquarters in Washington, D.C., call the Office of Personnel at (202) 482-3301.

Overseas Opportunities

The U.S. Commercial Service, International Trade Administration, of the U.S. Department of Commerce (DOC) is a corps of American and foreign employees dedicated to helping American companies expand sales in overseas markets.

The Overseas Work-Study Internship Program was developed to provide college or university juniors, seniors, and graduate students of Economics, Business Administration, and related fields with "hands-on" experience working in the Commercial Section of a U.S. Embassy. The program is uncompensated and designed to encourage students to consider careers in the commercial field. Internships in the Work-Study Program are considered to be adjunct to an applicant's education. Students must be currently enrolled and taking at least one-half of a full-time academic workload. They must also plan to continue their education immediately upon termination of their internship.

Interns typically serve for one quarter or semester during their academic year, or for a minimum of 10 weeks during the summer. U.S. citizenship and good academic standing are required, along with the successful completion of a security assurance check.

Students seeking internships abroad with the U.S. Commercial Service are requested to correspond directly with the Senior Commercial Officer (SCO) or Principal Commercial Officer (PCO) in the particular country in which they are interested in serving. Correspondence should include a cover letter to the SCO along with a resume, SF-612, or SF-171 (Application for Federal Employment form).

U.S. FOREIGN AGRICULTURAL SERVICE

The Foreign Agricultural Service (FAS) of the U.S. Department of Agriculture (USDA) works to improve foreign market access for U.S. products, build new markets, improve the competitive position of U.S. agriculture in the global marketplace, and provide food aid and technical assistance to foreign countries.

FAS has the primary responsibility for USDA's international activities—market development, trade agreements and negotiations, and the collection and analysis of statistics and market information. It also administers USDA's export credit guarantee and food aid programs, and helps increase income and food availability in developing nations by mobilizing expertise for agriculturally led economic growth. FAS also enhances U.S. agriculture's competitiveness by providing linkages to global resources and international organizations.

Representing U.S. Agriculture Abroad

FAS has a global network of agricultural economists, marketing experts, negotiators, and other specialists that few organizations can equal. FAS agricultural counselors, attachés, trade officers, and locally employed FAS staff stationed in over 90 countries support U.S. agricultural interests.

In addition to agricultural affairs offices in U.S. embassies, agricultural trade offices also have been established in a number of key markets and function as service centers for U.S. exporters and foreign buyers seeking market information. FAS's overseas offices serve as the Department's "eyes and ears" for monitoring international issues. Counselors and attachés work hand-in-hand with the country's ambassador and other components of its team. They work to ensure that agriculture's market access, food aid, capacity building, biotechnology, and information gathering remain at the forefront. When problems arise in export markets, counselors and attachés play a critical role in providing immediate assistance to exporters.

International Trade Policy

FAS coordinates and directs USDA's responsibilities in international trade negotiations, working closely with the U.S. Trade Representative's office. Trade policy experts at FAS help identify—and work to reduce—foreign trade barriers and other practices and policies that hinder U.S. agricultural exports.

FAS is the enquiry point for World Trade Organization (WTO) sanitary and phytosanitary issues and technical barriers to trade. As such, the agency serves as the official conduit for notifications and comments about these measures.

Trade information sent to Washington, D.C. by FAS personnel overseas is used to develop and hone strategies to increase market access, monitor trade agreements, and improve programs and policies to make U.S. farm products more competitive.

Complete information about a career with the Foreign Agricultural Service is available at www.fas.usda.gov.

NOTES